God, Guns, Grits, *and* Gravy

MIKE HUCKABEE

🦁 ST. MARTIN'S GRIFFIN 🦁 NEW YORK

www.stmartins.com

Designed by Steven Seighman

The Library of Congress has cataloged the hardcover edition as follows:

Huckabee, Mike, 1955–
    God, guns, grits, and gravy / Mike Huckabee.
        p. cm.
    Includes index.
    ISBN 978-1-250-06099-0 (hardcover)
    ISBN 978-1-4668-6671-3 (e-book)
    1. United States—Civilization.   2. Social problems—United States.
3. Social values—United States.   4. United States—Social conditions.
5. United States—Moral conditions.   6. United States—Politics and
government.   I. Title.
    E169.12.H75 2015
    973—dc23

                                                        2014032165

ISBN 978-1-250-06100-3 (trade paperback)

Our books may be purchased in bulk for promotional, educational, or business use. Please contact your local bookseller or the Macmillan Corporate and Premium Sales Department at (800) 221-7945, extension 5442, or by e-mail at MacmillanSpecialMarkets@macmillan.com.

First St. Martin's Griffin Edition: January 2016

10 9 8 7 6 5 4 3 2 1

I've never been ashamed of where I come from or the way I grew up. I wouldn't trade it for any amount of money. I learned to be resourceful and resilient. Only in the last few years have I earned the kind of money that empowered me to give away more than I used to make. It's given me mobility, opportunities, and comfort that I couldn't have imagined as a child. The people who taught me the great lessons of life were largely hardworking, humble, and simple. They had the sort of common sense that was born out of necessity, and were the kind of folks I would hope would show up if I got sick or needed a neighbor to help me hunt for my dog if he got loose.

My life has been largely molded by people that some might not consider to be "sophisticated." They're my kind of folks.

My wife, like me, comes from such stock. She's now weathered forty years with me, and has done it quite well. Our marriage has produced three now-grown children, and the four most beautiful grandchildren on the planet, and I say that with all objectivity. To my wife, children, grandchildren, and all my friends who have been part of this journey in the land of God, guns, grits, and gravy, I dedicate this book.

Contents

Acknowledgments

When you see a turtle sitting on a fence post, you can be pretty sure he didn't get there by himself. And though a book may be the product of one author's thoughts, rest assured that a lot of other people are involved. It certainly is true in the case of this precious tome you hold in your hands.

I owe a lot of gratitude to my family, who accepted my being unreachable many times while I was holed up in my office or my balcony and belting out another chapter to stay on deadline. This is the first of twelve books I've written without the companionship of my beloved black Lab, Jet, who died in January 2013 after fifteen years together. I still miss him, but Toby and Sonic, our Cavalier King Charles spaniel and Shih Tzu respectively, have done their best to provide inspiration and companionship when my wife has long since gone to bed.

St. Martin's Press has been great to put their trust in me and turn me loose. It's been wonderful working with their entire team and their editor in chief, George Witte, and editorial assistant Sara Thwaite. And Sally Richardson, president of St. Martin's Press, won me over at "hello." Her enthusiasm, depth, and vision for the book have been better than a bowl of grits with cheese and shrimp, and where I come from, that's good. As a writer, I have loved that I've been allowed the freedom to say what I felt and do it in my own voice.

My agent, Frank Breeden, has been more than an agent. He is a trusted friend who has helped guide me through the turbulent waters of the publishing world.

Two indispensable partners in the project were Pat Reeder and Laura Ainsworth, who have worked with me for several years as writers and researchers for my daily radio commentary, *The Huckabee Report*, and who helped research a lot of the material in the book that illustrates the message inside. They not only were of great assistance, but provided tremendous encouragement and gave their opinion when they thought a chapter was good and when something didn't float the boat.

Duane Ward and Josh Smallbone of Premiere Marketing, working along with my son David—who runs several of the companies I own—have put together the effort to get me on the road to promote and sign the book in venues across the country.

Most of all, thank *you*, for buying (or stealing) this book and investing some of your precious time to read it. I really do want you to enjoy it. I've written it for you to easily understand and enjoy. I didn't write it for academics and scholars because I think it would be over their heads. I truly hope you enjoy reading it as much as I enjoyed writing it!

New Preface
for This Edition

WE HAVE A SAYING in the South that "when you throw a rock over a fence, the hit dog hollers." For those needing a translation, it means that when the rock is thrown blindly over the fence, the dog that was actually hit by the rock is the one who whimpers or barks.

The original release of *God, Guns, Grits, and Gravy* was like a rock tossed over the fence, and the dogs went to hollerin' for sure! I knew for certain that I had hit a few dogs when the reaction from "Bubble-ville" validated the message: There is a huge cultural chasm between the people living in the "bubbles" of New York City, Washington, D.C., and Los Angeles, and the people living in "flyover" country, or "Bubba-ville" as I call it. It's what I refer to as the land of God, guns, grits, and gravy because in the red-state world of Middle America, those four things are normal and common.

I was challenged as to the accuracy of my claims that there is a culture clash by Bill Maher when I was guest on his HBO show, by Jon Stewart on *The Daily Show*, by the ladies of *The View*, and even by some of the New York–based Fox News Channel hosts. Almost universally, I was derided by the left for asserting that there is a cultural chasm in this nation. But as I traveled the country to sign copies of the book (mostly in flyover country), people stood in line to tell me that the book has described in detail just how they felt. I repeatedly was told "it was as if you were speaking for me."

And the fact is, I was. I told people in the South and the Midwest that they would be able to read the book without a translator. We would share a laugh, but it was in fact true, and the response and reaction from those who read the book validated my message. In many ways, those living in the bubbles are like folks trying to listen at the United Nations without a headset when it comes to recognizing the disconnect between cultures.

The current election cycle is another example of elitists just not "getting it." Though it's been hard to comprehend why truly "outsider" candidates would be so popular, the reason is pretty obvious—many Americans are in a seething rage because of their perception that the political class is oblivious to the struggles of the working class. It's not unusual for there to be a certain distrust of or even cynicism about political figures, but what has exploded in the last year or so is derisive contempt for those who have held office. The net result is that for the first time in our nation's history, the more inexperienced a candidate is, the better. Any noticeable qualifications a candidate might possess are actually a detriment rather than an asset.

The equivalent would be a corporate board looking to hire a CEO and passing over several very qualified and seasoned individuals with stellar academic and professional backgrounds to settle on someone who is totally unfamiliar with the product the company makes and who has never worked in a corporation before. We would think it naïve to give the controls of an airplane to a person who had never actually been in a cockpit, but had played some video games. Would we allow a person who had never performed surgery, but had watched some doctor shows on TV, to do abdominal surgery on us? One might say that the notion of hiring someone for a job he or she is totally *unprepared* for is nothing short of irrational, but the anger and frustration that many Americans have for their government right now has led to a call for something that appears illogical because they see government as irrational and illogical. The electorate is in no mood to take the time for a remodeling of the structure—they are ready to "burn it down!" and leave nothing but smoldering remains.

Of course, taking a can of gasoline and a book of matches and burning it to the ground is the easiest of all responses. No skill required—a twelve-year-old can burn a house down! But the elitists on Wall Street and in Washington underestimate the depth of disgust emanating from people whose livelihoods, culture, and very way of life have been upended by the ruling class whose response seems less compassionate than "let them eat cake!"

Watching Washington act shocked by the political earthquake that is shaking the ground under them, and the Wall Street donor class be startled that the hundreds of millions that they have tossed at the feet of candidates who will dance according to the tune are not having the desired effect, and the Hollywood elites go apoplectic that the great unwashed would rise up in rebellion at open borders and the criminalization of Christianity, is further evidence that the bubble-dwellers are totally out of touch with those in Bubba-ville.

The case of Kentucky County Clerk Kim Davis is a prime example of the dichotomy of values. Kim Davis, a Democrat (at the time) elected county clerk, declined to issue marriage licenses to same-sex couples because the Kentucky constitution specified only traditional marriage, and issuing such licenses would cause her to violate her faith. She pleaded with the legislature and governor to address such a situation even before the Supreme Court's utterly irrational decision to order states to redefine marriage. Neither the governor nor the legislature lifted a finger to anticipate the train wreck of this overreaching act of judicial tyranny. When Davis rejected a request to issue a license under her signature, an appointed federal judge took the drastic step of ordering her jailed—without bail!

It was a seminal moment in America for an elected official to be placed in jail for believing exactly what Barack Obama and Hillary Clinton believed in 2008. In fact, it was exactly what even Supreme

Court Justice Elena Kagan said in 2009 during her confirmation hearing to become the solicitor general.

Over at the blog *Legal Insurrection*, law professor William A. Jacobson reminds us of this answer Elena Kagan gave to Senator John Cornyn in her confirmation hearings to be solicitor general in 2009:

1. As solicitor general, you would be charged with defending the Defense of Marriage Act. That law, as you may know, was enacted by overwhelming majorities of both houses of Congress (85–14 in the Senate and 342–67 in the House) in 1996 and signed into law by President Clinton.

a. Given your rhetoric about the Don't Ask, Don't Tell policy— you called it "a profound wrong—a moral injustice of the first order"—let me ask this basic question: Do you believe that there is a federal constitutional right to same-sex marriage?

Answer: There is no federal constitutional right to same-sex marriage.

b. Have you ever expressed your opinion whether the federal Constitution should be read to confer a right to same-sex marriage? If so, please provide details.

Answer: I do not recall ever expressing an opinion on this question.

So did someone amend the Constitution between the time Elena Kagan gave that answer in 2009 and 2015 when she somehow "found" a constitutional right to same-sex marriage? The fact that both Kagan and Justice Ginsburg had performed same-sex weddings meant they should have recused themselves from even participating in the same-sex marriage case, but they declined to do so. Instead, they participated in issuing a majority opinion that led to a Kentucky county clerk being forced to choose between violating her faith and going to jail.

It was a wake-up call for many people who live in the heartland. I spoke by phone with Kim Davis when I first heard of her refusing to issue the licenses. Later that same day, the judge jailed her. I was stunned and told my team, "We're going to Kentucky!" Eight hours later, I had a team in Grayson, Kentucky, to plan a rally of support for her, and 5 days later, over 5,000 people overflowed a town of 3,500 to "Stand with Kim." The media elites sniffed at the event and at Kim and her family with derision and contempt. They portrayed the entire episode as a bunch of hillbillies and hayseeds fighting the "gummit" and showing a lack of sophistication. They failed to understand that the jailing of a Christian for following her faith was for many the last straw. Who would be next? Their pastor? The president of a faith-based university or private school?

The divide between the ruling class and the working class has only grown more pronounced since the original publication of *God, Guns, Grits, and Gravy*. And if the events of 2015 are any indication, the message will be even more relevant in the coming years. Far from walking back the original message, I proudly stand behind the story and would even proudly turn up the volume. And in the background, I hear the "hit dog holler"!

Introduction

THE THREE MAJOR "NERVE CENTERS" of our culture are New York City, Washington, D.C., and Los Angeles. The nation's finance and fashion center is New York City; D.C. is the epicenter of American politics and government; and Los Angeles is the nexus for entertainment, whether movies, television, or music. They are the three "bubbles" of influence in our modern culture and they are indeed "bubbles." I call these cities "Bubble-ville." I intentionally live in what I call "Bubba-ville." It's where "Bubbas" live, and where a lot of people are called by two names: Mary Elizabeth, Katherine Grace, Jim Bob, and Darryl Wayne.

I travel to New York City every week to host my TV show on the Fox News Channel. Because the show originates from there, most people think that I surely must live there. I'm quick to say, "I don't live there and won't unless they will let me duck hunt in Central Park." I'm quite certain that isn't going to happen since it's all but impossible to *own* a gun in New York City, much less legally use it. Unless you're a cop or a crook, you probably don't possess a firearm in New York City. In fact, you've probably never seen one in person.

But it's more than guns. Have you ever tried to order grits in a fancy Manhattan restaurant? Good luck. Not even for breakfast! And you'll get some real weird looks if you ask for "sawmill gravy" on your potatoes or biscuits—that is if you can find real biscuits. And I'm sorry, but gravy on a bagel just doesn't work for me. If I want to chew that hard, I'll take up chewing tobacco, which I won't. I'm not even *that* rural! I can somewhat understand that New York restaurants might not typically have red-eye gravy or chocolate gravy as those might be a bit regional, but how can an eating place that fancies itself fancy have the audacity to open its doors and not have biscuits and gravy or grits on the breakfast menu?

And while there are some really wonderful churches in New York City, I get the impression that the total number of the people who faithfully attend church is a small fraction of the population. It's not completely Sodom and Gomorrah, but the traffic at 3 a.m. Sunday is more intense than at 11 a.m. That ought to tell you something.

Don't get me wrong—New York is an exciting city and there's always a lot going on. It's full of energy and it has a unique "vibe" all its own. But it's crowded, loud, hurried, intense, and it just seems like its streets are filthy. Even when the trash gets picked up, you always want to burn your shoes after you've walked the New York streets because of all the "stuff" that is ever present on the sidewalks. I can't find a Walmart in Manhattan, either, and people stare at my cowboy boots when I'm on the subway. What's up with that? I prefer boots over Birkenstocks. Does that make *me* weird?

I feel out of place in Washington, D.C. as well. I really spend very little time in our nation's capital and only go there when I have to. It's a lovely city with all those monuments and stone buildings, but if ego could be turned into electricity, Washington, D.C. would have electric power in unlimited levels and never have a power outage. But for a city where everyone sure is in a hurry and acts busy, nothing productive ever happens there. Some people think that because I'm involved in politics, I surely must live there. I don't. In fact, there's only one address in that city that I'd probably want to relocate to. ☺

And Los Angeles has great weather, but the weather isn't great enough to make me want to sit in traffic for two hours to go four miles on any given day. And getting grits and gravy there is maybe tougher than in New York. If you want to eat seaweed salad, kale, or granola, you can find lots of varieties. But I thought only North Koreans ate lawn clippings, and no one ever looks you in the eyes in LA or if they do, you're unaware of it because they wear sunglasses all the time—even indoors. I don't know how they can see well enough to keep from stumbling all over the place.

So let me make it clear—I'm a proud son of the South, but I can easily relate to folks from the Midwest, Southwest, and most of rural America. I feel a bit more disconnected from people who have never fired a gun, never fished with a cane pole, never cooked with propane, or never changed a tire. If people use "summer" as a verb as in, "we summer in the Hamptons," I probably don't have much in common with them. If people don't put pepper sauce on their black-eyed peas or order fried green tomatoes for an appetizer, I probably won't relate to them without some effort.

This is a book about God, guns, grits, and gravy. It's not a recipe book for Southern cuisine, nor a collection of religious devotionals, nor a manual on how to properly load a semiautomatic shotgun. It's a book about what's commonly referred to as "flyover country," the vast portion of real estate that sits between the East Coast and the West Coast and which more often than not votes red instead of blue, roots for the Cowboys in the NFL and the Cardinals in the National League, and has three or more Bibles in every house. It's where there's nothing unusual at all about God, guns, grits, or gravy. It's not a novelty; it's not strange or weird. It's a way of life.

It's where I was born, raised, and have lived my entire life. I like it. I feel at home there. I'm a catfish and corn bread kind of guy, not a caviar and crab salad connoisseur.

This book will be very encouraging to people who live in Bubbaville. And to those who live in Bubble-ville, it will be very enlightening. After you've read it, you'll probably still want to live in your same bubble, but you might at least for the first time really understand those of us you fly over and look down on when you make the LA to New York red-eye flight and wonder, "Just what kind of people live there?"

Because most of the movies and television shows portray people living in one of the bubbles, we know you pretty well. We get your unique phrases, attitudes, and even know something about your various neighborhoods. But I don't think you know *us* very well. We really don't live in Bugtussle and we do have indoor plumbing and electricity. So let me introduce you to the land and the people for whom God, guns, grits, and gravy all make perfect sense. After you finish the book, you might just say, "Dang, those good ol' boys ain't so dumb after all."

1

The New American Outcasts

PEOPLE WHO PUT FAITH AND FAMILY FIRST

IT ALL STARTED OVER a simple chicken sandwich.

On a Saturday in July 2012, Truett Cathy, the ninety-one-year-old founder of the family-owned Chick-fil-A restaurant chain, was a guest on my Fox News Channel television show to talk about his book, *Wealth: Is It Worth It?* I had been trying to schedule him for months, ever since appearing with him on the speaking roster for a couple of events and finding his personal background to be one of the great American success stories. I'd read his book and found quite compelling its admonition to use wealth as a means to be generous and not just as an end in itself. Finally, the July date worked out for him to be in New York on a Saturday afternoon when we were taping my show.

But between our booking of Mr. Cathy and his appearance on the show, his son Dan Cathy, chief operating officer of the company at that time and now the CEO, gave an interview to the Ken Coleman radio show on June 16, 2012, and another on July 2 to the *Biblical Recorder* newspaper, which is published weekly for and about Baptists in North Carolina. Dan's comments in support of traditional Christian teachings that marriage is between one man and one woman were blunt, but not unusual or outrageous. He said, "We are very much supportive of the family—the biblical definition of the family unit. We are a family-owned business, a family-led business, and we are married to our first wives. We give God thanks for that. . . . We want to do anything we possibly can to strengthen families. We are very much committed to that." Cathy continued: "We intend to stay the course. We know that it might not be popular with everyone, but thank the Lord, we live in a country where we can share our values and operate on biblical principles."

Wow! That was really outrageous of him! The very idea that someone would publicly spout the view that a family has value to our society! Dan even had the audacity to talk of a family that included a father, mother, and children all living in the same household and husbands and wives who married and stayed that way. Scandalous!

And that's when the chicken hit the fan! By the time Truett was in New York for my show, the controversy over Dan's remarks had fired up the same-sex marriage advocates—even big-city mayors like Rahm Emanuel of Chicago and Thomas Menino of Boston, who publicly vowed to run the Chick-fil-A businesses out of "their" towns because they disagreed with personal comments made by an executive of the company! [*The Ken Coleman Show* on WDUN, June 16, 2012] There would have been less controversy had Dan Cathy slaughtered live chickens on the steps of Chicago City Hall at lunch hour. But what we witnessed instead was the slaughter of the basic American principles of freedom of speech, freedom of religion, and free enterprise. I was shocked that elected officials in America actually believed they could goose-step on top of the Constitution and use the power of government to squelch a viewpoint that they personally didn't like (but one that, incidentally, was consistent with the will of the electorate in thirty-four states that had voted on the issue of same-sex marriage). It was especially hypocritical in Emanuel's case, in that same-sex marriage was illegal at the time in his own state. But facts and the First

Amendment didn't seem to get in the way of the bigotry and intolerance directed toward Dan Cathy.

In fact, the viewpoint expressed by Dan Cathy was the very position held by none other than candidate Barack Obama in 2008. At California's Saddleback Forum in August 2008, when Pastor Rick Warren asked Obama's position on same-sex marriage, the then-candidate expressly said he was opposed to it because, as a Christian, he found it not in keeping with his biblical view of marriage. After he was elected President, Barack Obama not only changed his view but went on to become the cheerleader-in-chief for all things gay. (One might even say his opinion was "fundamentally transformed." Who knew that the "change" in "hope and change" would actually come to describe Obama's own views?) It's a reflection of how sloppy and biased "journalism" has become that I cannot find evidence of any reporter asking the simple question, "Mr. President, if your reason for opposing same-sex marriage in 2008 was because of your Christian belief that the biblical definition of marriage meant one man and one woman, has there been an update or revision to the Bible since then, or did you base your decision to change your position on political expediency? If so, were you being dishonest in 2008 . . . or now?" Still waiting on that one!

Truett had been scheduled to speak about his book, not the controversy over his son's remarks, and I wanted to be faithful to that purpose. Besides, it really wasn't his controversy, and it was obvious that the book's publicist, who was with him that day, was nervous that the interview would ignore the book and focus on same-sex marriage. But it has never been my practice to ambush guests on my show. I was raised in the old-fashioned traditions of the South—a guest is to be treated with gracious hospitality. The role of a host is to meet the needs of the guest, not to use that guest to serve one's own interests. The host offers food, beverage, and the most comfortable chair in the house. When I was growing up, even poor people in the South would dig up something for their guest in the way of refreshments, but criticism and confrontation were never on the menu. If a host had unkind words to say, they would be held until after the guest had gone. Then the first thing said would be, "Bless his heart . . ."

Of course, that signaled that someone was about to get filleted like a cheap fish. But while the guest was present, you treated him or her with great kindness and deference. I always assume that's the way it should be on TV, just as it is in my home. I believe this is why I've been able to get some guests on my show who most certainly didn't share my political views. They were comfortable on my show because if they were there to talk about their movie or book or television special, I didn't try to force them into an unwanted debate on some hot political topic. Yes, surprising a guest with confrontational questions for which the guest is not prepared might make for "great TV," but my dear late mother would find a way to come out of her grave and yank me by the ears if she ever thought I was acting like the south end of a northbound mule.

Truett Cathy passed away in September 2014 at the age of ninety-three. He was a delightful guest and spoke of his humble beginnings, his commitment to treating every customer with respect and kindness, and his resolve to stay true to his convictions, such as keeping his stores closed on Sunday so his employees could go to church if they wanted to. In his nineties, Truett was sharper and quicker than most men half his age. As the interview came to a close, I simply mentioned I was appalled that Dan's comments were being portrayed as hate speech, and expressed my dismay that a person speaking for himself and not for the company was coming under attack and being threatened with economic retribution and censorship by government officials like Emanuel and Menino. These two mayors somehow thought that they had been elected to be dictators who could use the power of their offices to punish businesses whose executives expressed a personal opinion that didn't reflect theirs. As I closed the interview, I suggested that people around the country who thought that free speech ought to be protected—not threatened—by the government should join me on Wednesday, August 1, for what I spontaneously labeled "Chick-fil-A Appreciation Day."

Importantly, this was intended not as a protest against same-sex marriage but as an affirmation for a chicken sandwich company's executives to enjoy the same rights of free speech as have been afforded to Tim Cook, CEO of Apple; Howard Schultz, CEO of Starbucks; Jeff Bezos, CEO of Amazon; and others who've been as outspoken *for* same-sex marriage as Dan Cathy has been against it. To emphasize the double standard even more, it might be noted that Apple, Starbucks, and Amazon are all publicly held companies, while Chick-fil-A is a private company.

With the date of August 1 just a couple of weeks away, I shared the plan with several other key political and faith leaders, requesting that they ask their constituents to simply show up at a nearby Chick-fil-A on August 1 and buy a sandwich in appreciation for their food and service and to quietly take a stand for their executives to have the same right of free speech as Cook, Schultz, Bezos, and others. We urged "don't carry signs, don't scream or argue. Just enjoy a sandwich and say thanks."

What happened on August 1 was nothing short of historic. We knew something was surely brewing because my Facebook page "blowed up," as we say in the South. It must have spooked the Facebook censors, because they blocked my Facebook event page for over twenty-four hours, leaving people unable to "sign up" and indicate they were "going." Not one dime was spent promoting the day. No high-dollar New York PR firm guided the process or advised it. There was no budget, no staff, and no formal organization. The entire effort was completely organic and self-igniting. I talked about it on my daily radio show and mentioned it briefly the next two Saturdays on my Fox News Channel show. I shared it on social media like Facebook and Twitter and urged others to do the same, and they did. Not a bit of coordination or even communication of any kind occurred with the people at Chick-fil-A. There must have been people who assumed the executives at CFA had suggested it, helped promote it, or encouraged it. None of the above. I'm not even sure the corporate office approved it or wanted me to do it. I never asked them. (For the record, I didn't hear from them or have any contact with them before, during, or after the event. To those who might surmise that I got a "free Chick-fil-A for life" card, you would be quite wrong!)

At this point, for me, it was not about what Dan Cathy said. It was about whether America was now going to have two completely different sets of rules: one for those who would be free to speak with ridicule and contempt toward those with a Christian worldview, and then a very different standard for people of faith, who could be told, "Sit down, shut up, and go away—or else!" I felt that if such hatred for religious liberty and the people who believed in it and practiced it went unchallenged, then people of faith would have no one to blame but themselves for losing every last vestige of freedom. The left seems intent on shutting down any viewpoint that differs from theirs. Ironically, this is done in the name of "tolerance" and "diversity" when the left has *zero* tolerance for a different point of view. With the left, "diversity" means "uniformity." (I'll cover this more fully in Chapter 3.)

Facebook apparently was inundated with screams from the left when the event page went viral. Their initial explanation for blocking the page was that someone had complained about the content. When we pointed out that the content related only to people eating chicken sandwiches, they must have realized they could hardly classify that as "offensive" (except to chickens), so then they claimed there had been some mistake and it would be back up soon. This apparent attempt to quash the momentum probably stirred it up even more, fueling the outrage from people in "flyover land" who were up to their necks in disgust and were ready to do something.

I had already decided to take an early-morning drive on Wednesday, August 1, to the Chick-fil-A restaurant closest to my house, about twenty miles away. I got there at 7 a.m. and people were already getting in line. Cars had started coming and never let up. Even though the stores had reportedly stocked more food than normal and expected an uptick in business, no one could have predicted the groundswell nationwide as millions of Americans waited patiently in line, in their cars, and on foot, simply to buy a sandwich to show support for a fellow American who had dared to voice his own opinion. Every national news network was forced to cover the event, as it blocked traffic around the stores in most cities. Most fascinating was that the response in Rahm Emanuel's Chicago and other major urban areas was equal to that of the communities in the Bible Belt. Skeptics had predicted a barely appreciable increase in the consumption of chicken sandwiches that day—an embarrassment not just for the Chick-fil-A stores but especially for the people like me who had urged our fellow citizens to take a stand.

The results were quite different. Many of the local restaurants completely ran out of food by mid-to-late afternoon, but people continued to arrive, some purchasing whatever the store had left or even buying gift certificates to come back on another day. There were hundreds of heartwarming stories flowing to my Web site and Facebook page of customers showing their kindness and courtesy despite long lines. In Des Moines, Iowa, a police officer on his lunch break was passed through the line to the front so he would be able to get his food within his limited lunch break time. Others sang hymns, visited with those around them, and made new friends. Some, as an act of "paying it forward," purchased the food for the customer behind them. There was no violence, no screaming or profanity, and no reports of "sandwich rage" from people having to wait up to three hours in line to get a piece of chicken on a bun. Some churches (including my own) bought a large number of sandwiches and took them to a local homeless shelter.

There were almost 19 million visits to my Facebook page during the process, and over 600,000 signed up to "attend" just on my event page alone—not to mention the hundreds if not thousands of other similar pages created by churches, organizations, and individuals. For just that one day, sales at many Chick-fil-A locations increased by 200 percent or more beyond their best-ever performance, and the 2012 sales increased by over 12 percent for the year, with most analysts attributing the dramatic sales jump to the August 1 "Appreciation Day." When I visited their communities in the months following the event, many local franchisees told me that not only did they have record sales that day beyond anything they'd ever had, but that overall sales had gone up and stayed up from that day forward.

I would be asked numerous times in the following weeks why there was such a strong outpouring of response. My answer would always be the same: Frustration for many people in the heartland of America had reached a tipping point. Those who lived their lives quietly and without a lot of confrontation had been pushed to the limit by those who angrily shouted them down as "haters" simply because they held to biblical standards on issues like marriage and the sanctity of life. Their values were mocked, sneered at, and distorted by the entertainment elites from Hollywood and New York and from the political ruling class in Washington.

These are not the kind of people who burn tires in the street, paint graffiti on bridges or buildings, camp out to protest in front of businesses, throw paint on people, walk naked down Main Street (Thank God!), or chain themselves to furniture in government office buildings. They're people who get up early most days and make a lunch for their kids before they catch the bus for school; they come home tired at the end of the day from a hard day's work; they mow their own lawns, watch their kids perform in music recitals and church pageants, and attend their children's baseball and soccer games. They pay their taxes on time and typically give generously to their church and to charities. They are believers—in God, or at the very least the sacred concept of religious freedom. They really don't want much from the government other than to be left alone. When they do want something from the government, it's simple stuff: getting the trash picked up on time, having a policeman show up promptly if their house is being broken into, seeing the potholes fixed, and little things like keeping terrorists from walking right over the borders and into the country. And for that, they're treated as if they're uninformed and unscientific backwater buffoons, lacking in the "hipness" factor and living in a world that ended with the last episode of *Leave It to Beaver*. (Why, I'll bet some of them even wash their hands before dinner and think Russia is still a threat! What rubes.)

And on August 1, 2012, they decided to show up and eat a chicken sandwich.

One missed opportunity on that day was the public position of Mitt Romney, who by then was the Republican nominee for President. He apparently took the advice of his Boston-based campaign brain trust and declined to weigh in on the issue at all. When asked about the huge turnout around the nation, he simply said, "Those are not things [. . .] that's not part of my campaign" [*Washington Examiner*, Romney: "Chick-fil-A Controversy Not Part of My Campaign," August 3, 2012]. And I believe that across America, many who would have been enthusiastic Romney voters were saying, "Then his campaign is not my campaign." I continued to support Mitt and vigorously campaign for him right up until Election Day, because I think he would have been a great President who'd have made major corrections to the direction we'd been going for four years. Though we were opponents in 2008, I believe him to be a good man with impeccable integrity in his personal and business life. There is no finer model of kindness and commitment than Mitt and his family. But I heard repeatedly from voters that it would have been nice for someone in the Romney campaign to simply say, "It's always good to see Americans stand for free speech." For many voters looking for someone to take a stand for *them* and speak a word of affirmation, it was curtains down and lights out.

That many would-be supporters cooled off at that point was unfair, as I give credit to Mitt for being a tireless campaigner and running a very disciplined and focused campaign. I feel that voters should rarely give up on a candidate over one comment or action. I will always believe that Mitt, a man of strong faith himself, was probably blindsided by the question and not aware of what a landmark event that day was for many values voters. Still, little crumbs from the table sometimes satisfy the hungry birds, and for this "take a stand moment," the birds got nary a crumb.

Speaking of birds, thanks should be given to the vast numbers of yardbirds (i.e., chickens, but it also means city folks who've never seen a chicken in their yards) who'd sacrificed their lives like turkeys on Thanksgiving to handle those hungry crowds—crowds that quickly dispelled the notion that only those in favor of redefining marriage were willing to take a stand. The idea that a person expressing views that are quite ordinary and common among evangelical Christians, Catholics, Orthodox Jews, and, for that matter, Muslims, would be excoriated by the press and, more significantly, by government was a bridge too far. Most people of faith are nice people. They don't typically want to scream, carry signs, march in a protest, or shake their fists in public.

(There are exceptions, to be sure—some of the meanest people I've ever known were "church people." And, truth be told, a lot of Christians like to do their fussing and cussing as "prayer requests," as in, "We need to pray for Robert; he is drinking again and Martha is going to divorce him if he doesn't get out of rehab all dried out." But I digress.)

But believers do have a sense of justice and understand the difference between right and wrong. And watching a fellow believer being threatened, abused, and trampled by a loud, intolerant minority of same-sex marriage advocates was not something they could sit on the sidelines for. We simply asked them to stand up for the right of free speech and the opportunity to express a viewpoint without threats of retaliation from those who had a different opinion. For most Americans, "free speech" means we'd welcome *more* voices into the mix, not try to silence the ones that didn't scream the loudest. Surely it would shock the Founders to think that the First Amendment—a legacy they risked their lives for—would one day be subverted in order to close the marketplace of ideas to those unsanctioned by the elite ruling class.

It was a seminal moment for many faith-friendly people across America. All those people in line for a chicken sandwich looked around and, for the first time in a *long* time, didn't feel alone. The power of that was palpable. A feeling of courage welled up within us. The faith community, like the conservative political movement, is often divided, but the act of sharing a Chick-fil-A sandwich with millions of others was comforting and reassuring to us that we could stand as one.

On the other hand, many who stood in line for hours that day would later be disappointed to learn that their overwhelming outpouring of support for Dan Cathy and Chick-fil-A was seemingly spurned. Eighteen months later, in a March 2014 interview with the *Atlanta Journal-Constitution* newspaper, Cathy said he regretted his 2012 comments about same-sex marriage but claimed to still hold his beliefs personally. In a subsequent article in *National Journal*, the headline screamed, "Conservatives' Favorite Chicken Wants Out of the Culture Wars." The tone of the article implied that Cathy had raised the white flag of surrender. "Consumers want to do business with brands that they can interface with, that they can relate with," he was quoted as saying. "And it's probably very wise from our standpoint to make sure that we present our brand in a compelling way that the consumer can relate to."

My inbox was quickly stuffed with emails from disappointed and dispirited people who felt that Chick-fil-A had caved—that they'd gone the way of most major American companies and acquiesced to the public pressure to either be supportive of same-sex marriage or at least remain silent about it. Ironically, the throngs of people who had filled Chick-fil-A's stores and cash registers had done so to encourage people of faith to resist that very pressure, and to defend them from it. The "I wouldn't do *that* again" comment from Dan Cathy was a gut punch to many of those hardworking and God-fearing Americans who had hoped to see someone in the corporate world refuse to sit down and shut up when it came to their most heartfelt beliefs. For many who had stood for free speech in showing appreciation for Chick-fil-A, it seemed that the company was choosing to abandon them and opt for "no speech." For them, silence wasn't golden.

It was a completely different story for the Green family of Oklahoma City, Oklahoma, who own the family-held company Hobby Lobby. When Obamacare was passed, a provision would have forced companies to provide twenty different methods of birth control, four of which were abortifacient, meaning that the effect of them pharmaceutically was to end the life of a post-fertilized egg in the womb. The Green family is a devout and very committed Christian family, who, like Chick-Fil-A, close their stores on Sunday and are known for their philanthropic endeavors for many Christian causes. They already provided a very generous health insurance plan for their 13,000-plus employees, and were willing to fund sixteen of the twenty drugs mandated by Obamacare. They were not willing to provide those that constituted a medicinal abortion and asked for a waiver from the Obama administration. It seemed like an easy ask, since over forty exemptions had been meted out to unions and other big businesses that were pals of the President when they had asked for them. But in the Hobby Lobby case, the government said no. The decision was effectively to tell the Green family that it was fine for them to believe, but their religious convictions were limited to the government's tolerance. The ruling was a shock to people of faith across America. Hobby Lobby sued, and the case wound through the lower courts, making its way eventually to the Supreme Court. In June 2014, the Supremes ruled in favor of Hobby Lobby. Had the Green family lost, they would have been subject to fines of up to a $1.5 million a *day*. It would have put them out of business. The government expected that the threat of bankruptcy would cause them to fold. They greatly underestimated the authenticity of the Green family and the fact that their convictions were not for sale, rent, or surrender. It was indeed a "teachable moment," in a profile of courage. Christians across America cheered for a corporation which put Christ above cash.

Another very public dust-up in the culture clash involved the runaway hit reality show *Duck Dynasty*, which (for the uninitiated) followed an eccentric Louisiana family as they shared their lives hunting, fishing, making game calls, and just living day-to-day in a small northern Louisiana town where going to church is not considered radical. A firestorm erupted in December 2013 when *Duck Dynasty* patriarch Phil Robertson was quoted defending traditional marriage, albeit in graphic terms. *Duck Dynasty*—a certified money machine for A&E—was promptly and publicly dumped by the network after complaints from gay rights organizations. The network officially said it was "suspending" Phil from the show, but the family quickly made it clear that "If Papa is out, we're all out." It was apparent that A&E wasn't used to dealing with people for whom family was more valuable than money.

This conflict isn't just a matter of faith—it's a matter of class. During the 2008 election cycle, the serial adulterer, notorious liar, and all-round con man John Edwards spoke convincingly of "Two Americas," in which one America was blessed with prosperity, opportunity, and plenty while the other America was a land of poverty, need, and hopelessness. Edwards and I would certainly disagree as to the remedies for this problem, but he did describe it well, despite the scorn he got from some of the finer tables at Republican gatherings, where they couldn't imagine anyone actually living in poverty in the United States. *They* certainly didn't know anyone like that, not personally. Their seeming indifference to the struggling class had far more to do with why Republicans lost elections than did awkward, inopportune, or even indefensible comments from candidates.

But as much as there is a great divide in this country between the "haves" and the "have-nots," there is also a great chasm between the "believes" and the "believe-nots." And, increasingly, the "believes" in America have come to feel like cultural lepers—untouchables and undesirables—and an embarrassment to their fellow Americans who equate the holding of traditional views on marriage, religion, family, patriotism, and even the rule of law and the Constitution with ignorance and superstition. The snobbery and bold bigotry aimed at the "believes" goes unchecked and unchallenged by "believe-nots" who call themselves "mainstream." But such condescending attitudes toward people of faith are hardly mainstream in the geographical center of America.

The disconnect between the two can be jaw-dropping. When the

Duck Dynasty controversy erupted over the impulsive decision at A&E to "suspend" Phil for his views on marriage, some genius PR hack working at the popular Cracker Barrel restaurant chain jumped forward to declare that their stores would yank those dastardly *Duck Dynasty* products from the shelves. Yes, it's noteworthy when a New York-based company such as A&E reflexively shuts the lid on a "cash cow" like *Duck Dynasty*, but shockingly brain-dead for Cracker Barrel to drop *Duck Dynasty* products, given its Southern middle-class customer base. Accordingly, when that little announcement was made public, the reaction was nuclear. A torrent of raw outrage fell on Cracker Barrel, who appeared to have nothing but chicken on their menu. Their monumentally stupid decision was a kick in the groin to their core customers who eat meatloaf, corn bread, and black-eyed peas, and who may have considered what Duck Commander Phil Robertson said to be on the mild side.

Threats of boycotts lit up the Internet, and phone lines to individual stores were burning hotter than the pepper sauce they keep on the tables. It was only a matter of hours before someone decided to bring a brain to work at Cracker Barrel corporate headquarters and announce that the *Duck Dynasty* products would stay. Whoever in the Cracker Barrel organization made the original lamebrain decision is a mystery, but I'm pretty sure he wasn't born and raised in Montgomery, Alabama, or Jackson, Tennessee! It was yet another reminder of the growing gap between those in the catfish-and-corn bread crowd vs. those in the crepes-and-caviar set. The very fact that a large company made such a boneheaded decision so impulsively is indicative that losing the faith community is seen as less of a problem than ticking off the militant secularists. It defies logic and defies demographics.

While corporate America touts "tolerance" as the basis for its policies, there is very little tolerance for views that provide respect for the "believes." In April 2014, Mozilla, the online giant that runs the Internet browser Firefox, accepted the resignation of CEO Brendan Eich because he had donated all of $1,000 of his own money to the successful, voter-approved Proposition 8 campaign that affirmed natural marriage between a man and a woman in California. Gay rights activists demanded his firing after his six-year-old donation was made public. So much for tolerance! In fact, the chairwoman of Mozilla, Mitchell Baker, crowed, "We have employees with wide diversity of views. Our culture of openness extends to encouraging staff and community to share their beliefs and opinions in public" [The Mozilla Blog, April 3, 2014]. Amazingly, she said it with a straight face (no pun intended), and few in the mainstream press acknowledged the utter hypocrisy of Mozilla's position, which may be interpreted as this: "We are very *tolerant* as long as you hold the views of the loudest voice demanding conformity, which happens to agree with our own. We are utterly *intolerant* of people whose views on marriage reflect a major portion if not a majority of the American public. And we encourage people to share their beliefs and opinions as long as they aren't biblical and if they are, we demand they shut up or we'll fire their butts from our tolerant and diverse workforce." Equality has come to mean "sameness." Religious and personal freedom will not be tolerated!

Incidentally, Phil Robertson hasn't stopped talking about the dictates of his faith; he occasionally does so at his own church, before his own congregation. But a trip online will show comment after nasty comment that he and his "homophobic rant" should be silenced. (The "homophobic rant" in question was Phil's accurate quoting of Scripture during an Easter sermon.) In other words, he's not even allowed to express his personal religious views *behind the doors of his own church.*

American Christians used to hear about the "underground church" in totalitarian countries like the old Soviet Union, Cuba, and Communist China. But the times they are a-changin'. As those countries become increasingly open to freedom of religion, America is becoming more and more openly hostile. At the rate we're going, churches will one day have to go underground *here* to protect themselves from a totalitarian government and a "tolerant" culture that shamelessly censors dissent and acts with open bigotry and hatred toward people of faith . . . all in the name of "diversity" and "tolerance."

2

Guns and Why We Have Them

WHO ARE THE "GUN NUTS"? If you live among the urban elites (in Bubble-ville), you probably think gun owners are. If you live where I do (Bubba-ville), you probably think the real gun nuts are those firearm-fearing folks who, despite years of research to the contrary, still think a so-called "gun-free zone" makes life safer for the people in it. We know the truth of that bumper sticker whose common-sense message has long been the object of their scorn and ridicule: WHEN GUNS ARE OUTLAWED, ONLY OUTLAWS WILL HAVE GUNS! Anyone who thinks we can simply ban guns and—*poof*—make them all disappear, even from the hands of criminals, is deluded. Maybe on drugs (we have laws against those, too).

Clearly, city slickers who are more afraid of guns than of the criminals who might use them have a serious mental condition rendering them incapable of critical thinking. A February 2013 headline in the liberal *Boston Globe* pretty much sums it up: GUN CRIMES INCREASE IN MASSACHUSETTS DESPITE TOUGH GUN LAWS. It reminded me of the classic obtuse liberal media headline that always cracks up conservatives: CRIME DOWN DESPITE RISING PRISON POPULATIONS. Gee, how could putting more criminals in prison possibly make crime go down?

It's always a surprise to the progressives that if you take protection away from law-abiding people, you virtually assure criminals that when they go on a shooting rampage, they'll be the only ones armed. A gun-free zone is really just a *defense*-free zone: a designated area where law-abiding citizens have agreed—however reluctantly—to be defenseless. They accept that if a bad guy starts shooting up the place, he'll be the only person armed until the cops can get to the scene. As the saying goes, "When seconds count, the police are just *minutes* away!" Depending on where you are, they might even be hours away. (This is not just a Southern rural concern: The New York rap group Public Enemy had one of their biggest hits with "911 Is a Joke," a song about the slow police response time to calls for help from inner-city African Americans.) So, who ya gonna call? Try Smith & Wesson.

If you still think it's safer to wait around for the police than to allow law-abiding citizens to have concealed carry permits, consider this: Blogger Davi Barker analyzed thirty-two shooting rampages that were stopped by outside intervention. Among the roughly half where an armed citizen happened to be on hand and stopped the shooter, the average number of fatalities was 1.8. When the victims had to wait for the police to arrive, the average number of deaths was 14.29. "Car 54, Where *Are* You?!"

I have never known a time in my life when there were not guns in my house. I had my first BB gun, a Daisy Model 25, when I was not more than six years old. I remember how proud I was to have my very own air rifle (an actual thing, not like an "air guitar"). My parents gave me the Daisy BB gun for Christmas, but the deal was that I'd have to buy the BBs for it. They came in little round tubes that I could purchase at the local Western Auto store in Hope, Arkansas. I collected pop bottles in a little red wagon and turned them in for deposit at the nearby Piggly Wiggly supermarket so I'd have money for BBs. Early on, I couldn't shoot the gun without my dad there to drill into me all the safety lessons—drill them so hard that I remember them to this day! Over the years, I would graduate from the Daisy BB gun to a pump model pellet gun. The idea was to pump in air to increase velocity—the more pumps, the more firepower. It was basically a souped-up air rifle. By the time I was around nine years old, I'd bought my first real gun—a Springfield single shot .22-caliber rifle. A few years later, I would obtain a used .20-gauge shotgun.

I still have all those guns. Actually, one of my sons does, and I suspect he'll pass them on to his son. The BB gun and the single shot .22 rifle are in mint condition, but the air bladder on the old pellet gun is pretty well worn out, and the .20-gauge shotgun has seen better days. Even so, every time I see or handle those guns, I'm taken back to some of my fondest childhood memories. I grew up with guns, ammo, and shooting, but never considered murdering anyone. When I hear people with a profound ignorance of firearms say idiotic things like "children shouldn't grow up in a house where there are guns," I want to say, "More people are killed by cars than guns each year, so maybe children should grow up in a house with no cars around."

I knew where Dad's more powerful guns were kept and actually had access to them. If I had wanted to get to them, I could have, because we couldn't afford a gun safe; they took up a corner on the upper shelf in my parents' bedroom closet. But getting a chair or ladder to reach those guns never crossed my mind. Not once was I tempted to get one down and play with it or, worse, use it for the commission of a crime. I knew what those guns could do, and—foremost in my mind—I knew what my *dad* would do if he ever caught me even *thinking* about touching those guns without his supervision. I grew up with a very healthy respect for guns, but I had an absolute fear of my father! The guns at worst could kill me. I'm pretty sure my old man could do far worse than that to me.

It still catches me off guard when I have a conversation with an adult who has never owned a firearm, never fired one, and yet who speaks so passionately against them. How does this staggering lack of knowledge result in such an abundance of opinion? I can see the look of horror on the faces of friends of mine who have spent their lives in New York City when I talk about owning a wide variety of firearms. It's the look one would get announcing in a synagogue that one owns a bacon factory.

In the world I come from and choose to live in, "gun control" means that you hit the target.

Yes, guns can be dangerous. And in the wrong hands, the hands of someone who has a nefarious purpose or is careless and fails to respect the power of the firearm, or is mentally ill, they *are* dangerous. Fire in the hands of a cook is useful; fire in the hands of a pyromaniac is deadly. Water can be for bathing or drowning. A pair of scissors can be for opening a box or stabbing someone. An airplane can be an incredibly efficient vehicle to travel between distances, or it can be a missile to be flown into buildings. I don't, however, hear any suggestions that we ban fire, water, scissors, or airplanes. Well, schools have banned scissors, or even holding up two fingers in the shape of scissors, but that's another chapter.

Before I even touched a BB gun, I knew the fundamentals of handling a firearm: Always treat any firearm—*any*—as if it's loaded and cocked. Many people are accidentally killed by "unloaded guns" because some bright individual assumed the gun was unloaded. The most famous case was Terry Kath, the great original guitarist for the band Chicago. He was playing with his pistol and had just shown a nervous friend that the magazine was empty. Kath assured him that the gun wasn't loaded, then pointed it at his own head and pulled the trigger. Those were his last words. He'd overlooked the bullet already in the chamber.

I was taught that *all* guns are loaded; that is to say, even if you can see daylight through all the chambers, you are still to act as if the gun were loaded. *Just in case.* You never, ever point a gun at someone you don't intend to shoot. All my friends during my childhood and adolescent years were raised the same way.

So, let's review:

1. All guns are loaded (even if they aren't).
2. Never point a gun at any person, animal, or object unless you plan to shoot it.
3 Before you squeeze the trigger, know the target (and know what's *behind* the target).
4. If you aren't absolutely certain of what you're shooting, then *don't shoot.* (Shooting at leaves rustling or at a figure that "sure looks like a buck from here" would've cost me the use if not the ownership of my gun. I think my dad was looking more at me and whether I was safely handling my weapon than he was scanning the woods for things to hunt.)
5. Never leave a gun unattended; always know where it is and immediately put it back in its place when finished.
6. Never shoot an animal you don't plan to eat.

After every horrible mass murder involving a gun, political opportunists race to the microphones to make the strongest possible emotional pitch for watering down the Second Amendment—and weakening the liberty and safety of law-abiding citizens. Even if it's indisputable that their proposals wouldn't have had the slightest effect on the latest bloodbath, the gun-hating left and a sympathetic media team up. Together, they crank up the volume to "11" in calling for—no, *demanding*—immediate "action." It's understandable that emotions would run high; these incidents are heartbreaking and families are shocked and grieving. They want to do . . . something! Typically, they punctuate their urgent call with phrases like, "If just *one child* can be saved, it will be worth it!" We're supposed to go wobbly at that and acquiesce to expanded liberal legislation that punishes people who didn't break the law to somehow stop people who *did* break the law. I can't explain that rationally, because it isn't rational. The real "gun nuts" are the ones who know the *least* about firearms or freedom, but who *most* want to make sure the good guys are unarmed when the bad guys decide to murder a few.

A study by Mark Gius of Quinnipiac University, published in *Applied Economics Letters*, showed what Left Coast bubbleheads and East Coast bubble-dwellers just can't believe—that if guns are taken away from people who haven't broken the law, gun violence will *increase*. Conclusions were based on data gathered between 1980 and 2009, so this represents one of the most significant longitudinal surveys ever done on the effect of gun laws on gun violence.

Overall, the study showed that gun-related murder rates were 10 percent higher if a state had *more* restrictive laws relative to concealed carry. Perhaps even more startling to the Hollywood hypocrites who fill their movies with violence and their pockets with profits, but who think Southern gun owners like me are the problem, is this inconvenient truth: Banning so-called "assault" weapons results in murder rates that are 19.3 percent *higher* than when no such laws are in effect.

FactCheck.org revealed that from 2001 to 2007, gun ownership in the United States rose from 84 to 88.8 guns per 100 people. Yet in 2011, there were 50.8 gun-aggravated assaults and 45.8 gun robberies per 100,000 people, the lowest rates since 2004. The murder rate from guns was 3.59 per 100,000, which marked the lowest rate since 1981. Granted, gun suicides were up to 6.28 per 100,000, the highest rate since 1998, but was that a gun issue or a mental health issue?

Most of the incidents of mass carnage that sparked calls to "take action *now!*" have occurred in gun-free zones. Makes sense, in that the shooter is relatively assured that there won't be an armed citizen around to fight back. Good citizens tend to obey a law, even one they don't like. A criminal doesn't abide by the laws we already have, so why should we expect him to adhere to any new and more restrictive ones we pass?

Forget the assumption that a gun-free zone will lower the risk of falling victim to a gun crime. John Lott, former chief economist with the U.S. Sentencing Commission and noted expert on gun laws, has noted that, with just one exception, every mass shooting involving three or more deaths since 1950 has happened in a gun-free zone. That one exception was the attack on Congresswoman Gabby Giffords in a shopping center parking lot in Arizona. Every other one happened in a gun-free zone, in large part because "gun-free zone" translates to bad guys as "sitting duck zone."

Mother Jones is an ultra-leftist magazine, and it's fair to say that their position on guns is about as supportive as Michelle Obama would be of passing out free candy and soft drinks to school kids in the cafeteria. But even in their attempt to justify new restrictions on law-abiding gun owners, *Mother Jones* ["A Guide to Mass Shootings in America," July 20, 2012] found that of the sixty-nine mass shootings in the past thirty years, the majority were committed by people who "were mentally troubled—and many displayed signs of it before setting out to kill." (And I'm thinking that maybe we just didn't *notice* the signs in other cases.) Yet there is little said by the elites about the need to ramp up "brain control." Ironically, many on the left strenuously oppose mental health intervention on the principle that it violates the privacy rights of the patient.

One of the most fascinating guests I've interviewed on my Fox News Channel television show was Dr. Suzanna Gratia Hupp, a victim of the Luby's Cafeteria shooting in Killeen, Texas, back in 1991. A crazed gunman killed twenty-three people and wounded twenty others after crashing his truck through the window. Dr. Gratia Hupp was dining there with her parents when it happened. At the sound of the gunfire, they all dived for cover. She started to reach into her purse for her pistol, only to remember that because she was a good, law-abiding citizen, she had dutifully left her gun in her vehicle instead of carrying it in. She watched helplessly as both her parents were murdered. She would go on to say that she wished she'd broken the law that day and kept her pistol in her purse, for she felt that her parents might still be alive if she had. Her compelling story helped pass a concealed carry law in Texas, and she was elected to the state legislature in 1995.

Opponents to the concealed carry law in Texas pointed to a coming "wild, wild West" and predicted that the increased bloodshed from gun violence would be staggering. So, what really happened? Gun deaths in the Lone Star State went *down* from an all-time high of 1,835 in 1991 to fewer than 1,000 in 2013.

One of my worst days as governor was March 24, 1998. While flying home on the Arkansas State Police airplane from a governors' meeting in Washington, D.C., I received a call that there had been a shooting at the Westside Middle School in Jonesboro, Arkansas. We landed shortly after that, and the details started coming in: Two boys, aged thirteen and eleven, had stolen guns from the young boy's grandfather, taken a van from the older boy's mother, and gone to Westside Middle School. One of the boys went into the school, pulled a fire alarm, and then ran to join the other in a wooded area close to the enclosed school playground. After the students exited the building for the fire alarm and the door locked behind them, the two boys opened fire with high-powered rifles, killing four of their classmates and a teacher and wounding ten others. I spent the rest of the day and evening in meetings with the State Police director, the Department of Education director, and legal counsel in my office and in phone contact with local officials, including the school superintendent. I spent the entire next day at the school, speaking with faculty and staff in a closed-door meeting, and then went to the hospital to visit with survivors of the shooting, their families, and as many of the victims' families as were available to see me. The entire state was in shock.

The shock turned to rage when it became known that under Arkansas law, the two boys could be held only until their eighteenth birthdays. Even though they had committed one of the most heinous crimes in the state's history and were among the youngest people in American history to commit mass murder, they were, by legal definition, juveniles. At no time in the 162-year history of the state—not at any time since the writing of the state constitution in 1874—had it occurred to anyone that we should enact laws to cover the possibility that eleven- and thirteen-year-olds would commit mass murder. Federal charges were brought against the boys that would allow them to be held until the ripe old age of twenty-one, but that was small consolation to families of the victims—or to anyone else, for that matter.

Jonesboro was one of the first school campus shootings in recent times, and the international news media swarmed there, overwhelming the town with coverage of the two boys and their cold-blooded killing of innocent classmates and a teacher. I was asked by Katie Couric on the *Today* show if I thought the shooting was indicative of some kind of "Southern gun culture." Frankly, I found the question condescending and insulting, as if to suggest that Southerners were predisposed toward senseless killing and had a reckless disregard for responsible gun ownership. I told Katie that while Southerners frequently owned guns, they were most certainly not predisposed to murder people. I also noted that when Colin Ferguson boarded a train in December 1993 and started firing, no one suggested that he was part of a "Northeastern murder culture." I then said, "Katie, last time I checked, that happened on Long Island, New York, not Long Island, Arkansas." When I said that, Katie cut to break and my interview was over.

I'm still a bit sensitive when someone from Bubble-ville tries to portray those of us in flyover country as being "in love with guns." I'm not at all in love with guns. I love freedom. I love my country and the Constitution. I love my family and would sacrifice my life to protect them. I would sacrifice someone *else's* life if that person tried to harm them. If a gun helps me protect them better than I could with my bare hands or a knife, or by swinging a bat, or flailing away with a zucchini squash, then I'll unapologetically use a gun. Any questions?

Unfortunately, much of the discussion over firearm ownership centers on hunting, with anti-gun activists always insisting their new restrictions would not infringe on hunting. Well, I'm a hunter. I hunt ducks, deer, and turkey and have also hunted antelope in Wyoming and pheasant in Iowa. But the Second Amendment isn't about hunting. The Second Amendment is about preserving all the rights we possess as citizens. The Bill of Rights is not about restricting the activities of *the people*. There is absolutely nothing in the Bill of Rights that tells a citizen what he or she is prohibited from doing. The Bill of Rights explicitly tells *government* what it can't do. The First Amendment tells the government to back off and leave people alone when it comes to their inherent right to free speech, freedom of the press, freedom of religion, freedom to assemble, and even the freedom to protest the government. And to make sure the government didn't dare try to take those rights away, our Founders followed up the First Amendment with the Second, which grants citizens the right to "bear arms" (not to be confused by my spelling-challenged redneck friends as "*bare* arms," though we still have no federal law against that, last time I checked). As radical as it sounds to us today, the purpose of the Second Amendment was not to guarantee us the right to hunt deer, but to make sure we can protect our freedoms from those who would take them away—including our own government, should it become as tyrannical as the one that launched the revolution in the first place.

If you watched the first season of the mesmerizing AMC television series *Turn*, about spying for George Washington during the Revolutionary War, you saw the occupying British forces in Setauket, Long Island, manufacture a pretense to round up all the guns of the people who lived there, to keep them helpless in case the rebellion came to their town. Anyone disobeying the British command would be hanged for treason. Americans who fought to free themselves from this kind of tyranny would have been the *last* people to restrict gun ownership within the populace!

On three different occasions I've been to Auschwitz and Birkenau, the infamous Nazi death camps about an hour from Krakow, Poland. I've made repeated trips to Yad Vashem in Jerusalem, the memorial to the victims of the Holocaust, and to the Holocaust Museum in Washington, D.C. A haunting question has always been, "Why did the Jews obey the Nazis and march from their homes and businesses to the train stations, boarding cattle cars so they could be hauled off to camps of mass murder and torture?" The inescapable conclusion, at least in part: because the Nazis had guns and the Jews didn't. The Nazis had systematically removed all firearms from Jewish homes. Ownership or possession of guns by Jews was outlawed. From *The New York Times* on November 8, 1938:

> The Berlin Police president, Count Wolf Heinrich von Helldorf, announced that as a result of police activity in the last few weeks, the entire Jewish population of Berlin had been "disarmed," with the confiscation of 2,569 hand weapons; 1,702 firearms; and 20,000 rounds of ammunition. Any Jews still found in possession of weapons without valid licenses are threatened with the severest punishment.

On November 9, Adolph Hitler, Propaganda Minister Joseph Goebbels, and other Nazi chiefs took the next step by issuing this order:

> All Jewish stores are to be destroyed immediately. Jewish synagogues are to be set on fire. The Fuhrer wishes that the police do not intervene. All Jews are to be disarmed. In the event of resistance, they are to be shot immediately.

And on November 10, headlines read, NAZIS SMASH, LOOT, AND BURN JEWISH SHOPS AND TEMPLES. *Kristallnacht* (Night of Broken Glass) shattered more than glass. It shattered the last vestige of freedom held by the Jews.

But how did the Nazis know which Jews had guns? It wasn't hard to figure that out. In 1928—before Hitler came to power—the Weimar Republic had passed a gun law requiring the police department to keep detailed records on gun owners. Hitler had passed even more gun control laws in the first part of 1938.

What little resistance they met was from those who'd kept their weapons despite the demands or who had found a way to secure more weapons by bartering or stealing them. The most significant resistance was the uprising in the Warsaw Ghetto in 1943, when a handful of

Polish resisters fought valiantly with a limited number of handguns. Of course, they were vastly outgunned and outnumbered by the Nazis, but their resistance was a setback to what the Nazis had planned as a simple mop-up operation.

My friends in anti-gun cities like New York typically give me strange looks if I talk about guns. I've had conversations that became awkward because I knew that my owning guns—quite a few of them, actually—made them uncomfortable. You'd think I had an opium den in my home! These experiences leave me wondering how people can hold such definite views on something they know so little about.

The late actor and former NRA president Charlton Heston must have had that feeling constantly, living in the limousine liberalism of Bubble-ville. Many of his showbiz colleagues who knew nothing about firearms (but hated them passionately and supported every new gun law) were slapped hard by reality during the 1992 LA riots. Heston loved to recall how his anti-gun friends called and frantically begged to borrow one of his guns to protect their homes and families. They wailed, "I tried to buy one, but they have this waiting period!" [GunsEditor.word -press.com. April 17, 2010] I guess it had never occurred to them that anyone who really needs a gun for self-defense probably needs it *now*, not two or three weeks from now.

In the 2008 Presidential campaign, I had a meeting/interview with the executive news staff of the Associated Press in Washington, D.C. One of the editors turned the conversation to gun control, saying matter-of-factly and with a certain tone of harrumph in her voice, "Well, *surely*, you agree that we ought to ban 'semiautomatic' weapons because no one needs a semiautomatic gun to go hunting." Stunned at her ignorance, I replied, "Ma'am,"—the use of "ma'am" as a way to express contempt in the nicest possible way is another Southern thing—"Ma'am, I duck hunt with a semiautomatic shotgun, a Benelli Super Black Eagle .12 gauge." The shocked look on her face didn't reveal that she'd been caught with her brains in her back pocket (although she had), but that she imagined me shredding ducks on the wing with something akin to an anti-aircraft gun. I asked if she knew what "semiautomatic" actually means. Her silence was a very loud answer. So I tried to explain that semiautomatic simply means that the gun automatically loads the next shell to save me from having to manually pump, cock, or reload the gun, but that my squeezing the trigger is still necessary for each individual round fired. I tried to explain that something being "semiautomatic" has nothing to do with lethality or power. It's just a type of gun. In fact, it's practically *every* type of gun. The concept has been around since 1885. I don't think she got it. But then, most of the media people writing or blabbing about guns have no clue what they're talking about.

The term "assault weapon" is one of the most misunderstood designations for a firearm. In a sense, *all* weapons are "assault" weapons— even a rock, if it's being hurled at someone! When people throw out that term, they typically mean a rifle that looks scary because it resembles the military-style rifles carried by soldiers and SWAT teams. Immediately after the Sandy Hook tragedy, I was in a meeting in New York when the subject of "assault rifles" came up. The general consensus among those in the meeting was that such a weapon was way too powerful for individuals to own. When I mentioned that I owned more than one, I thought people were going to dive under the table for protection. I explained that an AR-15 shoots powerful shells for sure, the .223 or 5.56 caliber, but it's actually *less* powerful than the Weatherby .300-magnum rifle that I hunt deer with. Most people expressing their disdain for the AR-15 do so on the basis of it being called an "assault rifle" or because its various features give it a serious or even sinister appearance. Most all those "scary" features are actually quite practical, like the adjustable stock or the flash suppressor on the barrel, or various options such as a pistol grip on the stock. None of those features have a thing to do with making the gun more deadly. Some even make it safer. They are practical features that offer better stability and make the rifle lighter, more adjustable for people of various sizes, and less likely to overheat. There are many rifles more powerful, but the popularity of the AR-15 is due to its versatility and adaptability—not because it's more dangerous than others.

I'm not trying to sell the AR-15. My point is that the breathless attempt by the "Bubble" crowd to ban it is based on ignorance and fear—the very things that the "Bubbas" are accused of being driven by. What irony!

I remember when GOP Presidential candidate Phil Gramm, then a U.S. senator from Texas, was asked how many guns he had. His classic reply, delivered in that characteristic Texas drawl of his, was memorable: "I own more shotguns than I need, but not as many as I want." [CBS News, December 19, 2012].

I don't expect that everybody living in urban areas will come to understand life in the land of God, guns, grits, and gravy. But if you don't understand it, and have no clue as to why we live or believe as we do, then, please, just leave us alone and let us go on believing that the Second Amendment exists not so we can "hoard guns," but so we can hoard liberty.

Do us that favor, and when the barbarians show up at your door and you frantically phone us for help, maybe we'll loan you a gun.

3

The Culture of Crude

IN THE 1960S, the then-avant-garde television show *Rowan & Martin's Laugh-In* was a groundbreaking mix of political satire and wacky comedy, with recurring features like the "Flying Fickle Finger of Fate" focusing attention on some quirky news story of the week. Millions tuned in each week to see how far the ensemble cast, led by comedians Dan Rowan and Dick Martin, would push the boundaries of topics and taboos. Dick Martin would "bet [his] sweet bippy" as the laugh track went wild and we all speculated as to what a "bippy" might be. The talented cast included Goldie Hawn (who danced innocently in body paint and a bikini), Henry Gibson, Arte Johnson, Jo Anne Worley, Ruth Buzzi, and Lily Tomlin. It was cutting-edge humor but done with a light touch, occasionally controversial for the late sixties but considered tame and sometimes even lame by today's standards.

Fast-forward to 2013, and the *MTV Video Music Awards*, where television audiences were treated to the "Flying Fearless Finger of Foam" as Miley Cyrus contorted her barely clad, barely legal-age body in a disgustingly pornographic performance that showed just about everything she had—except talent—and focused national attention on a new term, "twerking," which describes a vulgar movement better saved for a stripper pole than prime-time television. Her awkward choreography and intentionally nasty gyrations, which involved her use of a giant foam finger as a prop to simulate pleasuring herself, were her way of shedding not only her clothes but her Disney character "Hannah Montana" once and for all. In the very year that child stars from long ago like Shirley Temple and Mickey Rooney were dying off, the next generation of young "stars" were making their mark in the entertainment industry, not for any display of exceptional talent, but for the shameless and tasteless display of their quite ordinary private parts. Every human being has sexual parts, but not everyone is endowed with truly great talent for singing, dancing, acting, or playing an instrument. Removing one's clothing is not especially unique—most people do it every day. But to celebrate an especially vulgar and graceless way of undressing by making it the centerpiece of a stage act is a sad substitute for real talent.

Even sadder is that our culture has sunk so low that lewd behavior is rewarded in the marketplace with increased sales. The Miley Cyrus hit "Wrecking Ball" went to number one. (She also made a music video for that song in which she was *completely* naked.) Talentless young women become "famous for being famous" and get their own reality shows (truly a topic unto itself), contracts for product lines, and lucrative endorsement deals after turning up in sex tapes that "somehow" get "leaked." We truly have become the "Culture of Crude."

When I was growing up (admittedly a while back), the first hour of prime time TV was called the "family hour." Back in the day, most young children actually had bedtimes—now an outmoded concept for many— and it was assumed that they might be allowed to watch just that first hour or so before heading off to bed. So that hour had strict broadcast standards for—get ready—*decency*. Maybe some of the restrictions seem ridiculously quaint now, but we've gone 180 degrees in the opposite direction. It's during the "family hour" that the sitcom *2 Broke Girls* broke all barriers of good taste with the crudest and (by now) most predictable sex jokes imaginable. Really, you don't want me to quote even the tamest of these; trust me on this. And that's just one example; I could certainly cite others.

I love really funny, insightful stand-up comedy. It's great that women have come into their own in that field, both as stand-ups and as comedic actresses, and there are some fantastic examples. But today we have a number of female stand-ups who spout the crudest possible lines about their own sex lives. In fact, that's pretty much their whole act! Maybe they looked at some of the male comics who also work blue and decided that's what you have to do to succeed. They wouldn't want to work clean and become failed nobodies, like Bill Cosby and Jerry Seinfeld. (Funny women such as Rita Rudner, Elayne Boosler, and Carol Leifer also did pretty well without resorting to filth.) Is this what "equal opportunity" for female comics means now? If so, it's brought the whole profession down.

Some rare comic geniuses like George Carlin or Richard Pryor used dirty words as part of a satirical examination of societal taboos. But most comics just use them to get a cheap, easy laugh because creating witty, original humor is *hard*. Broadcast standards once forced comedians to be funny without being filthy if they ever wanted to land that big break on *The Tonight Show*. Today, smutty jokes that used to be relegated to smoke-filled clubs appear regularly on major networks during the former "family hour." If these comedians had to work clean, I don't know what they would say. Their "stand-up" would consist of nothing but them simply standing up on stage for twenty minutes.

I love movies. I especially enjoy the power of film to tell a story and to evoke emotion with a brilliant blend of acting, dialogue, and cinematography, backed by an equally brilliant soundtrack. But I must admit, there have been times when movies I loved for the story or the production quality or the sheer magnificence of the actors' performances were spoiled by incessant and gratuitous profanity that seemed to have nothing whatsoever to do with the content of the films. In some cases, it provided a total distraction from what could have been a powerful message. Understand, I'm no prude who wilts at the sound of a four-letter word; I've heard every term in the book and maybe a few that didn't even make the book. But I don't particularly enjoy having my ears used as a garbage can to substitute for some screenwriter's lack of creativity. I've often left a theater saying, "Why is there so much unnecessary profanity in that movie? No one actually talks like that!"

Then I started working each week in New York. Guess what? People *do* talk like that! Even in business settings and in mixed company of men and women, I realized that some people's vocabulary was clearly limited to a small inventory of nouns and verbs with large doses of the "f-bomb" interspersed throughout. It must have seemed like maturity to those who found a way to make every third word a profane utterance, but it's always struck me that the ultimate definition of profanity is the forcible expression of a feeble mind.

In 2014, the release of the Oscar-nominated *The Wolf of Wall Street* sparked a lively discussion about the amount of over-the-top profanity and sexual activity that's required to portray the hedonistic lifestyles of those real-life wolves, whose self-absorbed, predatory financial activities broke the economy and ruined the lives of millions of hardworking Americans. It was reported by *Time* magazine that in the Martin Scorsese epic, which clocked in at an excruciating three hours, the "f-word" was used a staggering 506 times, which averages out to the vile reference being said 2.81 times a *minute!* There's not enough soap in all of New York City to wash out a mouth so polluted.

For those of us who grew up in the South, there was a basic code of conduct that a man didn't "cuss" in front of a woman. (In the South, it was "cussing," not "cursing.") Cussing in the presence of a lady was considered trashy. Of course, if the "lady" wasn't much of a lady and did her own share of cussing, all bets were off. But it was really not a compliment to a female for guys to freely let their verbal manure fly within her earshot. There was, for some guys, a kind of attraction to girls whose language would fit in just fine in the men's locker room, but that was not the kind of girl you took home to "meet Mama." Over the years, those conventions of speech and behavior have gradually become less common, but sadly so. There was a certain dignity about a lady conducting herself publicly in a way that let you know she felt deserving of respectful treatment. And the word "gentlemen" used to be a title men aspired to, not just a sign on the bathroom door at upscale restaurants.

Such regard for women wasn't confined to a particular socioeconomic circle, either. The difference was not rich vs. poor. A person might be poor, but that didn't excuse him or her from good manners. Some very affluent people engaged in coarse speech, and some who were desperately poor would never have been heard grinding out language better suited for a barnyard than a ballroom. Propriety and class aren't economic conditions, but *moral* conditions as evidenced by a person's conduct.

Perhaps I shouldn't be surprised that our culture has descended to the lowest levels of linguistic slime, given the fact that we're bombarded constantly with the antics of celebrities trying to outdo each other with their exhibitionism. (I've seen dusty pickup truck windshields that were less see-through than the mesh "dress" Rihanna recently "wore" on the red carpet at a fashion show. One fashion critic said that if she weren't so famous, that dress might have been seen as a trashy bid for attention. Well, good thing famous people never do that!)

Along with the rise in narcissism and exhibitionism, the anonymity provided online has certainly prompted the proliferation of the disgustingly crude. People who would *never* say such things about another person to his or her face feel unrestrained in their ability to spew snarky sneers in blogs or tweets—especially when they use cyber-pseudonyms that allow them to hide behind an electronic mask of cowardice.

I've had people say unkind and rude things right to my face, but that's fairly rare. Most people wait until they can get home, fire up their keyboards, open the spigot, and let the verbal sewage flow. In that medium, I've been accused of just about every crime imaginable. I plead innocent: For the record, I didn't kidnap the Lindbergh baby, I didn't sink the *Titanic,* and I wasn't standing on the grassy knoll in Dealey Plaza in Dallas on November 22, 1963. But I've probably been associated with all those things and more on someone's silly little blog.

Facts aren't necessary in order to post, and there is no editor between the originator and the end user. When I speak to students and they ask me about journalism, I sometimes say that there's no such thing anymore. Journalism, in the ideal sense, is a noble profession in which objective people gather facts that are verified by multiple sources, questioned and checked by an editor, and then presented dispassionately to the reader to allow the end user to form an opinion about them. In today's so-called "information" society, there are often *no* sources ("experts say . . .") and no editor—or else the information is an agenda-driven one—disseminated with a very deliberate spin.

During the Grammy Awards of 2013, the opening musical act was Jay-Z and his megastar wife Beyoncé, pushing the limits of network television with a "song" called "Drunk in Love." Beyoncé must have been confused when she agreed to humiliate herself by performing in a way that prompted this comment from author Charlotte Hays (whose book *When Did White Trash Become the New Normal?* says it all): "Honestly, I didn't want to watch Jay-Z and Beyoncé's foreplay."

The song contains words and imagery so graphic that they would never make it through the editing process of this book. (Not that I would want them to!) But the onstage gyrations, bare flesh, and (most of) the lyrics did make it onto CBS, again during the smoldering remnants of what used to be the "family hour."

My reaction: "Why?" Beyoncé is incredibly talented—gifted, in fact. She has an exceptional set of pipes and can actually sing. She is a terrific dancer—without the explicit moves best left for the privacy of her bedroom. Jay-Z is a very shrewd businessman, but I wonder: Does it occur to him that he is arguably crossing the line from husband to pimp by exploiting his wife as a sex object? Like other once-wholesome young stars such as Justin Bieber and the aforementioned Miley Cyrus (who responds to critics by giving them "the finger" of foam), Beyoncé has traveled far, far, far from her days as a part of the girl-group Destiny's Child. Yet she was a huge, breakout star before going X-rated. She proved she doesn't need to lower herself to this type of crude exploitation to be a megastar. She must know that millions of young girls look up to her as a role model to emulate. And she even has a daughter herself now. So *why* has she done this?

Jay-Z and Beyoncé are BFFs with President Obama and the First Lady. I've generally admired the parenting instincts of the First Couple, so it's hard for me to believe they've actually listened to those lyrics. Jay-Z and Beyoncé have been to the White House numerous times, but how can it be that the Obamas let Sasha and Malia listen to that trash? Apparently they do, since President Obama made this comment in a 2012 interview with *Glamour* magazine:

> We actually share tastes in hip-hop and rap music but we don't listen to it together, because some of the language in there would embarrass me—at least while I'm listening to it with her.

Oh. I see. The important thing is for him not to be *embarrassed*. (Guess he has enough to be embarrassed about, every night on the news! But I digress.)

It's no small wonder why the culture has become so crude when fathers and mothers allow and even encourage their children to devour vulgar, misogynistic, and violent material when it's performed by "cool" people like Jay-Z and Beyoncé. With the First Lady so concerned about making sure her daughters' bellies don't ingest unhealthy food, how can she let their brains ingest obnoxious and toxic mental poison in the form of song lyrics? If lived out, those lyrics would be far more devastating to someone's health than a cupcake.

Where are the feminists in all of this? Why do most remain silent in the face of such hateful and exploitive treatment of women? Do they really think it's okay to treat women with contempt and reckless disregard for them as persons? How can they not be screaming that women are reduced to mere objects whose primary function is to serve as sex slaves to violent, narcissistic men? Is it okay to objectify women and treat them as toys, with body parts to be played with and tossed aside? Apparently so, if the one doing the exploiting is liberal; that is to say, "right on the issues." If there is any greater display of hypocrisy than that of liberals who pretend to be all about "empowering women" while remaining silent as women are treated with less respect than some people give to a rental car, or some other piece of disposable property, I can't imagine what it would be.

Most people exhibiting crude behavior or language aren't doing anything illegal, but they're contributing to a culture that is abrasive, rude, obnoxious, and just plain mean. When we treat others with reckless disregard for their personhood and act as if human feelings don't exist—or don't matter—we create an atmosphere in which it becomes much easier to damage them *physically*. Once we dehumanize someone, we feel much less sensitive about what we say or do. This was one of the tragic lessons of the Holocaust. It would have been difficult if not impossible to abruptly march ten million Jews, disabled people, elderly people, and mentally ill people to their deaths, but the first order of business was to create a climate in which certain people could be singled out as inferior beings. As such an abominable notion becomes ingrained into the culture, it's not that far a journey to believing that some people are not fully human, that they're disposable and expendable and don't deserve the same rights and protections as "us."

The same false premise was used to provide the permission for and the defense of slavery. And the same root evil that created slavery, genocide, "honor killings," and the Holocaust is growing in our society today, with some people deemed "less than" others, whether it's because they are unborn children, people of other ethnicities, or increasingly, people of faith.

My mother would have slapped me silly if she ever thought I was mistreating someone. It was one of the absolutes that she hammered into me. (Okay, maybe "slapped" and "hammered" are poor word choices in this context, but I think you know what I mean.) She'd say, "You don't make fun of people!" And even though my mother was raised and lived in a segregated South for most of her life, she insisted that I treat all people with respect. If she had ever caught me saying something disrespectful of a black person or speaking to a black adult with other than "Yes, Sir/No, Sir; Yes, Ma'am/No Ma'am," I would have been on the wrong end of one of those little green twigs off the bushes in our backyard. "Switches" were a common way for my legs and my butt to experience the full authority of my parents' sense of propriety. I'm sure that many modern parents and child experts will be aghast that I experienced corporal punishment at home (and at school, for that matter). But the temporary pain those switches inflicted did me no discernible harm, and, to this day, I wouldn't dare speak disrespectfully to someone for fear my mother would find a way to leave Heaven, come back to Earth, and give me Hell!

4

"Uniform Diversity" —An Oxymoron

"Variety is the spice of life!"

At least that's what we've been told. Diversity training is now standard at large corporations, to ensure that everyone joins our pursuit of the Holy Grail of diversity! Except that the goal doesn't appear to be diversity at all. When we say we want diversity, what we *really* seem to want is uniformity. God help the poor soul who utters an opinion that isn't politically correct or that doesn't jibe with what Hollywood thinks. There's plenty of room for opinions—as long as they conform to those held by members of the left who control the media and entertainment industries. We've seen the heavy hand of Hollywood and the noose of New York used repeatedly whenever someone surfaces from flyover country with a view that's perfectly normal in rural America but scorned on both coasts as if it were the belief in a flat Earth or unicorns.

In May 2014, brothers David and Jason Benham were recruited by HGTV to star in a reality TV series called *Flip It Forward*. These two young and handsome brothers had made millions flipping houses, and the show was to feature them teaching others how to buy, fix, and sell for profit. But Right Wing Watch, a hate group which exists to make sure no one utters an opinion that's out of line with the left, threatened to force a boycott of the show because the two siblings are devout

Christians who had expressed pro-life and pro-traditional marriage views in their *personal lives*. Though nothing about the show would have touched on their spiritual beliefs or sexual politics, the fix was in. HGTV folded like a cheap tent in a tornado and pulled the plug on the show. David and Jason had attended pro-life rallies and had been outspoken about their belief in marriage, but since *Flip It Forward* had not even aired yet, no one could say they were using the show as a platform to talk about their faith or their politics. In fact, their comments were made two years before *Flip It Forward* was even announced. But in today's climate of "believe like me or we'll put you out of business," HGTV joined other cowardly corporations and capitulated to the pressure of the bullies. To their everlasting credit, the Benham brothers, despite possibly losing millions of dollars in potential TV and endorsement income, took it all in stride and commented, "If our faith costs us a TV show, then so be it."

Wow! It was refreshing to see two young men put the value of their convictions above the value of money. They offered no apology—no public promise to attend sensitivity training. They didn't agree to meet with Planned Parenthood or GLAAD and have a "dialogue" about why their views were so offensive and wrong. They just said, "Too bad if we can't be on TV, but God is more important to us than a bigger paycheck."

The controversy over the Benham brothers escalated a few weeks later when their banking partner, SunTrust, bowing to pressure from the anti-Christian activists, announced that they would sever ties with them. Well, that didn't go over very well with the customers of SunTrust who either *were* Christian or who at least had read the First Amendment and thought that destroying people's livelihoods because of their religious beliefs seemed more like the practices of North Korea, not North America. Within hours, SunTrust danced the Emily Litella Shuffle ("Never mind!"), pinned the blame on a third party vendor (who insisted it was SunTrust's idea), and announced they were reversing the decision. Gee, that was quick! This time, the lion woke up and roared.

But is this what "diversity" looks like? Have we moved toward *fewer* voices and viewpoints rather than more? How is that making our culture more diverse? Let's face it, diversity is "code" for *uniformity*. The goal of the PC police and the zealots on the extreme left is to eliminate any voice that *is* diverse and to insist on compliance and acceptance of the words, definitions, actions, and attitudes that they have crafted around their own lifestyles and beliefs.

We are truly living as if we were characters in the novel *1984*. In the classic 1949 George Orwell book, words mean the opposite of what they say. "Newspeak" may as well be the official language of the United States. I'll not be at all surprised to go to an ATM someday and on the screen where it asks me to select a language, see that my options no longer include English but *do* include Newspeak! We are audaciously living the novel, and, sadly, just like the good doublethinking Party members described in the book, we see it but we don't. We accept the destruction of clarity and variety in our language and the utter contempt toward common sense. By conforming to these changes, we are unindicted co-conspirators.

For example, consider the word "racist." If one ignores President Obama's race and criticizes his policies or tells jokes about him, treating him exactly the way every other President has been treated, one is called a racist. Wouldn't it be racism if we treated him *differently* because of his race?

If one insists that women, by virtue of their gender, comprise a victim class needing and deserving special assistance from the government in all walks of life in order to be "equal" and for life to be "fair," then how is this feminism, which insists that women are identical to men and should be treated as such? Shouldn't women be incensed that instead of being regarded as equals, they are assumed to be helpless victims waiting for rescue by a government run mostly by men?

For instance, if you question the wisdom of sending women into combat, you are a sexist who refuses to acknowledge that women are as physically strong and psychologically tough as men. But the same "women-empowerment" activists also want all printed matter to come with a warning label if it includes "trigger words" that might even subconsciously remind delicate females of sensitive subjects such as sexual assault, forcing them to seek the nearest Victorian-era fainting couch.

Calling a communist a communist is "hate speech." Calling a conservative a Nazi is "free speech." A Christian who espouses traditional biblical doctrine is a "bigot," but the people who tell Christians to shut up and go away are the "open-minded" voices of tolerance.

"Pro-life" people like me are identified with the negative-sounding term "anti-abortion," while those who support abortion get the positive label "pro-choice," even though the only "choice" they really get behind is the choice to abort the baby. Know who doesn't get a choice at all? The baby.

If employers and colleges are forced to accept candidates of certain races over better-qualified candidates, based solely on their race, that's "affirmative action" against "racism." So let's make sure we understand: In order to keep an employer or college admissions office from preferring one person over another because of race, we *order* them to prefer one person over another because of race. Got it?

Consider the word "affordable." Congress passed the "Affordable" Care Act, but many people who had been able to afford their health insurance discovered that Obamacare was quite *un*-affordable when their rates, deductibles, and co-pays dramatically increased. The *Los Angeles Times* reported on the story of Maria Berumen, who was advised to see a specialist for numbness in her arm. She tried four different specialists, all listed by her insurer and the state's "Cover California" Web site as Obamacare participants, but all four turned her away. She started digging, and this led to the exposure of so-called "phantom networks," lists given to the public of "participating" doctors and hospitals that actually weren't participating at all. (Fake lists in a government healthcare system? Who would have thought?) So, what happens when a private business takes money for promised services that it has no intention of providing? We call this fraud, and it's supposed to result in prison and big fines. But under Obamacare, we call it the "Bronze Plan," and we reelect the person who sold it to us.

The essence of science has historically been to question, to search, to challenge results by attempting to replicate them, and to be open to new discoveries—not to accept a prevailing view as final. In other words, the debate is *never* over, and to make such a claim is anti-science. But in today's demand for uniformity, one who *questions* the politically driven agenda of global warming is labeled as "anti-science," even though there are many legitimate scientists on that side. The very term "global warming" has had to be replaced by "climate change" (and yet again in some circles to "climate chaos" or "climate disruption") because it was simply too much at odds with Americans' perception that the planet isn't consistently warming but rather going through temperature cycles, as it has done throughout its history. I recall that in the early seventies, my college classes and articles in *Time* (June 24, 1974) and *Newsweek* (April 28, 1975) magazines warned of the imminent threat of global *cooling*. We were told that "the science is settled" and that without drastic and urgent action, the planet would enter a deep freeze and we'd all become human popsicles. This was the cold hard truth—at the time.

The term "family" once meant people related by blood, marriage, or adoption. The notion of family was generally accepted to be a father, mother, and children. As divorce rates climbed to the 40–50 percent level and new forms of "family" emerged, the term has come to mean pretty much anything one wants it to mean.

Perhaps we are now truly living life "through the looking-glass," as novelist Lewis Carroll wrote in this exchange between Humpty Dumpty and Alice:

> "When *I* use a word," Humpty Dumpty said in rather a scornful tone, "it means just what I choose it to mean—neither more nor less."
>
> "The question is," said Alice, "whether you *can* make words mean so many different things."

"The question is," said Humpty Dumpty, "which is to be master—that's all."

And so we now make words mean what we want them to mean. How very convenient!

Once upon a time, a person who came to America illegally was called an "illegal alien." Admittedly, the term "alien" sounds a bit like the title role in the Sigourney Weaver movie blockbuster. Still, it was the term on all the government forms, and the dictionary defines "alien" as "an un-naturalized foreign resident of a country." So the word was both clear and accurate. Even so, that term was changed to "illegal immigrant." Then, because the use of the word "illegal" seemed harsh to some (even though it was true), the acceptable term became "undocumented im-migrant." But then "immigrant" made some people uncomfortable and seemed pejorative for some reason or another (it isn't), and the term be-came "undocumented worker." The Associated Press formally announced this change in a 2013 blog post by Executive Editor Kathleen Carroll. But, alas, the mention of "undocumented" implied that a person was lacking something (like a passport or visa maybe?), so the term was mod-ified yet again by many writers and organizations, this time to "guest worker." But some found even "guest worker" to be too impersonal (be-sides, the word "guest" implies an invitation, but calling them "unin-vited guests" might hurt their feelings). So now we're dealing with the problem of illegal immigration with warm and fuzzy euphemisms like . . . "dreamers." This recently led to a bizarre *Drudge Report* head-line about the Border Patrol being helplessly overrun by thousands of "dreamers." I pictured them all as resembling Kermit the Frog. Maybe we should also rename the Border Patrol the "Dream Police" or just "Dream Catchers."

Don't misunderstand—I have no interest in making people feel bad or in being harsh toward people who came here for the very same rea-son my ancestors did. (Truthfully, some of my ancestors were dumped out of debtors' prisons in England, put on ships, and dropped off on the shores of Georgia, so they did get freedom, but they didn't exactly come here for altruistic purposes and to one day join hands and sing "We Are the World.") But where does it all end? Can words mean anything when we've done everything we can to strip them of meaning?

The university campus was once the epicenter of free speech, free expression, and, sometimes, outrageous utterings. In the sixties, American campuses became the "hotbeds of hotheads" and pushed the limits of restraint. Remember the catchphrase, "Speak Truth to Power"? Today's Ivy League motto is "Speak Only Power-Approved Truths." One has to wonder what aging hippies think now when they see campuses becoming the headquarters of stifled speech and restricted language. Is this what they were fighting for?

Nowhere is this more obvious than in the traditional commencement speech on major college campuses. In May 2014, former Secretary of State Condoleezza Rice withdrew as the commencement speaker at Rutgers University because a group of really tolerant students (and faculty!) wanted her to be arrested for "war crimes" when she appeared on campus, over her acts as National Security Advisor and Secretary of State during the Bush administration's management of the wars in Iraq and Afghanistan. One of the most accomplished and remarkable women of her time—a woman who rose from the ashes of her Birmingham, Alabama, church where friends of hers were killed in a church bombing to become the first black woman to serve as National Security Advisor and Secretary of State—was somehow not good enough for some of the little snots at Rutgers. Secretary Rice certainly didn't miss anything by opting not to go, but the students surely did by not hearing her. When they refused to allow her to speak, they deprived *themselves.* They didn't even give themselves the chance to find out whether they liked her or not. Maybe they were afraid that they would.

If the value of diversity is exposure to multiple points of view to enable the free examination of a full range of ideas, then we are going the wrong way by shutting down those whose beliefs aren't in sync with the elites. The only beneficiaries: *elites* who want to stay in power. One wonders if George Orwell was an author or a prophet!

Despite the image some have of me, I think of myself as a pretty sensitive guy. I'm not callous or cold. I've been known to cry at movies, particularly when a dog dies or a kid gets hurt. That's why I couldn't even see *Marley & Me* and had to sit in the theater until everyone left before I exited after sitting through *My Dog Skip*. I mist up hearing stories of heroism from Medal of Honor recipients and even get *verklempt* watching the rerun of *The Andy Griffith Show* where Opie shot a bird with his slingshot. So, yes, I have feelings that can be touched, but I don't go around looking for ways to *have* them hurt.

These days, everyone seems to be nursing a deep emotional wound that can be torn open by even the slightest expression of honesty. In February 2014, Sally Mason, the president of the University of Iowa, had to apologize for a remark she made about sexual assaults on the campus. The offending comment was preceded by a laudable statement that "the goal would be to end that, to never have another sexual assault." So far, so good. But then she had to go off and say, "That's probably not a realistic goal just given human nature, and that's unfortunate."

The speech police sprayed the equivalent of electronic pepper spray in her face for including the term "human nature." There were demands for her to apologize, and she did. I guess it's unacceptable to suggest that since the days of Cain and Abel, there have been all sorts of deplorable and utterly indefensible acts of violence and selfishness, including sexual assault. The female university president wasn't in any way suggesting that sexual assaults are acceptable or insignificant. She was saying something about the fact that human beings often act in their own selfish interest and that does include exploiting others, abusing others, even killing others. If it were acceptable to say it, we would call those actions a reflection of what the Bible calls "sin nature," but that would really be taboo to say. After all, the modern narrative is that we are all wonderful, full of goodness and kindness, and that if we do act

in a way that injures others, it's just because we didn't have enough coun-
seling or had a bad Little League coach or maybe ate too much sugar
in our cereal. God knows it couldn't be because we never were subjected
to discipline that would have addressed our disgusting behavior.

Being offended is a full-time job for many. It's a tedious task, for it
requires enormous amounts of imagination and creativity, relentless pursuit of an audience willing to swallow the notion of the offense, and
then a never-let-go nursing of the manufactured hurt until the protag-
onist actually begins to believe his or her own grievance. (Recently, creative campus complainers have protested that all-you-can-eat taco bars
are insensitive to Hispanic culture, that a "Hump Day" party with a
live camel might harm the sensitivities of Middle Eastern students, and
that a fraternity committed an outrageous "act of cultural appropria-
tion" against Asian-Pacific Islanders by holding a charity luau where
guests wore grass skirts and coconut bras [TheCollegeFix.com. "'FIJI'
Frat Stands Firm After Its Longtime Nickname Attacked, Called
Racist," June 27, 2014]. Don't eat Neapolitan ice cream, or you might
offend three cultures at once!)

Sadder than the proliferation of the perpetually offended is the reaction from what should be a sane and rational public. Wouldn't it be
great if they could simply laugh out loud at the absurdity of it all and
refuse to be cowered into a catalog of words that will placate the whining class? But it's impossible to satisfy the whiners. People who live off
their self-inflicted emotional wounds don't want a resolution, or even a
true conversation to help them understand the feelings of another.
So the attempt to accommodate them creates a never-ending retreat on
the part of common sense and a surrender to irrational demands.

In January 2014, I spoke to the mid-winter meeting of the Republican National Committee (RNC). I was in California the day before
and took the red-eye from LA to D.C., arriving in time to get to the
hotel, shower, change, and go and make the speech. The moment it was
over, I rushed back to the airport, took another flight right back to California, and returned to the event I was part of there. Not an easy

logistical endeavor, but one I felt was worth the effort because of the opportunity to address the members of the Republican National Committee. The meeting and the speech were covered by much of the insider D.C. political chattering class of reporters—the ones who chase each other around town listening to the same speeches and who make a living mostly by cozying up to the regular cast of characters who enjoy being chased by them as much as *they* enjoy being courted and called by name by the "who's who" of our nation's capital.

The Democrats had invented a narrative and were really pushing that Republicans were waging a "WAR ON WOMEN!" It was beyond ludicrous, yet quite the clever masquerade, to equate the prevailing pro-life view of Republicans to a lack of respect for women. It was, in fact, a profound regard for women that was at the heart of the Republican view that women are truly equal in worth—that they deserve, in a true meritocracy, the same opportunity and rewards that a male would receive. The Democrats had tried to portray women as helpless victims of their gender, able to survive only if the government would step in and rescue them, subsidize them, and assist them economically and socially. Women I knew and talked to felt utterly exploited and were outraged to be painted as victims because they were female. The very idea directly contradicts liberal feminists, who believe they can do anything a man can do, as well as conservative women, who believe that their equal value is a gift from God and totally reject the idea that they're helpless without Big Government saving them from their poor, delicate selves.

My wife is a strong woman and quite independent. So are my daughter and my daughter-in-law. They are all well-educated, savvy, tough, and capable of thinking for themselves and holding their own in any circumstance. They reeled at the Democrats' phony message that portrayed them and women in general in the way they'd presented such characters as the fictional "Julia" in the web page, "Life of Julia," which chronicled the entire life cycle of a helpless victim of womanhood named Julia whom government had to subsidize and prop up from cradle to grave with every imaginable assistance and promise of security. It was obviously supposed to laud the value of Big Government, but it came across as a condescending and even comedic depiction of women: helpless, dependent creatures attached to a leash by which various government programs would lead them through their diminished little lives.

In my remarks to the RNC, I referenced the insulting idiocy of the Democrats' strategy, and—for the sake of color and clarity— I asserted that Democrats must think that women don't care as much about jobs, education, and safe neighborhoods as they do about being able to get free birth control, and also that it was sad that the Democrats must think women are incapable of "controlling their libido unless Uncle Sugar" comes forward to save them. Within seconds, Dana Bash of CNN and Kasie Hunt of NBC News tweeted that I had said "women couldn't control their libido without Uncle Sugar helping them."

Of course, what they furiously rushed to tweet was the *exact opposite* of what I had said! They were 100 percent incorrect. An hour later, when someone who'd actually been listening to my speech (and understood English) pointed out to them their blatant misrepresentation, the left-wing blogosphere was already on fire—not reporting or quoting my comments, but repeating a totally false tweet from a couple of inattentive reporters who were clueless as to what I had said. The two things that went viral were my use of the word "libido," which for reasons I still don't understand seemed to titillate the press, and my employment of a term that I've used for twenty-five years and heard all my life as a Southerner, "Uncle Sugar." Uncle Sugar is a term used commonly to describe Uncle Sam morphing into our "sugar daddy" and buying us off with his gifts and material things. The combination of "Uncle Sugar" has never been gender specific nor pejorative to the sugar industry— just a classic and colorful rhetorical expression from my beloved Southland. There was a firestorm, but not so much from what I had said as from what the inaccurate reporters tweeted that I had said. Even when they later corrected their original mistake, the ever-offended left wouldn't hear the truth. The inaccurate report served their purposes far better than the truth, so why correct a story with facts when that would fail to fit the already decided-upon attack?

There were calls for me to apologize. Some even came from Republican officials, who unfortunately became "nervous Nellies" (another expression from my beloved Southland) and feared the Dems would score points off a story that was full of the warm pile left behind by an adult bull. I was reminded why the Republicans often lose the rhetorical battles of our culture. Instead of demanding accountability for truth and pushing back against distortions, deceptions, and outright deceit, we peddle backward and allow the looniest and loudest lungs on the left to create the lexicon of words we can and cannot use. No wonder we come off looking bad! The one thing I learned from my competitive debating days in high school and college was that the debate can't begin until a definition of terms has been agreed to by both sides. Allowing one side to dictate the definition of the terms means a default victory for the side that sets the terms. Control the definition of terms, and you win the debate before it begins. When Republicans allow the other side to define the terms and determine which words we can and can't use, we may as well not show up.

In a climate of free speech, we must assume that people will sometimes say things that hurt others' feelings. It should never be acceptable to intentionally injure someone with slurs, stereotypes, or slander, but I find it hard to believe that our culture has created such a sensitive society that every utterance has to be sanitized so as to be sterile, which is to say "boring." The essence of "diversity" is, after all, celebrating differences. Not only celebrating them, but accepting them and understanding them. There is no celebrating, accepting, or understanding when opinions at variance with the word police are pulverized and punished.

5

Salt, Sugar, Soda, Smokes, and So Much More

PART OF MY GROWING UP Southern, as compared to kids who grew up in other parts of America, was the very different way of cooking and eating we had. I didn't really think about our Southern-fried culinary customs until I became an adult and had to deal with personal health challenges due to weight gain and subsequent weight loss and then gaining back and then losing again and then putting some back on and then . . . you get the picture. I even wrote a best-selling book about my experiences, *Quit Digging Your Grave with a Knife and Fork*.

It's one thing for my doctor to ream me out about my weight, triglycerides, or blood pressure, but I'm not too keen on good ol' Uncle Sugar getting in the middle of my dinner plate, picking through it, and scraping off what is deemed "not good."

Let me be clear—crystal clear. Clear as the pure and organic bottled water from the natural springs in my home state. I believe we should practice good health habits. Not because the government tells us to but because, first and foremost, our bodies belong to God. We don't own them—we just get to use them as our "temporary temple" while on Earth. Abusing them and ignoring the possible effects of our choices in eating or exercising is no different from throwing trash on the floor of our church during worship services or propping our muddy shoes on the pews. But the point is precisely that while God has a right to tell me to take care of my body, government is *not* my God, and it takes a treacherous "fork" in the road when it turns our dinner tables over to government regulators.

I consider myself a "health crusader," in that I believe public policy should promote the good health of Americans. But government oversteps when it goes beyond the effort to inform, lead, and encourage, and creates a kind of "Supernanny" that forces steamed and unsalted Brussels sprouts down our gagging throats.

I grew up eating the food that was simply part and parcel of my own culture. We fried everything. *everything.* I would later understand the Southern habit of frying, and it's quite practical. In a poor family, food needs to stretch to feed a maximum number of mouths at minimum cost. Breading and frying allows one to take pretty much anything and add to the caloric content and "fullness factor" without adding to the cost. Got a cheap piece of meat? Beat the daylights out of it to tenderize it, then bread it and fry it. Smells delicious, tastes great, and if you smother it (and some potatoes) with cream gravy—made with the pan drippings and a little flour and milk at virtually no cost—and pass the biscuits and corn bread, you've created a culinary masterpiece that will feed more people. *Voilà!* (Although I don't remember my mother ever saying *"Voilà!"* or using any other French words or recipes.) It was all *sooooo* good, I'm salivating just *writing* about it. As a kid, I thought we were eating fried foods because we were lucky. It wasn't until my teen years that I realized we ate those "rich" foods because we were poor!

Frying had another advantage. In homes where poverty meant not always having refrigeration or reliable ways to protect from spoilage, especially in the summer, it took food to such a high temperature that any bacteria were also crispy-cooked. On a 2008 trip with the ONE Campaign to Rwanda, over breakfast with former U.S. Senator Bill Frist, I discussed with him the challenge of eating safe food in developing countries like Rwanda. Prior to his being an outstanding senator from Tennessee and serving as Senate Majority Leader, he was Dr. Bill

Frist, renowned heart surgeon. I'll never forget his turning to me and saying that when one travels to places where sanitation is questionable, the fallback is simply to eat french fries and a Coca-Cola. *What???* A heart surgeon encouraging me to have an order of fries and a Coke? My first thought was, "Now, that's my kind of heart surgeon!" But the advice was not about nutrition—it was about food safety.

French *fries* are *fried* long enough, at a temperature high enough, to kill off most germs. Pair the fries with a nice bottle (any vintage) of Coca-Cola, which is surprisingly available even in the most remote places on Earth. I've seen Cokes sold out of makeshift "stores" in Afghanistan that were nothing more than shipping containers turned on their sides to serve as a "building." I've seen them peddled along dusty desert pathways in the interior of Egypt, stored in an ice chest that hadn't seen ice in twenty years, but served as the "Coke box" from which one could buy the familiar beverage. (Have *you* ever tasted a Coke served at 120 degrees Fahrenheit? Yow.) The bottling standards are the same the world over, and the sealed cap keeps it fresh and pure. Wouldn't try that with a can, though—God only knows what the top of that can has been subjected to!

So there you have it. Eating fried foods—long before Paula Deen had a cookbook—wasn't just a cultural tradition for those of us who grew up in the South, though it certainly was that. It was a means of survival, both in terms of having enough calories to sustain a life of hard manual labor in the fields and also promoting food safety long before the FDA, the CDC, the NIH, local health departments, and even Michelle Obama told us how to eat.

Food safety has a certain value for society, especially now that people eat more of their meals away from home. Knowing that a restaurant has passed an inspection to make sure the roaches aren't bigger than the cooks and the rats confine themselves to leftovers—not food off diners' plates *before* they're served—offers some comfort as we sit at the table. We know we're consuming food prepared by people who work back there in the kitchen where we can't see, and we can only hope they heed the signs telling them to wash their hands after they go to the bathroom. So we're okay with a little regulation.

But just how much government do we need in our own grocery bags and our own kitchens? According to some, including former New York Mayor Michael Bloomberg, we shouldn't consume a single morsel that hasn't first been nutritionally analyzed, weighed, inspected, prepared, approved, served, and previously digested by Uncle Sugar himself. Because I work in New York each week to do my Fox News TV show, I have more than a casual exposure to life in the "Big Apple." Some people assume that because I spend so much time there, I must surely live there, but ironically, that's why I *don't* and *won't* live there. As I said before, the only way I'd consider living there would be if I could duck hunt in Central Park, and that's not going to happen!

New York is an amazing city, and I don't want to be dismissive of this marvel of energy, entertainment, excitement, and influence. That it functions at all is a testament to the hardworking, resourceful people who grit it out every day. But as independent as New Yorkers tend to be, it's surprising that they haven't been more resistant to the city's ever-increasing regulation of all they do, say, and, especially, consume.

Michael Bloomberg's twelve years as mayor may be remembered as much for his "nanny state" approach to governing as for anything else he did. When I hosted a three-hour-a-day radio show for a couple of years, one of the regular features that my producer Joey Salvia and I created was the character "Nanny Boy," with the tune of "Danny Boy" and fractured lyrics to remind our listeners of the many ways in which "Nanny Boy" had involved himself in the daily personal lives and habits of New Yorkers.

There was, of course, Bloomberg's famous ban on salt shakers on restaurant tables and in restaurant kitchens. That was largely ignored, but he preached it like Joel Osteen preaching a happy life. He banned trans fats. Yes, trans fats are bad, so that's a topic for debate, but it was just one plank in the mayor's full good-health platform. Perhaps most famous was his much-ridiculed ban on sugary sodas over sixteen ounces. He actually got that one passed by his hand-appointed city board of health. The rationale, explained Hizzoner, was that "no one *needs*" a soft drink larger than sixteen ounces. Gee whiz, Mr. Mayor, I'm not sure anyone "needs" a soft drink at all when you get right down to it. Not sure anyone "needs" a cold beer or would collapse and die without a big tall glass of sweet tea, either. Who gave the mayor of New York the divine insight to know precisely how many ounces of a soft drink are too many? It always seemed to me that the sixteen-ounce limit was arbitrary and that since people come in various sizes, maybe cups should, too. Sixteen ounces isn't the same for NFL lineman Michael Oher as it is for a teenage girl whose entire left leg doesn't weigh that much. Of course, the mayor didn't really *stop* people from drinking more than sixteen ounces of soda. They just bought two sodas, duh. And like most clunky government dictates, the ban arbitrarily targeted sodas but not other beverages, such as a calorie-laden frappe at Starbucks; or a fruity drink that can have more calories than a soda; or a milkshake, which can have *far* more calories.

So if the government's job isn't to order off the menu for me, does it have any role in trying to influence health habits? Sure, because it's the taxpayers' money going down the grease pipe when people don't care for themselves and then need help to foot medical bills for a heart attack, an amputated foot from diabetes, or expensive medication for chronic disease. Still, there's a huge difference between government encouraging healthy behavior and government force-feeding us an arugula salad because some bureaucrat sitting in a cubicle thinks his power to control is more powerful than our freedom to choose.

I've seen a number of cultural revolutions right here in America, in my own lifetime, and the government had a role—a limited one—in helping bring about these shifts. Let me mention a few ways in which I've seen government play a part in changing behavioral norms.

I can remember as a kid when American highways were cluttered with litter. People routinely threw trash out car windows as they drove our nation's roads. In the sixties, First Lady Lady Bird Johnson launched a campaign to "Beautify America." It was a simple awareness campaign to encourage people to take pride in the beauty of our country and not to toss litter on our sidewalks, streets, highways, and byways. Who could argue with that? There was no order to arrest or shoot a litterer, but rather just a straightforward, positive message to think differently about our surroundings.

I also remember when cars didn't have seat belts. They were an aftermarket item, but I didn't know of anyone who actually had seat belts in their car. Frankly, where I grew up, it would have been scandalous to go to an auto parts store, buy some seat belts, and then go to a local mechanic to have them installed. I can just hear it now: "You want me to do *what*? You want me to put these straps in your car so you can tie yourself down while you're driving??? Dang fool wants to strap himself in his car!" You would've been the talk of the town!

Another major change in our culture: the prevalence of smoking. It was virtually automatic for adults in the South to smoke. And, of course, kids would swipe cigarettes from their parents and sneak off to pretend to be "grown up." Heck, we had *candy* cigarettes. I can remember kids in my own neighborhood trying cigarettes as young as age seven, with some becoming hard-core confirmed smokers by age thirteen. The schools actually accommodated junior high and high school students who smoked by giving them their own on-campus "smoking zones." (I kid you not!) I suppose I'm lucky to be highly allergic to tobacco smoke, because I've never smoked a single cigarette and never wanted to. It was hard enough having it all around me! I found it repulsive even though it was normal and regular behavior for adults in virtually every walk of life.

So, what did doctors have to say about this? Well, doctors not only smoked—they smoked in their offices while treating patients. I remember my own family doctor puffing on his pipe as he examined me when I was just a tot. There were ashtrays in the waiting room, and if I wasn't all that sick when I got there, I sure was by the time I got in to see the doctor, thanks to my then-unknown and untreated allergies! Doctors were even featured in cigarette ads with slogans such as, "More doctors smoke Camels than any other cigarette." In today's world, that would be as absurd as an ad that says, "More chefs use arsenic than any other poison."

Ads for Virginia Slims, the first cigarette created for and marketed to women, told them, "You've come a long way, baby!" Likewise, our government has come a long way when it comes to cigarettes. It once all but insisted that we smoke. It literally *pushed* cigarettes by including them as part of soldiers' field rations, right along with food and water. That's right—a man had to have food, water, and a cigarette, said the government. But a boatload of research linking cigarettes to cancer, proving what we'd already suspected (check out the chorus of the 1947 "Tex" Williams hit, "Smoke! Smoke! Smoke! (That Cigarette)"; note also that the singer later died from lung cancer), sent us along the path to a totally different reality when it came to smoking.

Another cultural transformation: the total change of attitude toward drunk driving. Up through the seventies, drunkenness wasn't exactly promoted but still was fodder for entertainers such as Dean Martin and Foster Brooks. We laughed *at* Foster Brooks and *with* Dean Martin, who gave tipsiness a kind of Rat Pack cool. Then Mothers Against Drunk Driving gave names and faces to the victims of drunk driving, and being drunk wasn't so funny anymore. The culture shifted dramatically yet again.

So, changes can happen, but not by having the government *force* new behavior. (*Case in point:* prohibition.) There's a pattern common to all the examples offered here—litter, seat belts, smoking, drunk driving—but it's not one in which government was the entity that made them work. And it's certainly not one in which the government "nudged" an unwilling public with outright bans and punitive taxes and fees, as left-wing ideologues love to do.

In each case, three things had to happen to make the needle move: First, a difference in ATTITUDE, sparked by education and advertising to create an awareness that didn't exist before. For example, the emotionally powerful "Keep America Beautiful" ads put the issue of littering before the public in a fresh new way. I vividly recall the television spot featuring a Native American (we called them Indians in the sixties) looking at a river polluted by trash and turning to the camera as a single tear rolled out of his eye and down his cheek. I remember thinking, "Please, Dad, don't throw stuff out of the car—we don't want to make that Indian cry!"

Coincidentally, an awareness campaign featuring Native Americans was launched in 2014, sponsored by the Yocha Dehe Wintun Nation to help Washington Redskins fans understand why they'd like to see the name "Redskins" changed. The ads don't have to do much explaining. They simply present a series of video images featuring proud Native Americans celebrating their culture, and end on a picture of the Redskins helmet. A powerful point is made, very elegantly: We are proud people, and this trivializes our culture. I can't imagine a more effective way to change attitudes than this.

The second ingredient: an encouraging ATMOSPHERE. This was fairly simple to accomplish, but not without some cost. Signs were placed that said, DON'T LITTER, along with strategically placed trash barrels in public areas, along roadsides, in parks, and on beaches. (Took a real genius to figure out that if you had a convenient receptacle for your trash, you might be more likely to use it!) We changed the atmosphere so it became easier to do the right thing.

Finally, the third step: ACTION. Yes, there was and is a role for government, but notice that the "action" phase, in which government puts forth a rule or a law, happens *after* and not before the attitudes and the atmosphere change. Government can't make people behave differently; in fact, most Americans value their individual freedom so much that if the heavy hand of government says, "You can't," the public is likely to say, "Oh, yes, we *will*." But if the public has modified its attitudes and wants society to reflect that, they'll accept and even insist that this new norm be codified into law.

Had someone in 1964 said the day would come when people could be fined $1,000 for littering the roadside with a gum wrapper, he or she would have been laughed out of the room. Back then, the idea that seat belts would one day be mandatory in forty-nine of the fifty states and that in most states a motorist would be pulled over simply for not wearing one would've sounded insane. By the way, there's only one state that still has no seat belt law—New Hampshire. But then, the state motto of New Hampshire is "Live free or DIE!" so I guess that makes sense.

To change ATTITUDES on the value of seat belts, there first came an ad campaign and efforts to educate the public (remember the crash test dummies?). Then seat belts were mandated—not to be worn, mind you, but just to be in the car, creating the ATMOSPHERE. Finally, once the public knew the research and not only accepted but insisted that seat belts were a good idea, states took ACTION and codified the new cultural norm into law. Except for New Hampshire, of course.

The same thing happened with smoking: In 1964, the U.S. Surgeon General released his report definitively linking smoking with lung cancer. The release of this report made huge headlines and was named one of the top ten news stories for that year. Starting in 1965, warning labels on cigarette packs proclaimed the famous Surgeon General's warning that "smoking may be hazardous to your health." (Warning labels did come by way of congressional legislation, but this was still not the kind of law that specifically bans a product or behavior.) TV ads showed a dad picking up a cigarette and his little son wanting to pick one up, too, as if to say, "Pop, if you smoke 'em, so will your kid." And even back then, most smokers didn't really wish that habit on their kids. As attitudes changed, so did the atmosphere. Ashtrays were replaced in many public places with NO SMOKING signs. Hotels began offering a limited number of nonsmoking rooms. Airlines created separate smoking sections, as did restaurants. The question became, "Smoking or nonsmoking?"

Only then, as Arkansas governor, did I sign the Indoor Clean Air Act, which stated that all indoor public places were to be smoke free.

This law was overwhelmingly popular, and even opponents who owned restaurants later admitted it was a godsend to their businesses. Turns out, it didn't cost them customers since people come to eat, not just to smoke; their cleaning expenses were dramatically cut by not having to deal with smoke residue; and, to their delight, their tables turned over twenty minutes faster because nobody stuck around after the meal to *smoke*. That legislation could never have passed even a few years before, but when it did, it wasn't that controversial because the public had changed. Had the government tried to dictate behavior in 1968 simply by declaring America "smoke free," there would have been smoke all right—cities burned to the ground by raging nicotine addicts who would have torched city halls and the Capitol building with their lighters.

Drunk driving was probably easiest to change in terms of attitudes because it's hard to defend the notion of someone getting drunk, driving a vehicle, and killing an innocent person. Too many of us have personally known someone who was killed by a drunk driver, and there's precious little sympathy for such a reckless and selfish behavior. But the point remains: Law enforcement starting cracking down on this offense not to force a change in cultural norms, but in response to one. In fact, many still think the law needs to catch up to the public's desire for even stiffer punishment.

First Lady Michelle Obama launched the "Let's Move" initiative in 2009 to combat childhood obesity. Granted, some hardened libertarians were highly critical of Mrs. Obama for her efforts, but I frankly appreciated that as a mother and a personal practitioner of good health, she sought to lead a charge against what really is a scourge among the nation's children. Pretending that childhood obesity is not a major issue is blinding oneself, not only to the obvious health risks but also to the financial repercussions of providing care to a generation of sick, overweight kids.

These are issues I dealt with firsthand as a governor. Doctors at Arkansas Children's Hospital in Little Rock told me that fifteen years earlier, there was no such thing as type 2 diabetes in preteens. Diabetes was classified as either "juvenile" or "adult-onset" because these two different forms affected those in the respective age groups. Then, as many children went from being overweight to obese, something ominous happened. The age at which people were being diagnosed with "adult" diabetes dropped so stunningly that the terms had to be changed completely. They're now called type 1 and type 2 diabetes, to avoid any implication of an age-related diagnosis.

To illustrate the impact of preteens developing an adult disease, I'll quote my dear friend and the man I appointed as director of the State Health Department, the late Dr. Fay Boozman, who told me: "A child diagnosed with type 2 diabetes as a preteen will have vision problems by the time he's twenty, have a heart attack before he's thirty, be in renal failure by the time he's forty, and will never live to see a fiftieth birthday." Public health experts have said that, barring major changes or significant medical advances, today's generation of overweight, sedentary kids will be the first in the nation's history not expected to live as long as their parents and grandparents.

And today, according to the CDC's 2014 National Diabetes Statistics Report, nearly 10 percent of the U.S. population has type 2 diabetes. That's over 29 million people. So let's not be disingenuous and say there isn't a problem. There is one.

At the same time, let's remember that government can't act independently to force change. Government works best as a clean-up batter, not a lead-off batter. It's not the engine; more like the caboose. (Otherwise, it's the cart before the horse, the tail wagging the dog, and now I'm out of metaphors.) This is why Michelle Obama's well-intentioned micromanaging of school cafeteria menus has given us the most well-nourished trash cans ever to grace American schools! Government can't *force* kids to eat their spinach.

It's also clear that government isn't rational or science-based about issues, but purely political. For example, the same people who want to ban tobacco want to legalize marijuana. Get that? If you do, then explain it to me, because I sure don't. When Colorado and Washington

State became the first states to legalize "recreational pot," the rationale was that no one would be the worse off for it. So what, they said, if some mellowed-out stoners wanted to live in a purple haze? And just think: All those potheads with the munchies might give a big boost to the snack food industry. (We already know that pot is a gateway drug; it creates junk-food junkies!)

At the same time, there's a move toward banning even e-cigarettes, *electronic* cigarettes that emit vapor instead of tobacco smoke. Granted, not being a smoker, I don't understand nicotine cravings so intense that they cause people to go around sucking on what looks like a ballpoint pen but is actually a battery-operated device. It gives them a nicotine buzz and releases vapor that some claim contains carcinogens, but which some studies have shown are no different from outdoor air or human breath. (Frankly, I've smelled some human breath that *was* toxic, but I digress!)

We should certainly look at whether the vapor from an e-cigarette truly is harmful to those nearby, but why would any state ban e-cigarettes and legalize pot, which we *know* has carcinogenic chemicals? For this and many reasons, I'm sure people will someday look back on the early twenty-first century, scratch their heads, and wonder, "What were they *thinking*?"

And if the government were really interested in our health, why would they push to give a twelve-year-old girl the right to buy birth control pills without her parents' knowledge—let alone their permission (when a school nurse can be fired for giving the same girl an aspirin without her parents' permission)—or push for her to be able to secretly have an abortion? The "advocates" who think a preteen girl is adult enough to have an abortion, but child enough to stay on her parents' health insurance until she's twenty-six, confuse me.

When Big Government liberals from the ivory towers of the Ivy League demand that government not "come between a woman and her doctor" regarding abortion, but then put the government between *everyone* and their doctor with Obamacare, doesn't that seem a bit nuts to everyone with an IQ above plant life?

So here we have it—a government that wants to control salt, sugar, soda, smokes, trans fats, and much more in the name of "protecting" us, but not to protect a perfectly innocent unborn child from being dismembered in its mother's womb? If the government wants to "save lives," let it start with saving babies. There is surely some science in that.

6

"Can You Hear Me Now?"
(THE NSA CAN)

IN MAY 2014, my wife and I went to China to celebrate our fortieth wedding anniversary. Neither of us had visited before, so we decided to see for ourselves this booming economy and emerging world power. My second morning there, I awoke to a couple of attention-grabbing headlines on the front page of *China Daily*, the leading English-language newspaper of Beijing. The first story was accompanied by a photo of Russia's Vladimir Putin and China's President, Xi Jinping, both smiling as they announced the signing of a record forty-nine agreements between the two nations. The other big story was China's outrage over having some of its military leaders indicted in the United States on charges of cyber theft.

My first thought was "takes one to know one!" The United States had rightfully expressed its objections to any government hacking into the computers of our nation's private sector companies or government agencies. But there was a certain irony to it all, given that for the past two years America had been embroiled in a home-cooked controversy over whether our government violated the constitutional rights of its own citizens by capturing their phone calls and e-mails under the all-inclusive banner of "anti-terrorism."

I jokingly told an audience that I had lost my iPhone and really panicked, given all the information that was stored on it. But, hey, it all turned out fine! I just called the NSA (National Security Agency) and asked them where my phone was and they told me. They even restored all my e-mails and phone calls. The audience roared with laughter, but their appreciation was a solemn reminder that for something to be funny, it has to be somewhat believable or, at least, plausible. In the case of the government knowing exactly where my phone was and what was on it, that story was entirely believable. Ouch!

Edward Snowden, by all appearances a young, low-level tech nerd working for a private contractor and doing work for the U.S. government in Hawaii, somehow accessed a treasure trove of information on just how much data the government collects on its citizens and what it's capable of doing with it. Through Glenn Greenwald, an American journalist working for a British newspaper, he started leaking explosive bits of information on the extent to which U.S. government agencies collected data on our own citizens with no specific warrant or probable cause that a crime of any kind—much less terrorism—was being committed. Over the next two years, Snowden dribbled out more and more information, creating a severe headache for the Obama administration and for the intelligence community at large.

Snowden has been labeled everything from a traitor to a hero, but the truth probably lies somewhere in between. He's certainly not a hero, for instead of acting out of conviction and conscience and facing the consequences because he believed what he was doing was right, he took off running and eventually accepted asylum in Russia—hardly the mark of a true patriot. But to completely demonize his methods or his motives without thinking objectively about what he revealed to American citizens about the activities of our own government would minimize the shock of finding out that "Big Brother" really *is* watching us.

Verizon Communications built an ad campaign around a guy trying to get a good cell phone signal, repeatedly saying, "Can you hear me now?" The ad was effective because every person who'd ever used a cell phone had experienced walking a few paces in all directions and holding the device in all sorts of ways while asking, "Can you hear me *now*?" With all the advances in technology we've seen, most of us are singularly exasperated by the inability to get a clear signal on our cell phones to make a simple call. It truly appears that the more advanced our technology gets, the lousier the cell signals get. So the Verizon campaign struck a cultural nerve. Proves my earlier point: For something to be funny, it has to be believable.

Prior to the Snowden information-avalanche regarding our spying activities, most of us didn't think the range of government snooping to catch terrorists included capturing our phone calls to the local pizza joint to place an order for pepperoni with extra cheese or to our great-aunt's house to say "Happy birthday!" The "looking for the needle in the haystack" excuse was muddled when we saw that our own government, instead of focusing on the needle, had amassed a haystack the size of Idaho. They did this intentionally, so we have to ask: What was the real intent?

During my trip to China, I was constantly frustrated by the Chinese government's censorship of the Internet, blocking Facebook, YouTube, Twitter, and numerous Web sites that I usually took for granted as sources of news and opinion. When such Web sites did load, it often took longer than an AOL dial-up on a pre-Internet, dinosaur version of a PC from the late eighties. I had forgotten what it was like to hit a key to launch a command and go get a cup of coffee while it processed. While I waited, I realized how fortunate we are in America to have access to super-high-speed connections and open access. And then . . . and *then* . . . I remembered that our own government keeps toying and tinkering with the notion of more "regulation" (*translation: control*) over the Internet, and I shuddered to think that in addition to monitoring my every cyber move, my own government might just decide to commandeer it as well.

When I hear otherwise thinking people say, "Well, if that keeps me safe from terrorists, I'm willing to give up some of my freedoms," I wonder if they really understand what they're saying. If the ultimate goal of a terrorist is to intimidate a people into changing their behavior, giving up basic rights, and allowing tighter and tighter control, it would appear the terrorists are indeed winning—and they don't even have to launch a thousand suicide bombers on American streets. They can get us to do it to ourselves. Just get Americans completely comfortable with the government knowing everything we do and when we do it and how we do it and, while they're at it, maybe *why* we do it. Did our Founders really sacrifice their very existence to create a police state? Did our fathers and grandfathers fight enemies across the globe so we could be turned into the same kind of society they sought to stop? Do we want to become a nation whose government monitors us, records us, tracks us, and catalogs us?

Just for the record (which we know they're keeping)—*No!*

Under the Obama administration, government control of "free press" went to warp speed, but most of the establishment and traditional media organizations were so focused on defending President Obama that they seemed not to notice or complain.

On May 13, 2013, the Associated Press disclosed that twenty of their reporters had had their phone records subpoenaed by the Department of Justice. I can only imagine the outcry had George W. Bush's team been caught subpoenaing the phone records of the Associated Press in a fishing expedition to discover the source of AP news stories! There would have been calls for an independent prosecutor, criminal charges, and, for good measure, a guillotine set up in front of the U.S. Capitol, just in case. To provide themselves some cover, Obama's Department of Justice (DOJ), led by Eric Holder, the most blatantly and blindly partisan hack at the DOJ since John Mitchell under President Nixon, didn't issue the subpoena to the AP itself, but rather to the AP's phone provider. Same goal, same focus, same snooping for the information, but too cute by half in attempting to sneak it through the third-party private company that provided the AP with phone service.

Gary Pruitt, who was CEO of the Associated Press at the time, whimpered a bit and complained, "These records potentially reveal communications with confidential sources across all of the newsgathering activities undertaken by the AP during a two-month period, provide a roadmap to AP's newsgathering operations and disclose information about AP's activities and operations the government has no conceivable right to know" [AP Web site, May 13, 2013].

Pruitt spoke to the National Press Club on June 19, 2013, and decried the "bigness" of a government that goes after reporters who are trying to do their constitutionally protected duty to keep on eye on the people's business. He pointed out the chilling effect of having it known that talking to a reporter in confidence might not prevent a snooping government from tapping into the conversation. Said Pruitt, "Some longtime trusted sources have become nervous and anxious about talking with us—even on stories unrelated to national security. In some cases, government employees we once checked in with regularly will no longer speak to us by phone. Others are reluctant to meet in person. And I can tell you that this chilling effect on newsgathering is not just limited to AP. Journalists from other news organizations have personally told me that it has intimidated both official and nonofficial sources from speaking to them as well."

Well said, Mr. Pruitt. But after that, the AP pretty much shut up and went right back to their normal duties of lapdogging for the Obama administration, largely ignoring other abuses of the press by the "Big Brothers" in the Obama White House. In the tradition of Sergeant Schultz from the sixties television series *Hogan's Heroes*, they "say nothing!" when it comes to other outrageous violations, such as the phone hacking of Fox News reporter and my colleague James Rosen, who worked at the D.C. bureau.

When the Justice Department suspected that a State Department security adviser had leaked secrets to Rosen about North Korea, they tracked Rosen's phone calls and his comings and goings at the State Department and even got a search warrant for his private e-mails by naming him as a "criminal co-conspirator." Rosen was, incredibly, described as a "flight risk." Through all of this, he was never even informed that he was under suspicion.

Even liberal news outlets and columnists were rightly outraged over the treatment given to Rosen. Clearly, it was not a love for Fox News that helped them discover their voice, but the fear that it could easily happen to them. An editorial in *The New York Times* opined, "With the decision to label a Fox News television reporter a possible 'co-conspirator' in a criminal investigation of a news leak, the Obama administration has moved beyond protecting government secrets to threatening fundamental freedoms of the press to gather news."

Dana Milbank, liberal writer at *The Washington Post* wrote, "The Rosen affair is as flagrant an assault on civil liberties as anything done by George W. Bush's administration, and it uses technology to silence critics in a way Richard Nixon could only have dreamed of. To treat a reporter as a criminal for doing his job—seeking out information the government doesn't want made public—deprives Americans of the First Amendment freedom on which all other constitutional rights are based."

Here, here! I raise my glass of sweet tea to the fine minds at the *Times* and *The Washington Post* for having noses capable of smelling a skunk! This outrageous abuse of power should have resulted in the entire D.C. press corps launching a wolf pack–style attack against Obama's furtive little rodents. Sadly, that faint glimmer of journalistic integrity was visible only for a few fleeting moments. The media's outrage quickly faded away, like a lightning bug in a fog bank. As in any abusive codependent relationship, the mainstream media love Obama so much, they just can't stay mad at him, no matter what he does to them.

But Americans remotely concerned about the First Amendment need not worry their little heads about it, because in late May 2013, President Obama asked the Justice Department to "get to the bottom of it." In response, Attorney General Eric Holder did what any other completely objective and honorable public servant would do: He launched a thorough investigation of himself and found himself to be (surprise) completely blameless. For President Obama and Eric Holder, "getting to the bottom" of something has come to mean burying it at the bottom of the ocean and never letting it see the light of day. "The most transparent administration in history" isn't, according to its own estimation, answerable to us at all. So while the government thinks it's within their power to look through *your* e-mails, monitor *your* phone calls, and consider *you* a criminal for exercising *your* First Amendment rights, they don't want *you* asking any questions about what they're doing, why they're doing it, or how they're going about it.

Any questions?

If so, send them to the NSA. By now, they should have amassed all the information in the universe. Let's see if they can actually pull anything useful out of it.

7

Same-Sex Marriage and the Law (God's and Man's)

I WAS ELEVEN YEARS OLD before I ever heard the term "homosexual." I had no idea what it meant. There were no shows on TV like *Modern Family* or *Glee,* and it would be decades before movies like *Brokeback Mountain* became mainstream. Here's how it happened: As a member of a Boy Scout troop in my hometown of Hope, Arkansas, I heard rumors about the troop's Scoutmaster and his very odd practice of inviting boys from the troop, one at a time, over to his house to work on merit badges. One of my more worldly fellow Scouts bluntly said that the Scoutmaster was "queer." I had never heard the term applied to anyone and asked what it meant.

The answer he gave was way too descriptive and blunt for this book. I didn't believe at all what he told me, so that night I asked my dad what it meant. I'll never forget how my dad fumbled around—with a look of absolute panic—and then said that the term applied to someone who was homosexual. That was another term I'd never heard, so when I asked what *that* meant, he stumbled for a few moments before simply saying, "It's a man who loves another man."

That seemed really bizarre. It was so far from any concept I could imagine at that age that I hardly reacted at all. I couldn't even visualize how that might be lived out, so I said, "Okay," and went on my merry way. After the Scoutmaster was confronted about his extracurricular "work" with some of the Scouts in my troop, he was forced to resign and "go off and get some help." He was from a wealthy and influential family; there was no publicity and no criminal charges filed. After spending a few weeks "in the hospital," he came back and continued to live in our little community. People talked, but the boys he molested—a fairly sizable number—never went public, and he never had to register as a sex offender because in those days, the term didn't exist and no one would have known what it meant. (Even today, that's often unclear, but in this case it definitely would have meant *child molester/pedophile*.) To be clear, I am not equating all gay men with pedophiles; I'm just relating how this particular person was my introduction to the then-unfathomable concept of same-sex attraction. As I got into my teenage years, I would hear more about homosexuality, but it was far from mainstream and certainly wasn't openly promoted in the culture.

Things have changed.

If someone had told me then that there would be a day when the President of the United States would call a basketball player and congratulate him for "coming out" as gay, or push publicly for marriage between people of the same gender, I would have thought that person had been getting too deep into Boone's Farm Strawberry Hill. (For the non–baby boomers out there, this was a cheap fruit-flavored "wine," more like alcoholic soda pop, that was the rage for underage drinkers at my high school in the late sixties and early seventies. I never tasted the stuff; the kids who drank it were generally the type who acted a bit loopy even before downing the booze.) Today, those of us who still believe that marriage means a man and a woman are told we're "homophobic," "gay haters," or "on the wrong side of history." Some things we're called are much worse and quite unprintable in a book of such class and distinction as this one!

Of course, as I noted earlier, President Obama was not always for same-sex marriage. He was against it before he was for it. In August

2008, during a nationally televised Saddleback Forum with Republican Presidential candidate John McCain and hosted by Pastor Rick Warren at the Saddleback Church in California, President Obama was asked his views on same-sex marriage. In opposing it, his answer was clear and direct. He stated that he believed marriage was a relationship between a man and a woman and that "as for me, a Christian, it's a sacred union. God is in the mix." By 2012, he'd not only accepted same-sex marriage but was promoting it and accusing anyone who didn't support it of being against equality. Quite the turn in a short period of time!

Let's look at this logically. If the President opposed same-sex marriage in 2008 because of his Christian views and his belief that marriage is a sacred union, then only three possibilities exist to account for the dramatic change in his public position:

1. He was lying *then* and really supported same-sex marriage, but knew that view would kill him politically in his first run for the White House.
2. He is lying *now* and really believes in traditional marriage, but wants the political benefit he gets today from the left by "coming out" for same-sex marriage.
3. He's been told by God that the Christian teachings on which he'd based his opinion about same-sex marriage have been edited or revised. (Apparently God forgot to tell the rest of us.)

These really are the only options, and I haven't heard President Obama disclose which one is true. If you think I'm being too harsh, let me say that if he had simply stated in 2008 that he supported traditional marriage because of his personal views and traditions, he would've left himself the option to "evolve" on the issue. But once you invoke your Christian faith as the basis for your views, and then change them, you've got to admit being dishonest about your stated beliefs (then or now) or make a case for the Word of God changing somehow. It would be pretty bold for even a very confident and sometimes arrogant President to declare, "God has changed his mind! And he only told *me!*"

It might surprise people—and cynics on the left will no doubt roll their eyes to hear me say it—but I have friends who are gay. My wife and I have entertained gay friends, including gay couples, in our home; I do business with gay people and have had gay people working for me. My beliefs and convictions don't change with the people I'm around. I accept people who disagree with me and genuinely appreciate that they accept me as a friend and associate. I don't argue with them, berate them, or condemn them. They don't scream at me, call me homophobic, or tell me I'm a hater. It would be laughable to all of us if they did, since they'd be doing it while sharing my friendship and hospitality!

My personal views are indeed based on my faith and adherence to biblical teaching. They are not mere preferences, but unwavering convictions that I don't have the right to revise. I realize that to an increasing number of people, especially those living in Bubble-ville, some of my views are archaic, even the stuff of bigotry or hate. I find that discouraging because it's an argument built on fear and intentional misrepresentation. Critics standing on such shaky ground have no alternative but to attack the motives and character of those who disagree with them. A rational debate, based on logic and facts, becomes impossible.

There are numerous issues involved in a discussion of same-sex marriage, some based in God's law and some based in our Earthly law. I'll seek to address it from the perspective of one whose orientation is God-centered and not man-centered. The points below reflect considerations from Bible-believing Bubba-ville:

1. First, there is the issue of homosexuality and other types of sexual preference. Are such variations normal? Which ones? Are there any limits on what is an acceptable attraction? If so, what is the objective basis for those limits, and who gets to draw that line?

2. There is the issue of marriage itself. What *is* marriage; what are its historical, biological, psychological, sociological, and theological roots? Is marriage merely a contract to accommodate a social bond between people? Are there any limits to how we define marriage? Why does it matter to heterosexual married people if homosexuals wish to marry? What difference does it make?

3. Then there is the issue of constitutional law and the balance of powers. If there are changes in the law regarding the definition of marriage, who should make them? What role, if any, should the judicial branch play? How much power should it be able to exercise? (These particular questions should be very important to *all* Americans, not just Bible believers like me.)

A God-centered worldview is considerably different from one that is man-centered. Either there is a God or there isn't. If there is, either He's knowable or He isn't. If He's knowable—and, come to think of it, even if He isn't—either He's involved in our world or He isn't. If He's knowable *and* involved, then either He has boundaries and purpose for us, or He doesn't. If He does, then we need to be aware of them, for without them we cannot know what true success and fulfillment is.

Winning at any game is possible only when we understand its objective and play by its rules. Either the "endgame" is knowable or it's not. If it is, we need to live according to that knowledge or accept that we will come to regret making up our own rules.

I believe we live in a God-centered world and that all the definitions of success, fulfillment, morality, value, family, and life are His to give and ours to follow. They provide a roadmap for us. They also are immutable, meaning *unchangeable.*

In a man-centered world, it's "every man for himself." Each person acts as his or her own god. Rules exist according to either an agreement among the people or the will of the strongest against the weaker. In fact, the very *existence* of the weak is determined by the will of the strong. This is essentially social Darwinism, in which moral law boils down to "survival of the fittest." Those who are weak and unable to convince the strong of their value have no recourse or form of appeal. They live at the whim and mercy and ultimately for the utility of the strong. In a world with no acknowledgment of a higher power, no one answers to a moral authority that is fixed and absolute and applied equally to all. Any canons of right and wrong can be moved without being measured against such an authority. In the biblical era of the Judges, it was said that "every man did what was right in his own eyes." The same could be said of our culture today.

Those with a man-centered worldview are free to think, feel, and believe in their own way, and it would be utterly improper for others to question any of it. Indeed, America is not a theocracy, and we have the right to our own thoughts, feelings, and beliefs. But those who try to reflect a God-centered worldview accept that their own behavior will be judged against a higher standard. For such a person, the ultimate test of authority is, "Did God say anything about this, and, if so, what did He say and how should it affect what I do?"

To those of us for whom biblical and historical orthodoxy matter, same-sex marriage is just part of a much larger issue: the definition of marriage. In recent years, for example, the trivialization of fatherhood has contributed greatly to the confusion within our culture as to what constitutes "marriage" and "family." We've been bombarded in movies, television, and pop culture with the message that a father is expendable to both marriage and parenting. When a Hollywood "A-lister" has a baby without bothering to marry or chooses artificial insemination so that the "father" is only a sperm donor, the only thing we wonder about is how soon after giving birth she's going to be bikini-ready. The father is not viewed as an integral part of having or raising a child. It's no surprise that people are confused about the purpose of marriage when it's seen as a separate issue from having children.

Earthly fathers have become so marginalized that even when believers speak of "God the Father," it's hard to know what that means.

(Same with "Founding Fathers.") The word seems diminished some-how.

It's hard to convince people that the monogamous marriage of a mother and father matters when the divorce rate approaches 50 per-cent, births to unwed mothers equal or exceed those to married couples, and cultural role models cohabitate and have children without the commitment of a lifetime marriage. This is why—and I'll bet you didn't expect to hear this from me—the claim that same-sex marriage is de-stroying society is actually greatly overstated. Christians who themselves abandoned the primacy of lifelong marriage to follow the divorce and remarriage customs of a secular society have as much to answer for as do those who militantly push to redefine marriage. Sadly, many church leaders already have loosened the definition to allow for unrestricted divorce and remarriage and now feign to be "Shocked! Shocked!" when even more versions of marriage are proposed.

The dominant culture of Bubble-ville is based on the man-centered view that all people are basically good, that everyone gets to follow his or her own set of morals, and "if it feels good, do it." The dominant culture of Bubba-ville is based on the belief that there is a God, we can know Him, and the rules we ought to live by are His. The difference shines through clearly in the arguments one hears in support of same-sex marriage: "Why can't I marry the person of *my* choice? Who has the right to tell *me* I can't?" I, me, mine.

The arguments for ignoring the history of nearly every civilization in recorded time and insisting on a redefinition of marriage are almost always expressed in very personal terms—what "best" satisfies the feel-ings and passions of the person desiring to marry within his or her own gender. Rarely is there cited an objective source of authority, whether it be the experience of past cultures; a religious source such as the Bible or Koran; or, for that matter, the teachings of Confucius.

It's not my intent to be combative or to appear to be uncaring or indifferent to what are true desires and passions. But the attempt to tar those who don't support same-sex marriage (still a majority in

Bubba-ville) as homophobic bigots is simply disingenuous; it's a tactic to cut off rational debate by impugning the motives of the other side. This isn't a matter of hating or fearing gay people; it's a matter of loving God, seeking to honor the clear descriptions of marriage as repeatedly revealed in Scripture, and maintaining faithfulness to the institution of the family.

Let's examine the first question I posed: Are there limits on which combinations of relationships are allowed and which are not? If man/man and woman/woman marriages are considered normal and acceptable, what about marriage between a man and multiple women? Or multiple men? Are women limited to marrying one man or one woman, but not both at the same time? By what standard has this been determined? Who has the authority to decide? No one? Okay, then, should we include *any* relationship?

When I have posed such a question to gay activists, I've often found myself at the receiving end of angry, profanity-laced rants that same-sex marriage is only about two people loving each other. They're missing my point: Why limit marriage to just two people? If we're going to accommodate one sexual preference, isn't it only *fair* to accommodate any and all preferences? If mere consent of the participants makes something right, then any combination of consenting adults should be absolutely legal, moral, and defensible.

As for the broader context of marriage, there are historical, psychological, sociological, theological, and biological aspects of a marital relationship. I fully understand that it's awkward to bring some of these up, but if we want a legitimate and honest assessment of whether it's in the best interest of society to make a radical change in what marriage means, then it's imperative that we have a full conversation about it.

Some of the objections to same-sex marriage are biological (this is the awkward part, but here we go). Male and female bodies were designed by the Creator (that's my God-centered view and I'm sticking to it) so that they complement each other physically. It's truly a wonder that the male body has the capacity to physically unite with the female body for the purpose of copulation and procreation. In the act of conceiving a child, a man and woman literally do become "one flesh," as it's described in the Bible, in that they create a new individual with unique DNA. (I love that the "one flesh" description of sex was written thousands of years before we knew anything about genetic code.) Sex is also a way for husband and wife to strengthen their emotional connection. And, yes, it's obvious that sexual union also has a recreational value. Even so, while two bodies of the same gender can engage in a variety of sexual activities, which can certainly involve a deep emotional connection, none of them fit the natural physical expression that is the male/female union as I believe God designed.

When advocates of same-sex marriage say, "What's the harm?" the honest reply is that at this point, we simply don't have enough reliable accumulated data to be able to say. While homosexuality has been around throughout recorded history, with references to it even in the Old Testament, one has to be more imaginative than Pixar to claim that the Bible approves of homosexual behavior, much less homosexual marriage. One would have to say that the traditions as well as the biblical texts are simply *wrong*.

If a person doesn't accept a God-centered worldview, and with it a God who establishes the "ground rules" for life, then it's possible to accommodate pretty much any lifestyle imaginable. This is not to say that nonbelievers can't see the wisdom of following many faith-based traditional norms; many do, and strive to lead a moral life just for the sake of doing good and making the world a better place. Nonbelievers can certainly commit to lifelong fidelity, just as Christians can, because they grew up with those "ground rules" and see the Earthly benefits of having them.

But if we lose those "ground rules" and start redefining marriage, where do we stop? *Can* we stop? Are there any limits on what marriage can mean? For example, if a person is self-described as bisexual, equally comfortable relating to members of either gender, then by the very nature of the mandate to allow people to love anyone they want, shouldn't a bisexual be able to have both a male and a female spouse? Wouldn't restricting that person access to both genders be denying the bisexual his or her marriage "equality"?

While I realize that the biological and historical aspects of marriage are grounded in some level of objective research and data, the psychological and sociological components are more complicated. Until the 1970s, homosexuality was considered a disorder. Was the change in the definition based on sound science and objective research, or was it in part the result of political pressure? Is Lady Gaga correct when she sings about being "Born This Way"? We know that some people appear to transition from straight to gay, and sometimes back again, but others seem extremely unlikely to do this. It's apparent that numerous factors are involved in sexual orientation; as with global warming and virtually every other issue being studied, the science is not settled! Someday we'll look back on this time and marvel at how little we knew.

The most controversial and contentious aspect of homosexuality is theological. If one doesn't consider Scripture to be the last word in moral absolutes, then this area of the discussion is irrelevant. But for the sake of explaining to those outside the land of God, guns, grits, and gravy why this issue is not malleable for Bible-believing Christians, I will clarify.

To believers, marriage is not merely a secular institution; if it were, it would naturally reflect the contemporary culture of any given moment. As I mentioned earlier, true adherents of Scripture recognize that homosexual marriage is not the only departure from the ideal. Divorce, adultery, and cohabitation also fall short of the biblical standard. But it's not because God is the great cosmic killjoy in the sky who wants to clamp down on our pleasures. In God's creation, marriage is the natural relationship that two people experience as they join together spiritually, emotionally, and physically. It is also the "picture" of the relationship Christ has with His church. (Not the building, of course, but the body of believers.) The Bible speaks of "male and female created He them." And of the union, He said, "A man shall leave his mother and father, and a woman shall leave her home, and the two will become one flesh." Pretty clear on that. For believers, changing the definition of marriage is no more an option than it would be for observant Jews to serve bacon-wrapped shrimp or Hindus to open a steakhouse.

One striking irony is that while gays are fighting to get married, marriage as an institution in the rest of the population struggles. (Numerous stand-up comics do their own versions of the joke, "I think same-sex marriage should be legal! Why shouldn't gays have the right to be every bit as miserable as the rest of us?") Maybe when we create a culture in which marriage means anything and everything, it ends up meaning nothing. According to the Centers for Disease Control, the percentage of out-of-wedlock births stood at just under 41 percent for 2012.

In 2009, Janice Shaw Crouse penned a piece for the magazine *American Thinker* which stated that the incidence of cohabitation without marriage had increased 1,000 percent since 1970 and that nearly 50 percent of adults age twenty to forty had lived together without marriage. One-third of those households included children. Marriage as an institution is not so much threatened by same-sex couples as it is by heterosexuals' increasing indifference to it.

As for the argument that legalization of same-sex marriage would affect only gays, that has proven to be the utter nonsense most rational people knew it to be. *Case in point:* An engaged lesbian couple, Rachel Cryer and Laurel Bowman, wanted Sweet Cakes by Melissa—a bakery in Portland, Oregon, owned and operated by a Christian couple, Aaron and Melissa Klein—to make their wedding cake. The Kleins wouldn't do it, citing their Christian views. The lesbian couple filed a complaint with the state of Oregon, and the Oregon Bureau of Labor and Industries determined that the Kleins had violated the Oregon Equality Act of 2007, a law designed to protect gays from discrimination. The Kleins faced thousands of dollars in fines and penalties, plus a harsh retaliation from gay rights activists who picketed their bakery and threatened those who did business there. The Kleins closed their retail bakery and now operate the business out of their home, still facing what the state calls "reconciliation" (*translation:* a requirement to give up the expression of their devout religious faith). The Kleins didn't refuse service to the women because they were lesbians; they simply declined to make a cake for the express purpose of a same-sex wedding.

It was far from an isolated instance.

Jack Phillips, a Denver baker, was ordered by a judge to either provide cakes for same-sex weddings or face fines [CharismaNews.com. "Christian Cake Artist Sent to 'Re-Education' After Gay Marriage Flap," July 29, 2014].

In New Mexico, the state Supreme Court ruled that two Christian photographers who turned down photographing a same-sex wedding violated the state's Human Rights Act, even though same-sex marriage was illegal in New Mexico at the time! [Breitbart.com. "Same-Sex Marriage, Religious Liberty Collide in Case Presented to Supreme Court," November 8, 2013].

In Washington State, the attorney general filed a lawsuit attacking Arlene's Flowers and Gifts because owner Barronelle Stutzman had declined to provide flowers for a gay wedding [SeattleTimes.com. "State Sues Florist over Refusing Service for Gay Wedding," April 9, 2013].

So much for same-sex marriages not affecting anyone else. If these business owners had refused to let someone buy a cupcake or said no to taking a portrait solely because the customer was gay, it would clearly be a civil rights violation and obvious discrimination. But in the case of arranging flowers, making a cake, or taking photos, there is not only a business component but an artistic one. An artist should have the right to say, "I cannot express what you desire artistically because the statement it makes violates my own conscience and my free speech rights."

Imagine that a member of a socially liberal, mostly gay congregation owned a T-shirt shop and that someone came in to buy a custom T-shirt with the message PRAY THE GAY AWAY! Would the shop owner be taken to court for advising the customer that he should try *another*

T-shirt shop? Should the courts force a gay business owner to print such a shirt? And would the gay community say, "Oh, yeah, we're fine with it. He should have to make that shirt"?

The manner in which same-sex marriage is being implemented should be of great concern even to those who support it. While the euphoria of seeing it made "legal" in numerous states tends to overwhelm a rational and thoughtful conversation about the process, we have a serious constitutional question on our hands.

At the time of this writing, no state has passed a people's referendum or initiative to allow marriage other than the traditional kind, one man/one woman. A very small number of states have passed laws to allow same-sex marriage, but most of the states where it was made "legal" were states in which the decision was made by judges. Here we have the judicial branch acting totally on its own, not only making the decision but prescribing and implementing the solution. Those of us who believe in a balance of powers have a problem with that.

Our government was intentionally designed with very thoughtful checks and balances. The three branches of government—legislative, executive, and judicial—are equal in power. Let me say that again: They are EQUAL. Judicial is not a "super" branch. Even the *Supreme* Court is only the supreme or highest part of the *judicial* branch and is not to be seen as having supremacy over the executive and legislative branches. The highest authority of government within our system remains *the people*, whose consent is required to govern at all!

When the people of a state vote to affirm traditional marriage, as has happened in thirty-two states at the time of this writing, the courts should respect that the ultimate voice has spoken. Should the Supreme Court find that the people have violated their own Constitution and created a law that exceeds the power granted to the legislative or executive branches, the most it can do is declare the law unconstitutional. I've been stunned that even some graduates of prestigious law schools believe that, just because they've gotten away with it before, courts not only can declare something unconstitutional but also exceed that authority, assuming the functions of the legislative and executive branches and prescribing the fix, all by themselves.

Judges can rule that the legislative branch has passed laws violating the Constitution and even advise the executive branch not to enforce them, but it cannot dictate to those two independent and equal branches exactly what they are to do. That is the practice of "judicial supremacy," and it's the equivalent of a coup d'état! If same-sex marriage is mandated by the courts, instead of by laws passed in the duly authorized legislature and signed and carried out by the executive branch, then the courts have trampled on the Constitution.

If that sounds just fine to you, keep in mind that if a left-leaning court can *give*, a right-leaning court can *take away*, and woe unto us if we allow politicized courts to become just another manifestation of partisan-driven government. The pendulum will swing back and forth, and "progressives" will rue the day they relied on a power-mad judiciary to achieve for them what couldn't or wouldn't be enacted through prescribed channels. Dependence on a "super branch" that lords over the other two is not to be celebrated but stopped in its tracks.

When Judge Chris Piazza, a local circuit court judge for one Arkansas county, decided that the amendment to the Arkansas Constitution affirming traditional marriage was invalid, he authorized all seventy-five counties to begin issuing marriage licenses immediately. It was outrageous enough that he had acted unilaterally and ignored a 70-percent vote of the people, but when he opened the gates not just for his circuit but for the entire state, his arrogance was stunning. Of course, he issued his opinion late on a Friday afternoon, after most courthouses and state and county offices had closed. His very calculated decision had been timed so that attorneys—even the attorney general—couldn't file for an injunction against same-sex marriage licenses. An injunction would've allowed time for appeal and review by a *much* higher judicial authority than a single circuit court judge in Pulaski County, Arkansas.

I will never believe we should create a form of marriage that by definition fails to meet the biblical ideal. Should there come a day in which *the people* of America vote to establish new versions of marriage—with their direct vote or through their elected representatives—those who oppose this change will face a choice: to either accept it, ignore it, or rebel against it. If a single judge can rebel against the people's law, has he not encouraged others to do the same?

8

All Grown Up! (Country Folks Can Survive)

IT WAS THE BOY'S FIRST experience playing baseball. He was only five, and he was invited to a birthday party for a boy from his church who was a couple of years older than he was. Being about the youngest kid there, he was already nervous and afraid. Now, he was being placed on the field to participate in a game that he had seen but didn't understand. He was being coached through each step by his friend, the other boys, and the boys' parents. As he stood at bat for the very first time in his life, he was told just to watch for the ball and swing the bat at it. That's exactly what he did. Miraculously, the bat and the ball connected, and as the baseball went sailing through the infield, the other boys screamed, "Run!" He made it to first base. When the next batter hit, he was told to run again—this time to second base. The next batter got a hit and the boy was told to go to third base, which he did. He hoped he was doing things right but was still a bit unsure about the mechanics of the game. When the next boy at the plate hit the ball, he wasn't sure exactly what to do but immediately heard screams from everywhere, "GO HOME! GO HOME!" With that, the little boy just started crying. "I can't go home. My mother's not here to take me home!"

That story is true. I should know, because the little boy who thought his friends literally wanted him to go home was me. I didn't know the terms or rules for baseball then. At age five, I was pretty sure that the only way I could have made it home would be for my mother to come pick me up and take me.

I'm happy to report that I know a little more about baseball now and could probably find my way home on my own from just about anywhere these days. If I couldn't figure it out, I'm pretty sure I wouldn't break down and cry. I'd just use my Google Maps app on my iPhone.

My parents encouraged me to do my best and wouldn't tolerate a half-hearted effort from me at anything, be it school, household chores, sports, or music. But I never faced some unholy pressure to speak six languages before I was seven, be a violin virtuoso at age five, or win every game I played. My parents certainly would have been proud of me if I had, but superachievement wasn't a condition of their love and approval. Like most kids in Bubba-ville, I grew up with a more relaxed, low-pressure way of life.

I'm so glad I didn't grow up with a dictatorial "Tiger Mom" or hovering "helicopter parents." To be sure, there are kids living in the land of God, guns, grits, and gravy—geographically speaking—whose parents raise them as if they were anointed from the moment of conception to go to an Ivy League school, but that's not the norm. One reason people choose to live and raise their families far away from the pressure pots of New York, Washington, D.C., and Los Angeles is to let their kids be kids.

I've known and talked to parents who started trying to get their children on waiting lists for the best preschools and elementary schools even before they were born. I do understand the desire of parents to make sure their child has the best opportunities possible, but perhaps we've become a bit obsessed with pushing the achievement bar higher and higher and expecting it to be reached at lower and lower ages.

Dr. Steven D. Levitt, coauthor of the best-selling book *Freakonomics,* has written that his research found no correlation between high-pressure early childhood education and high academic achievement later in life. In fact, he warned that forcing young children into intense learning environments and pushing them to exceed the norms for their age group can result in negative consequences—children who later in life burn out from being "all work and no play."

And play should be just that—*play*. If all play for children is mapped out, thoroughly planned, and choreographed; if "play dates" are executed with the precision of a NASA launch, it's really not play at all. It's duty. You know that something's gone askew when "play" is harder work than work. It ought to be okay for children's play to be largely self-directed and built on imagination. Creativity and resourcefulness are far greater tools for success later in life than being able to understand quantum physics before they're out of training pants.

In my neighborhood, most of us didn't have the latest and greatest in TV-advertised toys, but we made up for it with our imaginations. If we watched a movie about the Knights of the Round Table, we naturally wanted to be knights. Our bicycles were our horses, old metal trash can lids were great shields, and sawed-off broomsticks or yardsticks were very adequate swords. If we played army (which we did a lot in those days not far removed from World War II and Korea), sticks could be made into pistols and rifles, and we'd build "forts" with downed tree limbs, discarded cardboard boxes, and random scraps of lumber. It's a good thing we didn't have enough money to buy realistic toys or refuse to play until we had hundreds of dollars' worth of electronics in the form of an Xbox or PlayStation. Instead, we relied on being forced to create something out of nothing. Learning to make do with what we had rather than what we wished we had was a blessing. Of course, I was an adult before I realized this.

I can't remember the kids in my neighborhood ever saying, "We can't play policemen because we don't have electronic sirens and actual flashing red lights or real handcuffs and badges." We'd stick playing cards in the spokes of our bike wheels and secure them with clothespins to give our bikes the sound of a motorcycle, we learned to scream about as loud as a siren, we made "handcuffs" out of little pieces of rope, and our pointed index fingers were the pistols. (These days, kids are routinely expelled from school for pointing their fingers like a gun, though I don't recall anyone ever getting shot by a pointed finger in all the years that I pointed mine.)

Lest you think kids like me were horribly deprived by the lack of more elaborate, expensive, and realistic toys, please be assured that we developed a MacGyver-like penchant for coming up with solutions to various challenges because we spent half our time in imaginative play and the other half trying to create the tools and toys we played with. Growing up as I did meant that when I faced a problem, I focused on solving it with what I had rather than by trying to obtain what I didn't have and probably couldn't afford anyway. Rather than leading to material depravity and a deep despair over being a victim of poverty, my experience taught me to be resourceful. "Playtime" was, for me, a never-ending lesson in finding ways to solve problems based on the creative use of materials at hand.

When we wore out the only baseball we had and the cover came off, we didn't throw it away. We just put black electrical tape on it and went right on playing. If you don't know, that stuff is like duct tape; you can do just about anything with it! In fact, Jay Leno, in his days on *The Tonight Show,* used to do a segment called (sorry) "White Trash Repairs," showing pictures of highly imaginative fixes, some of them genius, some of them terrible, all of them fall-down funny. This sort of thing is common in rural America, where even if you have the money to do a slick repair job, it might be a pretty long drive to the nearest Home Depot. I probably played with as many "black tape" baseballs as I did with cowhide-covered ones.

As kids, we improvised a *lot.* When we couldn't afford to buy nice headlights for our bikes, we'd tape a flashlight to the handlebars. If we wanted to go frog gigging and cook the frog legs over a campfire but didn't have a "store-bought" gig, we'd tape the end of a garden tool onto a broomstick to make what we needed. There was no money for expensive artificial fishing lures, but digging up worms in our yards was easy enough, and if we couldn't find any real fishing hooks, a safety pin would work. Since this was Arkansas and none of us anticipated ever seeing salt water in person, we "surfed" by making a skateboard from a piece of lumber, attaching wheels from roller skates to the bottom, and finally attaching a rope to a bicycle and "skiing" behind the bike in a parking lot. Cowabunga!

Such creative solutions were good training ground for adult problem solving. A great example of this comes from my friend Nancy, a makeup artist in Little Rock who often did TV makeup for appearances I made while I was governor and later as a Fox News host doing live hits from Little Rock. She's a lovely and terrific person who moved about forty minutes away from Little Rock to a small community so she wouldn't have to put up with the hassles of city life. We've often talked about the joys of growing up in rural America where "heavy traffic" was three pickup trucks on our street in a single hour. Nancy is a hardworking lady who as far as I can recall doesn't have a college degree, but rather got her credentials by taking the jobs that came her way and doing them so well that she is often the first-call makeup artist for movies and TV commercials filmed in Arkansas and nearby states.

Nancy once told me about a time she and some of her friends went out to eat. They wanted to sit around and talk for a long time after the meal, but she had an early call the next morning for a commercial shoot and wanted simply to go home and get some sleep. She had ridden to the dinner in another friend's car, and when that friend didn't want to leave early, Nancy decided to find another way home. She was living in Little Rock at the time and called the local cab company, but they wanted to charge her almost $25 just to get home. She then noticed that next door to the restaurant where they'd been eating was a Papa John's Pizza. Nancy called and said she wanted to order a pizza for delivery. She gave her address and then said she was next door and would like to go with them when they delivered the pizza to her house. The boss said that was okay, and for $12, Nancy got a ride home *and* a pizza.

Nancy is a wonderful example of the difference between an educated person and a smart person. There are people with more education, and who certainly *think* they're the smart ones. But you'd be hard-pressed to find people with more "smarts" than someone like Nancy. Have you ever heard it said of someone that he was "educated beyond his intelligence"? Look around and you'll see, we've got plenty of people who are exactly that—especially in government. (We have so many Harvard and Yale grads in D.C. that if they all got tuition refunds, they could pay off the national debt—and judging from the results of this brain trust, most of them deserve a tuition refund.) Give me a smart person any day over one with an education who lacks the resourcefulness to solve problems with whatever is available.

In the governor's office, I often said I had two kinds of people working for me: people who would figure out how to get something done, and those who would spend more time explaining why it couldn't be done than it would have taken to get it done! I'm sure you've figured out that I preferred the kind who could figure out how to get it done.

One of my staff people, Gary Underwood, ran media operations for the governor's office. He had been with me for many years. We'd built a community television station together prior to my going into politics, and to stay within our shoestring budget, we had to be very creative when it came to making things work. Gary didn't have formal training in television, but he learned it the best way—by *doing* it. He came up with some really inventive solutions. For example, if we needed lighting and couldn't afford to buy a professional lighting kit for $5,000, Gary would go to Sam's Club and buy some work lights, the kind you'd use in a shop. Their "color temperature" was not a pure 3,200-degree kelvin— the ideal for TV—but the 3,000-degree kelvin of the work lights was adequate. He even figured out a way to hook the camera and the lights up to car batteries so we could be portable. We ran a TV station for a fraction of what it should have cost to do it, because Gary had more smarts than he had education about TV. Had he been too educated about it, he would have known that doing what we needed to do was simply impossible on the budget we had. But Gary, not being such an "expert" that he could simply throw up his hands and walk away, went ahead and made it possible.

This true story affirms the old tale about the aeronautical engineer who studied the bumblebee and surmised that due to its size, weight, wingspan, and dimensions, it was impossible for the bumblebee to fly. Case closed. The bumblebee, in its ignorance of these scientific facts, continued to fly anyway. The part about bees defying the laws of physics may not be true, but the part about humans declaring things impossible most certainly is!

So allowing children to be children may turn out to be the best education of all. Children in rural America whose parents might not be able to put them on a prebirth waiting list to attend a $30,000-a-year *preschool* aren't necessarily doomed to a life of failure and lost opportunity. William Doherty, professor of family studies and director of the marriage and family therapy program at the University of Minnesota, says, "The experiences we thought kids had to have before high school have moved down to junior high and now elementary. Soon, we'll be talking about leadership opportunities for toddlers [*The New York Times,* "Family Happiness and the Overbooked Child," August 12, 2011]. But it's mostly just talk, talk, talk.

There is enormous tension between those who rail against "the overscheduled child" and those who say children need to be pushed to excel and to achieve great things. The arguments from the experts miss the point that common sense ought to teach us: Kids are different. Profound, huh? Simply put, some kids are prodigies. Not only are they unusually gifted, they can comfortably handle a busy schedule, the pressure of deadlines, and the looming expectations of performance in the midst of intense competition. But it's simply wrong to measure a child's worth by these sorts of standards. The child needs to sense a balance to what clinical psychologist Paula Broom calls the difference between human "doing" and human "being." The value or worth of a child is not in what he or she can do, but in what he or she *is*.

Other kids may be smart and capable but, even at their "personal best," probably won't set the academic curve or break long-standing athletic records. Kids don't necessarily develop according to a timetable. They may have a particular talent or interest that won't be discovered for years—perhaps even late in life.

Parental anxiety may be best described by the term "helicopter parent," coined by Dr. Haim Ginott in 1969 in reference to parents who were so afraid of their little darlings being hurt or having a stumble that they "hovered" over them like helicopters, ready to swoop in and save them like a Black Hawk on a rescue mission.

Debate over parenting styles rages on. Amy Chua's controversial book, *Battle Hymn of the Tiger Mother,* gave rise to a national conversation over whether or not it's better to have Eastern-style parents who control every aspect of their children's lives and demand total obedience and perfection from them. This philosophy defines success incredibly narrowly—to the point of restricting the musical instruments one's child may study to piano and violin. It's fair to say that most Western parents would be downright horrified at the thought of such extreme authoritarianism, even if it resulted in straight A-pluses, perfect SATs, and a full scholarship to Harvard Medical School.

At the other end of the spectrum is the view best described by Lenore Skenazy in her book *Free Range Kids*: *How to Raise Safe, Self-Reliant Children* (*Without Going Nuts with Worry*). Skenazy takes the more laissez-faire approach, believing that parents need to relax and let children learn through their own mistakes, risk-taking, and independence. Skenazy once allowed her nine-year-old son to take the New York subway home alone from Bloomingdale's. Many Americans were horrified by this approach, too.

But unless it was at night, I can't honestly say I'm so shocked that a nine-year-old could get home safely on the subway in New York. I regularly ride the subway there, and unless it is very late at night or involves getting off in certain neighborhoods, I've never seen a reason to assume inherent danger on the subway. The streets of New York are a different story—not so much because of predators, but because of crazy cab drivers and bicyclists riding through stoplights and going against traffic.

In fact, the story of the nine-year-old made me reflect upon my own childhood and how completely independent we were at that age. We rode bikes all over town, stayed gone for hours, and never thought about going home before dark. Our parents weren't worried about us until "dark-thirty." And, remember, this was before cell phones; they didn't have that way to track us down. If my mom and dad had been helicopter parents, they would have run out of fuel and crashed, not while hovering over us, but while trying to *find* us.

Sometimes, it's not the kids I worry about, but the parents. When some parents in Colorado Springs, Colorado, couldn't stand the thought that *their* precious offspring might not find enough eggs at a community Easter egg hunt, they tore through the rope separating them from the children in the hunting area and proceeded to shove other parents and children out of the way so they could grab the eggs. One "exemplary" parent explained, "I promised my kid an Easter egg hunt, and I'd want to give him an even edge" [*The Huffington Post*, "Aggressive Parents Force Colorado Egg Hunt Cancellation," March 26, 2012]. The following year's Easter egg hunt was canceled.

A ninth-grade honors English teacher posted at Reddit a story about giving a D grade to a student for a paper. The mother of the student came to the school in a rage and argued the paper deserved an A. When the teacher asked her why, the mother huffed, "I have a college degree, and I wrote this paper myself" [Reddit.com. "Teachers of Reddit, What Is the Worst Case of 'Helicopter Parenting' You Have Ever Encountered," September 9, 2013]. I can just imagine this poor kid begging, "Mom . . . please . . . stop helping me!"

Somehow, even without parents getting their babies into the top private schools before they've left the delivery room, the human race has survived. And if I were in a roomful of people facing a real jam—a group including some farm kids, say, and some Ivy League grads—and I had to handpick the team to get us out of it, I'd take the kids from the farm.

Oh, and my friend Nancy, if I'm lucky enough to have her there. You never know when a pizza and a ride home will come in handy!

One of the great moments I've had hosting a TV show for Fox News Channel was when Hank Williams Jr. was on the show. I love his music, I love his genius for lyric writing, and I just love ol' Hank, period. His classic song may say it all . . .

A Country Boy Can Survive

The preacher man says it's the end of time
And the Mississippi River she's a goin' dry
The interest is up and the stock market's down
And you only get mugged if you go down town

I live back in the woods you see
Just my woman and the kids and the dog and me
I've got a shot gun, a rifle, and a four-wheel drive
And a country boy can survive
Country folks will survive.

I can plow a field all day long
And catch catfish from dusk 'til dawn.
We make our own whiskey and our own smoke too,
Ain't too many things these old boys can't do.
We grow good tomatoes make homemade wine
And a country boy can survive
Country folks will survive.

'Cause you can't starve us out
An' ya can't make us run
'Cause we're them ole boys raised on shot guns.
We say grace and we say Mamm
If you ain't into that we don't give a damn.

We come from West Virginia coal mines,
And the Rocky Mountains and the western skies.
And we can skin a buck and run a trot line
And a country boy can survive
Country folks can survive.

I had a good friend in New York City,
He never called me by my name just hillbilly
My grandpa taught me how to live off the land
And his taught him to be a business man.
He sent me pictures of the Broadway lights
I'd send him some homemade wine.

But he was killed by a man with a switchblade knife
For forty three dollars my friend lost his life.
I'd like to spit some beechnut in that dude's eyes
And shoot him with my old forty five,
And a country boy can survive
Country folks can survive.

9

Personal Freedom—
"GET OFF MY LAWN!"

CLINT EASTWOOD'S MEMORABLE PERFORMANCE with the empty stool at the 2012 Republican National Convention in Tampa was roundly criticized and even condemned by the chattering class. It was unscripted, impromptu, and authentic—totally unlike the overscripted, choreographed, and contrived *rest* of the convention. Full disclosure: I was one of the speakers at that convention, as I have been in other years, and I've always been completely exasperated by the "nervous Nellie" approach taken by convention planners to ensure that every syllable uttered from the stage is preapproved. It's exhausting to fight for every word in one's speech and be forced to go to "rehearsals" where "professional speech coaches" drill the speakers on the sometimes awkward and unnatural stage mannerisms that I uniformly ignored. While I don't claim to be the best public speaker in the world—by any stretch—I'm pretty sure I've done it more and had greater success at it than the people trying to tell me how to stand at a podium.

That's why I personally loved the Eastwood speech. He broke all the rules and went out there and was himself. (Who's going to tell *Clint Eastwood* that he can't?) That empty-chair symbolism, spot-on accurate as it was at the time, has turned out to be astonishingly and sadly prophetic. I had only one disappointment about his speech: I honest-to-God wanted him to go out there and reprise his role from the 2008 film *Gran Torino* and say in his iconic gruff voice, "GET OFF MY LAWN!"

For many of us, that pretty well sums up our attitude toward the nanny-state government that wants to make sure we live "The Life of Julia" that President Obama extolled in the online cartoon rolled out during the 2012 campaign. It depicted a woman named Julia who from cradle to grave was dependent on all things "government" and could live her life only with the ever-present and all-guiding hand of Uncle Sugar. (As I recounted earlier, the phrase "Uncle Sugar," popular throughout my lifetime and immediately understood by every Southerner as a descriptive mash-up of Uncle Sam and "sugar daddy," became controversial when I uttered it during a speech in D.C. in January 2014. Some media elites who must rarely venture forth from their comfortable confines in Bubble-ville thought there was something nefarious about the term.) To many self-reliant Americans, the notion of "Julia" was a disturbing combination of insult and laugh-out-loud revelation of how our "nannies" in government must think of the poor, feckless American people—or must deeply desire to train and condition them to be.

I actually felt sorry for the people who thought Julia's little life was something to be celebrated as a tribute to the wonderful, all-encompassing role government plays in our lives. In my own role as a parent, it was never my hope that I would raise my three children in a way that would make them dependent on *me* for their entire lives. I would be heartbroken and distraught if three able-bodied adult children felt unable or unwilling to leave the nest and try their wings; that my parenting had left them paralyzed and clinging to their mother and me for the rest of their lives would be unthinkable. Friends of mine who have children with incapacitating physical or mental disabilities have had no choice but to keep them at home for their entire lives. But they provide never-ending care out of necessity—not because it's the way they'd hoped it would be. The willing sacrifices they make are extraordinary, but they would be the first to say that it's not the life they would have chosen for their children.

"The Life of Julia" was in many ways a revelation of how proponents of Big Government view life. Intervention by government at each stage of Julia's existence makes her life possible. From food stamps to Medicaid to rent subsidies to tuition assistance to the Women and Infant Children (WIC) program to welfare checks to Medicare to even a government-subsidized community garden, just to name a few of the programs, good ol' Julia survives only because she is a ward of the state her entire life, as is her child. Where Julia's husband/spouse/partner/sperm donor/baby daddy is, we never know. In the minds of those who love all things government, a participating father is so irrelevant, he's not even worth mentioning. Government is both protector and provider. Who needs anybody else when you've got Uncle Sugar? (Maybe he even fathered Julia's kid through a Planned Parenthood grant.)

We've discussed "helicopter parents," who hover over their children to swoop in and protect them from every scrape, bump, and bruise. Today, we're also faced with the prospect of "helicopter government," which is similarly poised to swoop in and rescue us from life's trials and tribulations. Of course, the government also has to make sure that the staggering cost of "hovering" is passed on to the dupes they can force to pony up and subsidize the programs.

(Incidentally, it's a lot easier to dupe people who haven't even been born yet; this explains the stupefying national debt.)

But for many of us in Bubba-ville, we'd like to join Clint Eastwood in saying to the government, "GET OFF MY LAWN!"

The contractor who built our house has a plaque glued to the back of his government-mandated construction site hard hat. It says, GETTING WELFARE OUGHT TO BE AT LEAST AS HARD AS GETTING A BUILDING PERMIT. I understand this sentiment very well, thanks to my experience with both. As governor, I was responsible for making welfare available to those who needed it and even spent a day working in an office of the Department of Human Services as an intake clerk. I'd made it part of my practice during my ten and a half years as governor to spend a minimum of one day every six weeks working at the delivery level of state government. I also required this of my senior staff and cabinet officials so we'd understand from the ground up what we did, why we did it, and how we could do it better. I can attest that we intentionally made the process of helping truly needy citizens as painless as possible. I'm quite aware that some government programs are vital, filling gaps for people going through tough periods and struggling through no fault of their own. And while the ideal, arguably, would be for them to receive help from their families, their neighbors, or their church, mosque, or synagogue, sometimes the only fallback they have is a public assistance program.

At the same time, while I truly don't begrudge assisting people who are struggling with serious illness, unemployment, family crises, or unexpected calamities, I find it quite disheartening that accessing a handout from the government is typically much easier than getting it out of the way so one can build a house, start a business, or hire a new employee (which can require a roomful of lawyers and accountants and the patience of Job!). For example, before my wife, Janet, and I could build our house along the Florida Panhandle Gulf Coast, we needed a permit from the Department of Environmental Protection (DEP). Because the permit was being sought at a time of devastation in the real estate and construction markets, with virtually no construction going on, getting a building permit should have been a snap. The DEP had the same number of employees working that area as they'd had during the boom times in 2004 to 2006, when there were dozens if not hundreds of permit applications being submitted. The window for DEP to issue a permit, once requested, was ninety days. The contractor assumed that since there were few if any applicants ahead of us, our permit might be granted much sooner, probably in thirty days at most. He had several crews of construction workers who hadn't been on a job site in months, and this would give them their first real paychecks in quite a while. The sooner the permit was issued, the sooner these crews would go to work and get paid.

So, we submitted our application, and then . . . thirty days went by . . . forty-five days . . . sixty days . . . seventy-five days, and still no permit. A couple of times during this waiting period, DEP would ask our engineer or architect for some aspect of the plans that had already been sent. Our people would respond that the information *had* been sent, noting the date and even the acknowledgment from DEP that they'd received it. Their response was to channel the late Gilda Radner's Emily Litella character from the early days of *Saturday Night Live* and say, "Never mind." More days wasted. More days that working-class people were at home waiting instead of on the job, building. Finally, on about Day 88 of the process, the permit came. My contractor was understandably disgusted, as was I. It was costing everyone money—the contractor, the workers, me. The only people to whom it didn't matter were the ones determining the timetable: the brick-wall bureaucrats at DEP, who took eighty-eight days of a ninety-day window to issue a simple permit that shouldn't have taken more than a week.

Trying to bring some comfort to the contractor, or at least some explanation, I told him: "There's a reason why that office would slow-walk the permit and take it right to the limit. If it were known that permits could be issued in far less time than ninety days, someone might determine that maybe there were more people than necessary in the DEP office. After all, since so many construction workers and real estate people were laid off during that time because of the lack of work, it would stand to reason that government employees serving the industry might need to experience some layoffs as well, to save the taxpayers some money. But if you think that, you don't understand how government really works. Never mind how things work in the private sector, where money matters and if you aren't making any, then you have to cut expenses. In the public sector, you just slow everything down and continue to insist that you need *more* employees and a *bigger* budget.

Cutting expenses equals survival in the private sector economy, but suicide in the public sector economy. Never, ever forget that!"

Most Americans agree that some regulations are sensible and defensible. We would like to know that the airplane we're flying in has been inspected by someone other than Goober Pyle down at the filling station. We want to know that the drugs being injected into our child's veins for his Eustachian tube surgery were thoroughly tested first and are known to be safe. We feel better if someone inspects a suspension bridge over the Mississippi River before we drive a car full of grandkids across it. Yes, there are some things government can and should do as a way of providing some protection to those of us who might not have the time or expertise to test drugs, bridges, or airplanes.

I realize some of my libertarian friends would end pretty much *all* government regulation and let the market decide, but some of us fear that by the time the "market" figures out that a particular restaurant is serving salmonella, some of us might already be dead.

But even the most Big Government–loving, die-hard liberal Democrat should think about the unintended consequences of taking oversight to the level of over*kill*. An example from Florida illustrates: Fort Walton Beach is not too many miles from where I currently live and spend most of my time. In January 2014, the city council voted 3–2 to outlaw the practice of local churches allowing homeless people to sleep at the church without a permit from the city. The reason given was that it might not be safe for homeless people to sleep in a church facility that hadn't been inspected by the fire marshal, the health department, the building code inspector, and God only knows who else. City manager Michael Beedie said, "We can't allow them to sleep in the doorways. We can't allow them to sleep in the halls" [*Northwest Florida Daily News*, "FWB May Enforce Tougher Standards for Cold Night Shelters," January 15, 2014]. (No, of course we can't. So we'll just let them sleep on park benches or on the beach—that's much better.) At least six area churches were sent scrambling to get permits so they could continue their ministry to people nobody else really wanted to deal with.

The city council indicated that it was considering spending up to $30,000 to hire a consultant to study the issue of homelessness and make recommendations, which might include going out and building or buying a facility that would accommodate them.

Here's what I find hard to understand: Churches were already providing the services for free as a ministry, but the city would rather hire a consultant for $30K and then spend considerably more so the city could do at great cost what was already being done at no cost. Yep, that's how Big Government thinks and acts!

I don't mean to be overly critical of the city council. The council genuinely thought it would be helpful to have city inspectors check on the facilities to make sure they had good fire escapes, hot water that met the code, and safe food to serve the homeless. But if a person is eating out of dumpsters, sleeping on a park bench or in a car, and shivering under a donated blanket on a cold night, doesn't an unregulated church building where there's food, bedding, a shower, and some warmth represent an *improvement*? And the fact that it's being done by caring people who get paid nothing means it's not at taxpayer expense. The city did not address the amount of money churches might have to spend to comply with all the rules, but it did announce they would give the permits at "no cost."

Well, la-de-freaking-da! How very generous of the city not to charge the churches to do what *it* otherwise would likely have ended up doing in some form—including charging some of the homeless with vagrancy and locking them up in a nice, state-approved jail cell. If the churches were running the shelter as a commercial enterprise and charging homeless people for the beds, clothes, showers, and meals, then I'd be a bit more sympathetic to the city for wanting to make sure things were on the up-and-up. But if no one had filed a complaint and the homeless people seemed better off than they'd be on the streets begging for coins, one would hope that what the city would be saying to the churches is *Thank you.*

In Shreveport, the Louisiana State Health Department ordered 1,600 pounds of venison to be destroyed. This deer meat—worth $8,000—had been donated by hunters to give to the homeless, but health department bureaucrats rushed in and saved those hungry homeless people from putting their teeth into some of the leanest, healthiest protein that humans can eat because the state hadn't "approved" it. The homeless people *did*—they would have appreciated that meat. But it was taken to the dumpster, and those valiant and courageous protectors of the public poured bleach all over it to make sure it wouldn't be consumed. (Never mind that this bleach-contaminated meat might have poisoned scavenging animals.)

The bureaucrats' reasoning: This deer meat is not allowed to be served, even when it's been processed at a slaughterhouse permitted by the Louisiana Department of Agriculture, because government inspectors weren't there to verify how the deer were killed and how the meat was prepared and stored.

The Louisiana Health Department issued a statement that said, "We must protect the people who eat at Rescue Mission, and we cannot allow potentially serious health threats to endanger the public." Excuse me, but isn't hunger and starvation a much greater threat to the public than some deer meat? This was well-prepared meat; it's not as if someone had dragged in a pile of roadkill and said, "Here ya go!" Gee, I eat meat year-round from the deer I take during hunting season; I guess *I'm* not worth much to the government because they don't stop me from eating it or serving it to guests at my house. Considering the amount of venison I eat each year, it's a miracle I'm not dead already. And my dinner guests must get horribly sick!

Public outrage at this insane overreach resulted in legislation being introduced that would allow hunters to donate meat and game for the hungry and homeless. The only thing more absurd than dumping 1,600 pounds of perfectly good meat into a dumpster and pouring bleach over it is having to pass a law that allows generous hunters to share the very food they feed *their* families with people who are poor. That's right—we actually need laws that allow one to be kind.

I am a hunter and I eat what I hunt. I'm not an animal hater; I'm an animal lover. I love them baked, fried, roasted, grilled, sautéed, steamed, smoked, and poached. Kidding aside, I am very respectful of the life of the animal. I never take the shot without trying to make sure it will be accurate and the animal will go down immediately and not suffer. I'm also aware that without a deliberate harvest of certain animal species such as deer, they would overpopulate, become starved and sick, and ultimately face a cruel death. I know that part of the "circle of life" is hard to swallow (pun intended) for PETA members, but it's the way God made the natural world. One of the most awful things I ever saw was a severely diseased deer venturing into a field where I was hunting. He was a 10-point buck that normally would have been a real trophy for south Arkansas, but he was sick and wasting and obviously suffering. Taking down a deer is usually for the sake of putting meat on the hunter's table, but in this case, it was to end the irreversible misery of a once proud and strong buck. No one who sees a deer in that condition and wants such horrible suffering to continue can be called an animal lover.

In 1887, President Grover Cleveland vetoed a bill that would have sent all of $10,000 to farmers in Texas for seeds to help them through an especially hard drought. His reason? "I can find no warrant for such an appropriation in the Constitution," wrote Cleveland. This doesn't mean that he was hard-hearted and didn't care about the farmers. It means he knew it was his sworn job as President to preserve, protect, and defend the Constitution. He knew not to try to redefine the role of the federal government. He clearly would be appalled to see what D.C.—and specifically the President—is up to these days.

We've drifted quite a distance from the original design of our federal government. The Founders were scared senseless that government would try to grow and stick its national nose into the people's liberty, so they tossed in a few exclamation points at the end of the Constitution that we know as the Bill of Rights. They wanted to make it double-dog definite that future members of Congress wouldn't take it upon themselves to pull a "Captain Kirk" on the people and "boldly go where no man has gone before." The fact that Congress (and, incidentally, the other two branches) ignored their prescribed boundaries, not only veering off course but heading in the opposite direction of the original intent, is testament to their stubbornness and arrogance.

Our country was built on the bedrock belief that government was to be limited and local. Limited, because government can grow only by feeding on the liberty of the ones being governed. If government tells me how bright the lightbulbs on my porch can be, my liberty as it relates to my own property has been taken from me and transferred to the government. The classic lie, "I'm from the government and I'm here to help you," might well be translated, "I'm from the government, and I'm here to *control* you because we think you're too stupid to make decisions on your own."

Also, government was intended to be as local as possible, because the more local it is, the more accountable it is to the people who are being governed. Think about it this way: If you and your family sat down and decided what to have for dinner, that would be called a "family decision." If your neighbors all came over and you decided what to have for dinner, that would be called a "potluck dinner" where I come from. If the federal government sent you a decree and told you what to have for dinner, that would be called insanity, otherwise known as the official policy of the Democrat party.

Most people would prefer to make their own decisions about dinner and a lot of other things, but in this day of inviting Uncle Sugar to take care of you, more and more decisions will be made *for* you rather than *by* you, and they will be made by people so far from you that you will never know or even meet them. Worse, those people will never know *you*. This is why any power not explicitly enumerated in the Constitution is supposed to be off-limits to the federal government. How has that worked out for you?

The value of local decisions is that you will likely get to participate in them. A proposal to build a new park in your neighborhood probably requires that some meetings be held before your city council and planning commission. If you love the idea, it's probably within driving distance for you to slip into the meeting and say so. Try going to D.C. and getting your voice heard on Capitol Hill without hiring a high-priced lobbyist and/or making huge, strategic campaign contributions. You may as well howl at the moon!

Let's be fair in at least acknowledging that government grows because the people demand it. I found out as governor that even self-proclaimed libertarians and "*real* conservatives" are against more government until they are for it. We end up with laws being passed and boards, agencies, and commissions being created because people sit around whining about something or somebody they don't like and sooner or later someone pipes up and says, "There ought to be a law!" It might be a law to make people pick up their dog's poop on the sidewalk or a law declaring that when a pedophile molests a little girl, he has to serve life in prison. No argument there, but just know that when someone says "There ought to be a law," you'll need to reach into your wallet. It's going to cost you. Of course, no one thinks that the part of government *they* want is bad—it's "the right thing to do." But once we create a law, we have to hire someone to see that it's being obeyed. Then we need someone to enforce the law. And someone to adjudicate the law if it's broken. And someone to carry out the punishment of the person who broke the law.

Every law is like that. In a perfect world—if all people were naturally good neighbors who never did selfish things but always acted in the best interest of others—we wouldn't need nearly so many laws. The proliferation of laws is directly proportional to our failure to live by the "Golden Rule" that my mother drilled into me when I was growing up: "Do unto others as you would have others do unto you." Many of our laws exist to deal with those situations caused by people who just "do unto others."

No one wants to be beaten to a pulp by a thug, so if everyone abided by the Golden Rule, no one would get beaten by a thug. By definition, there would *be* no thugs. There would be no domestic violence because no one wants to be a victim of domestic violence. There would be no theft because no one wants to have his or her stuff stolen. There would be no littering because no one wants his own yard covered in someone else's trash.

We pass laws when people *don't* behave kindly toward others. By and large, that's what inspires someone to say, "There ought to be a law!" And the next thing you know, there is one. Soon there are pages and pages of them.

This is why I feel I must educate my hardcore libertarian friends who say, "You can't legislate morality. I don't want the government involved in moral or social issues." But that's exactly why we pass laws *at all*. When people act immorally or without regard for others, laws get passed to set a standard of behavior that would have existed naturally and organically if we all demonstrated a little empathy.

A free people can't exist in a moral vacuum. Liberty is more abundant when the personal behavior of the citizenry is abundantly moral. When people steal, attack, defraud, abuse, or kill, citizens *want* the government to crack down. Laws will be passed and government will grow to more clearly define the boundaries of acceptable behavior.

When someone violates our law, it costs money to investigate the crime, arrest the criminal, pay for his trial (and often for his attorney), and incarcerate him. The cost just for incarceration is staggering. In most every state, it costs more to keep someone in prison for one year than it would to provide college tuition, room and board, books, and even some spending money! The monetary burden created by people who act in contradiction to the morality of the community is far greater than most people realize. It's the cost of paying sandblasters to remove graffiti from buildings and bridges; the cost of juvenile detention homes; the cost of more expensive insurance premiums to cover theft; the cost of policing, surveillance, and enforcement on our streets; and the higher cost of products on the shelves to cover stores' losses due to shoplifting.

And while some call for longer prison sentences and the end of parole, those modifications dramatically increase a state's prison budget. It was my observation that some people who labeled themselves "fiscal conservatives" never saw the disconnect between their call to *increase* the cost of government and their pride in not raising taxes to pay for it. This is where priorities must come into play; an increase in one area of the budget means a decrease—a *real* decrease, not just a fool-the-eye accounting trick—somewhere else.

I don't think we need more money in government; I do think we need more morality and decency in our culture. Just as numerous cultural forces have brought our standards down—*way* down—other influences in society can surely reverse that trend. And if we really want government to "get off my lawn," then part of the solution is better citizens obeying the laws we already have so we don't have to pass new laws to further explain and expand the old ones.

The great writer Tom Wolfe said it best, in his satirical novel *The Bonfire of the Vanities,* through the character of Judge White (played in the movie by Morgan Freeman) as he speaks from the bench: "Let me tell you what justice is. Justice is the law, and the law is man's feeble attempt to set down the principles of decency. Decency! And decency is not a deal. It isn't an angle, or a contract, or a hustle! Decency . . . decency is what your grandmother taught you! It's in your bones! Now you go home. Go home and be decent people. Be decent."

10

Bend Over and Take It Like a Prisoner!

"SPREAD YOUR FEET and put your hands up!" shouted the federal agent. As my computer and wallet were taken from me and out of my sight, I asked, "Can I keep an eye on my wallet, please?"

"No! Don't move! Stay right there," the agent barked in reply.

You may be wondering, "Gov. Huckabee, when were you *arrested*?" Let me assure you, this wasn't an arrest; for me, it was just another day in the airport "security" line, undergoing the process we all endure just to get on a plane. Where else would I be ordered to stand still, put up my hands, and have my personal belongings taken and searched without a warrant or probable cause? After years of this indignity, much of the flying public thinks little of it, and they usually don't complain. They just dutifully stand there, bend over, and take it like a prisoner.

President George W. Bush created the Office of Homeland Security just days after the September 11, 2001, jihadist terror attacks on American soil. Former Pennsylvania Governor Tom Ridge headed up the office as of October 8, 2001. By the fall of 2002, it had become the Department of Homeland Security and merged a number of federal agencies into a single behemoth bureaucracy.

The USA Patriot Act was created even more hurriedly. It passed the

House 357–66, and the Senate 98–1, and was signed by President Bush just six weeks after 9/11. The "USA Patriot Act" is actually an acronym for the "Uniting and Strengthening America by Providing Appropriate Tools Required to Intercept and Obstruct Terrorism" Act. *Whew!* One has to wonder if it took more time to come up with the catchy name—or, heck, even to say it—than it did to consider whether Americans were being asked, in the name of freedom, to *give up* substantial freedoms and constitutional rights. A subtitle explained that this was "An Act to deter and punish terrorist acts in the United States and around the world, to enhance law enforcement investigatory tools, and for other purposes." We are all for punishing terrorists. Never met someone who thought we shouldn't. But did anyone anticipate that not many terrorists would really get punished as a result of this act, but that American citizens would? And isn't the tacked-on phrase "for other purposes" a little vague?

Government doesn't do things well, even when it takes its sweet time. When it acts in haste, it can *really* screw things up.

Many of the act's provisions were set to begin expiring in 2005, but Congress voted to reauthorize it. The Senate version made major changes due to bipartisan concerns about civil liberties violations, but the extension that came out of reconciliation was mostly the House version, which was substantially the same bill as in 2001.

Parts of it were due to sunset again in 2009, but Congress passed a one-year extension. Another attempt at a one-year extension failed, but then Congress passed the PATRIOT Sunsets Extension Act of 2011, a four-year extension of three major, controversial provisions: roving wiretaps (to track people who might be avoiding wiretaps by using multiple phones); allowing the feds to secretly search library and business records (known as the "library records" provision); and surveillance of "lone wolf terrorists" (people not known to be linked to terrorist groups but suspected of terrorism-related activities). The extension also finessed a few parts of the original law that had been ruled unconstitutional by the courts. President Obama signed the one-year extension in 2010 and let his autopen sign the four-year extension in 2011.

"Don't like the law? Blame my pen! It signed it, not me!"

Some Republicans questioned whether it was constitutional to sign with an autopen, but since nobody ever presses Obama beyond the initial question on any constitutional issue, that never went anywhere.

After the horrific attacks of 9/11, some cracks began to appear in the foundation of freedom upon which the United States of America is built. America hadn't suffered such a deadly attack from an outside force since Pearl Harbor. And like Pearl Harbor, 9/11 led to a vast expansion of government spending on defense and intelligence. But unlike 9/11, the attack on Pearl Harbor was carried out by a specific national government—Japan's, for those who dozed through history class. The Axis nations of Japan, Germany, and Italy were the targets of our shooting and spying, and we knew it was over when they formally surrendered and went back to selling us cars, ale, and expensive shoes.

With 9/11, the emotional impact was even greater than it had been with Pearl Harbor. This time, the victims weren't active-duty military and battleships, but thousands of innocent civilians in New York City and Washington, D.C. The office workers, airline passengers, and first responders who died could have been any of us, just going about our day. The horror was brought right into our homes—a shocking television drama that was real, live, and uncut. Such unprecedented atrocity required a response of unprecedented strength. But this shadowy enemy offered no clear target and no defined "end" to the fight. This was an entirely new type of warfare, so we had to feel our way in learning how to wage it. And as weasel-y politicians like to say, "Mistakes were made."

One mistake the government made was to assume that because the enemy hid in a crowd, it was okay to treat the entire crowd as suspects. And one mistake Americans made was to let the fear and paranoia generated by 9/11 lead them to forget Benjamin Franklin's sage warning about the slippery slope of trading freedom for security:

Those who would give up essential Liberty, to purchase a little temporary Safety, deserve neither Liberty nor Safety.
—BENJAMIN FRANKLIN, PENNSYLVANIA ASSEMBLY:
REPLY TO THE GOVERNOR, NOVEMBER 11, 1755

What would Ben say today? Would he cheerfully go through a full-body scanner that electronically strip-searched him and then allow a federal agent to put his blue-gloved hands inside his pants and over his thighs, crotch, and upper body for the sake of domestic travel on a privately owned commercial carrier? I'll bet you a Benjamin that he most certainly *would not*. (Come to think of it, though, kite-flying Ben would definitely be in awe of this and every other use of . . . electricity! Also airplane flight, but I digress.)

One can't blame Democrats or Obama for this intrusion. And one must concede that things done in the aftermath of 9/11 were carried out in the fog and fear that mark the launch of any war. But almost fourteen years later, have we made major adjustments based on common sense and that pesky little document called the Constitution, or do we just bend over and take it like a prisoner?

Almost certainly, I travel by air more than you do. Over the past few years, I've logged 300,000 to 350,000 miles annually. That includes roughly 200 flight legs a year just on airlines, plus numerous flights on private aircraft when I can't make an event by airline schedule or if someone offers to get me there on a private plane. I reach Delta's Diamond Medallion status (highest level of frequent flyer) by April or May of most years. All this is to make the point that I'm a seasoned traveler.

I will say that there have been some significant improvements in the TSA process, most notably the PreCheck program whereby one pays a fee to have an extensive background check done, be fingerprinted, fill out paperwork, and submit to a personal interview with a federal agent to qualify for expedited screening.

For my friends who say, "I don't want to give the government my fingerprints," I remind them that when you go through that full-body scanner, you're giving them far more than fingerprints—you're allowing them to take a peek "under the hood," so to speak. When a TSA agent comes running up to the security line laughing out loud and showing other agents something on his iPhone, you just hope it isn't the image of you that's got them chuckling. Despite the personal disclosures and fingerprints, PreCheck is a godsend to frequent flyers and well worth the money to avoid getting stuck behind someone who brings a thirty-two-ounce bottle of water through the line because, he says, "I didn't know *water* was a liquid." People that dumb must be the ones who actually *need* the flight attendant's demonstration of how to buckle a seat belt. (I kid you not, on a flight out of Panama City, Florida, I was seated next to a lady who didn't know how the seat belt worked and asked me if I could help!) Really, if you don't know water is a liquid or how to buckle a seat belt, you shouldn't be allowed to fly.

The PreCheck system and the Global Entry program for returning to the United States from another country are fantastic innovations, showing that at least someone in the federal government has a brain and some common sense.

But most of the procedures designed to "protect" us are there largely to protect politicians from accusations of political incorrectness. That's why we ended up with so many idiotic, inconsistent, and irrational rules being applied to American citizens who just want to take the kids to visit Grandma or get them to Disney World without having to reprise *National Lampoon's Vacation*.

Jason Edward Harrington did a six-year stint as a TSA agent in Chicago while trying to work his way through college. He wrote a couple of articles for *Politico* in January and March 2014 that went viral. Some excerpts:

> I hated it from the beginning. It was a job that had me patting down the crotches of children, the elderly and even infants as part of the post-9/11 airport security show. I confiscated jars of homemade apple butter on the pretense that they could pose threats to

national security. I was even required to confiscate nail clippers from airline pilots—the implied logic being that pilots could use the nail clippers to hijack the very planes they were flying.

Once, in 2008, I had to confiscate a bottle of alcohol from a group of Marines coming home from Afghanistan. It was celebration champagne intended for one of the men in the group—a young, decorated soldier. He was in a wheelchair, both legs lost to an I.E.D., and it fell to me to tell this kid who would never walk again that his homecoming champagne had to be taken away in the name of national security.

There I was, an aspiring satire writer, earnestly acting on orders straight out of *Catch-22*.

I quickly discovered I was working for an agency whose morale was among the lowest in the U.S. government. In private, most TSA officers I talked to told me they felt the agency's day-to-day operations represented an abuse of public trust and funds.

Charges of racial profiling by the TSA made headlines every few months, and working from behind the scenes we knew what was prompting those claims. Until 2010 (not long after the TSA standard operating procedure manual was accidentally leaked to the public), all TSA officers worked with a secret list printed on small slips of paper that many of us taped to the back of our TSA badges for easy reference: the Selectee Passport List. It consisted of 12 nations that automatically triggered enhanced passenger screening. The training department drilled us on the selectee countries so regularly that I had memorized them, like a little poem:

Syria, Algeria, Afghanistan
Iraq, Iran, Yemen
and Cuba,
Lebanon-Libya, Somalia-Sudan
People's Republic of North Korea.

People holding passports from the selectee countries were automatically pulled aside for full-body pat-downs and had their luggage examined with a fine-toothed comb. The selectee list was purely political, of course, with diplomacy playing its role as always: There was no Saudi Arabia or Pakistan on a list of states historically known to harbor, aid and abet terrorists. Besides, my co-workers at the airport didn't know Algeria from a medical condition, we rarely came across Cubans and no one's ever seen a North Korean passport that didn't include the words "Kim-Jong." So it was mostly the Middle Easterners who got the special screening.

I recently had a bad flashback. I was lying in bed trying to fall asleep when I was hit with a vivid memory from my time as a Transportation Security Administration officer at Chicago's O'Hare Airport. It was 2008, and I was conducting a bag check when three of my TSA colleagues got into an argument with a passenger at the checkpoint. Things got pretty heated.

The subject of debate? Whether mashed potatoes were a liquid or a solid.

In the end, of course, the TSA agents had the last word: Since the potatoes took the shape of their container, they were determined to be a liquid—specifically, a gel. That's the official TSA line. "Liquids, aerosols and gels over 3.4 ounces cannot be brought through security." The potatoes were forcibly surrendered.

If you're anything like me, you may have thought, "Well, mashed potatoes are technically gelatinous, so . . ."—which sends one down the rabbit hole of bureaucratic absurdity that ends with a passenger looking a TSA officer in the eye and saying, "Do you really think my mashed potatoes are a terrorist threat?" And the officer, if he or she is just an all-around tool, saying: "Ma'am, possibly. Rules are rules."

Another one: It's 2010, and a passenger is trying to bring her live goldfish through security. One of my co-workers informs her that the fish can go through but the water cannot. The woman is on the verge of tears when a supervisor steps in to save the fish's life.

And another: Working alongside a screener who always demanded that pacifiers be removed from infants' mouths and submitted for X-ray screening before the babies and their mothers were permitted to pass through the metal detectors.

Perhaps the biggest surprise to come out of what I now see as the life-changing experience of having my story go viral is the realization of just how much I still have left to tell about my six years at the TSA—the strange checkpoint happenings, the colorful passengers and the outrageous, real-life TSA characters.

Americans took my initial report as confirmation of what they always dreaded about a humiliating experience so many millions of them had shared. But I also realized that there was a part of the story I hadn't fully told: about a government agency and its leaders, and how they came up with the absurd policies that turned me and my colleagues into just-following-orders Mashed Potato Police [reprinted with permission from Jason Edward Harrington].

Jason is like many other TSA agents, who did what they were told because they needed the job and who knew full well that many of their tasks couldn't be defended in the name of "national security." Certainly, the majority of TSA workers are just people doing the job they're required to do, as well as they can and with a good attitude.

Because I encounter so many of them in virtually every airport in America, I can attest that it's not fair to blame security agents for the procedures they're *required* to follow. It's obvious that some are truly pained to have to go through certain machinations of "security check." On the other hand, some obviously enjoy bullying and bossing people around, reveling in the fact that there's not much a passenger can do if he really has to get to Cleveland tonight. As for filing a complaint with those little forms or going to the Web site to complain, fuggedaboutit! Waste of time.

Todd and Selena Drexel of Bowling Green, Kentucky, were trying to board a plane in New Orleans when their daughter was singled out for a pat-down. Her mom asked why and got no good answer. She asked for an alternative, like a rescan, but they refused. The parents had to stand by, powerless, as a screener rubbed their daughter's thighs and felt inside her pants waist. She cried when it was over.

Their daughter was six years old.

But there was one thing her parents had the power to do: They recorded it all and posted the video on YouTube, where it ignited a firestorm. The TSA responded that this was actually their proper, approved procedure for dealing with children.

A Destin, Florida, woman filed a formal complaint in June 2011 after her sick mother was subjected to a complete pat-down search. The woman is ninety-five years old, in the final stages of leukemia, and barely able to stand. But she was forced by TSA agents to get up from her wheelchair and undergo an extensive body search—including an examination of her adult diaper. Again, Homeland Security insisted that they followed proper procedures because *anyone* can be a terrorist [newstravel .aol.com, "TSA Pats Down Cancer-Stricken 95-year-old Woman, Removes Adult Diaper," June 26, 2011]. It might be worth noting, though, that if this 95-year-old, 105-pound, wheelchair-bound, leukemia-stricken Florida grandmother did turn out to be a terrorist, she would be the very, very first one, *ever*. It might also be suggested that such a waste of attention and manpower at the security checkpoint could only *help* a real terrorist slip through.

While many people complain about the Transportation Safety Administration, its defenders say all that groping, poking, and peeking is keeping us safer. But what does the man who actually created the TSA think about it now? Florida Representative John Mica is chairman of the House Transportation Committee, and he wrote the bill creating the TSA. Ten years later, he told *Human Events* that he gives it a grade of "D-minus." Representative Mica says the TSA was hijacked by bureaucrats and has mushroomed into a $9 billion "fiasco" that reacts to every threat by making us all remove our shoes or leave behind our shampoo, yet in ten years has failed to detect any real threat. The father of the TSA thinks it's time to scale it down, slashing it to five thousand people who monitor intelligence. Screening should be privatized and turned over to the airports, where they have a vested interest in both security and customer satisfaction. Thus, the father of the agency has taken Bill Cosby's approach to parenting: "I brought you into this world; I can take you out!" In Mica's case, he really means it!

Just when you think stories about the TSA can't get any sillier, along comes one that shaves a few more IQ points from their collective bureaucratic brain. In May 2012 at the Fort Lauderdale Airport, a couple who asked not to be identified were awaiting takeoff on a JetBlue flight when an airline employee told them they had to get off the plane. The TSA wanted to talk to them. They were baffled and asked why. They were told it wasn't about them, but their daughter, Riyanna. She'd been flagged as being on the terrorist no-fly list. Well, her parents were stunned. The dad pointed out that Riyanna is eighteen months old. How could she be on the no-fly list? Didn't matter: They were ordered off and spent half an hour with the TSA before being told they could reboard the plane, with no apology or explanation [ABC News 25, "Baby, 18 Months Old, Ordered off Plane at Fort Lauderdale Airport," May 14, 2012].

They chose to leave the airport instead. They're of Middle Eastern descent and figured that their flight would have been an uncomfortable one. They still want to know how a toddler got onto a terrorist no-fly list. (Although I bet a lot of us have flown next to some toddlers we *wished* had been on a no-fly list. Just for the record, it's not the toddlers who drive me nuts—it's usually their parents I'd like to ban. But I digress.)

Newark Liberty International Airport is one of America's busiest, and that means the TSA puts passengers through draconian security measures to make sure each one is the person he or she claims to be. But who's checking the checkers? For twenty years, Jerry Thomas worked in private security at the Newark Airport. He rose through four different security firms, passing background checks at every step until May 2012, when he was jailed on $75,000 bond. "Jerry Thomas" was accused of actually being Bimbo Oyewole, an illegal immigrant from Nigeria. The real Jerry Thomas was the victim of an unsolved murder in Queens two decades ago, and authorities believed Oyewole stole his identity. He'd been in airport security, scrutinizing other people's identities, ever since. Feeling safer now?

The TSA is but one of many ingredients in the "alphabet soup" of federal agencies that are supposed to protect our freedom but are in many ways threatening it. The worst abuser of all is the IRS, the Internal Revenue Service. Only in "government speak" can one call what they do a *service*. They remind me of a sadistic coach at my high school who used to enjoy "giving licks" to teen boys for any infraction of his rules. Just so you know, "giving licks" was the term used to describe the coach hitting the butt of a student with a short-handled boat paddle, riddled with holes to minimize wind resistance and enhance striking power.

Such activity would likely land a person in jail today, but in the sixties it was just part of the school day. The coach had a rule that if you got a "lick" you were required to say, "Thanks, coach, may I have another one?" And most often he would say, "Sure," and pop you again. One might get three or four before the coach finally said, "No, I think you've had enough," and stop his twisted abuse of a helpless adolescent. Whenever I think of the IRS, I see that coach standing with his paddle, expecting me to say, "Thanks, IRS, may I have another one?"

The IRS has become a criminal enterprise—yes, that's what I said—a rogue agency that abuses its power by harassing groups for political reasons and then destroying the evidence by pretending that "my computer crashed and I don't have a backup" and taking the Fifth Amendment to avoid answering questions as to why only conservative, or Tea Party, or pro-freedom, or pro-life, or pro-marriage, or pro-Israel groups were targeted for a level of harassment and bureaucratic bullying that, by comparison, could make mafia tactics feel like gentle massages.

Abuse of citizens by the IRS is especially pernicious. Unique among federal agencies, it can launch an investigation on its own without notifying the target, conduct the investigation, accuse a citizen of wrongdoing, require the person to prove his or her innocence, render a verdict, assess the punishment (plus interest and penalties), and impose it in virtually any way the agency sees fit—garnishing of wages, perhaps, or seizure of property. One-stop shopping! In the criminal justice system, a suspect must be notified of the charges, have the evidence presented before a fair and impartial jury of his peers, be considered innocent until proven guilty, have the case adjudicated by a member of another branch of government, and even have the cost of legal representation borne by the government, if need be. Not so with the IRS—it's cop, prosecutor, judge, jury, *and* executioner, rolled into one. Convenient, to be sure! Accountable and answerable to virtually no one, but feared by all. It's the closest thing America has to a goose-stepping Gestapo.

Even if the IRS ultimately can't nail someone's hide to its "trophy wall" and must find the accused completely innocent, it still may completely break a person or a company. It ruins lives—all in the name of being a "service." Calling the IRS a "service" is like calling your taxes a "voluntary contribution."

I've said it before and I'll say it again: The IRS is a criminal enterprise, it systematically violates our constitutional rights, and it has got to go. I mean it needs to cease to exist, and, yes, this can actually happen—if enough people decide it's time to stop bending over and taking it. To reference Monty Python's "dead parrot" sketch, the IRS needs to shuffle off its mortal coil, run down the curtain, and join the choir invisible. It needs to be an ex-IRS. We should repeal the Sixteenth Amendment allowing the government to tax our income, and replace income tax with the Fair Tax. No more IRS. No more intrusion. No more audits. No more lawbreaking. And they wouldn't be around to have any involvement in our health care, either.

In the summer of 2014, we witnessed a stunning cascade of revelations: Two years' worth of e-mails from one Lois Lerner, aka "Lois the Letter-Loser," had been lost in a computer crash. Neither she nor anyone else at the IRS had made hard copies of any of the e-mails that were lost, even though such copies are required by law. In an incredible coincidence, the crash had wiped out the records from the exact period being investigated by Congress for illegal targeting of political groups. And it had happened, very conveniently, after the IRS was notified by letter of the investigation. The IRS had a backup system, but those records were—gosh darn it—erased. Lerner's hard drive had been "recycled," meaning that IT experts wouldn't be able to recover the lost e-mails from it. It turned out that six other people had lost *their* e-mails in similar hard-drive crashes.

Okay, then . . . how about tracking down the e-mails from the other end, from the recipients? That's a great idea! Well, the IRS hadn't bothered to do that. Meanwhile, the President and his lackey press secretary claimed there wasn't a "smidgeon" of corruption at the IRS and that the White House wasn't involved in targeting groups that disagreed with the President's policies. At the same time, the head of the IRS was revealed to be a major Democrat party donor (another coincidence) who, in his appearance before Congress, defiantly personified utter indifference to the law, IRS procedures, abuses, and the people trapped in his spidery web.

I suspect that the revelations thus far have only scratched the surface of criminal conduct at the IRS. It appears that they've gone to a terrible amount of trouble to hide something. The IRS gets away with a level of corruption that would—and should—land others in prison for a very long time. Yet the head of the IRS stuck out his chin with firm resolve and refused even to apologize to Congress for any of this. And some of the very people at the heart of the scandal have collected bonuses, taken early retirement, lawyered up, and shut up.

This is the agency that expects me to produce a receipt from seven years ago if I claimed a charitable deduction but can't even follow the law to retain *their* records—of possible criminal behavior? For *three* years?

Will a citizen out in Bubba-ville be able to avoid an audit by saying, "My computer got 'Lernered'"? Everyone here in the real world knows the answer to that is a big fat NO. It's bad enough when government acts with disregard in the way they spend our money. It's worse when they force us to obey every "jot and tittle" of the law but recklessly, intentionally, and flagrantly ignore it themselves. And then they have the unmitigated gall to call themselves a "service."

If you ever wanted to see a textbook example of the Domino Theory as a reaction to bureaucratic overreach, just take a look at recent history. In December 2010, in Tunisia, a country smaller than the state of Oklahoma, one bullying civil servant confiscated a street vendor's merchandise and humiliated him. Tunisian authorities were so used to trampling on people's basic rights and human dignity that this one probably never gave the man a second thought. But he was in such despair that he set himself on fire in protest. His death by fire inflamed the long-festering anger toward the government into a massive protest that toppled the national leadership. From Tunisia, the anti-government protests spread throughout the Middle East. Egypt's leader toppled next, then Libya fell, and Syria and Iraq have been in a mess since. The violence and uncertainty caused the price of oil to leap, and the escalating unrest in that part of the world increasingly threatens all of us. But as the whole world rocks and roils, I think it would be a good idea to think back and remember the spark that set this wildfire. It all started with just one government bureaucrat, drunk on too much power, trampling on the rights of one individual.

America is not just a nation of immigrants—it's a nation of pioneers.

Our population is descended not simply from cultures around the world but from a very specific subset of those cultures: the people who looked at the situation around them—whether there was famine, dire poverty, religious persecution, totalitarian oppression, or just the general unfairness of a strict class system—and declared, "There has to be someplace better than this, and whatever risks I might face, I'm going to go find it." Think about it: If your ancestors were content to hold their tongues in front of the king and meekly accept whatever scraps of gold, food, or freedom (or kicks in the groin) he handed out, then you're probably still living in the same place they did. By and large, our ancestors came here to escape the tyranny of governments that treated their people as serfs of the state, subject to the whims of the king, dictator, or military functionary. The Founders were so paranoid about government getting too big and out of control that they added some clarifications to the Constitution that we have come to know as the Bill of Rights. As I've said, the Bill of Rights didn't tell citizens what they could do—it told the *government* what it could *not* do. And the Fourth and Fifth Amendments spell out some protections for American citizens:

> Fourth Amendment: The right of the people to be secure in their persons, houses, papers, and effects, against unreasonable searches and seizures, shall not be violated, and no Warrants shall issue, but upon probable cause, supported by oath or affirmation, and particularly describing the place to be searched, and the persons or things to be seized.

Read that over again. Slowly. Then again. Ask yourself if you feel that the NSA indiscriminately capturing your phone calls and e-mails (even if they promise not to peek!) can be reconciled with this. Would Thomas Jefferson or James Madison submit to a full-body scan at the TSA checkpoint and allow a total stranger sporting a federal badge and blue gloves to very intrusively pat him down?

Even the Supreme Court, in June 2014, struck down the notion that a police officer can take your iPhone and go through your e-mails, directories, phone logs, and photos just because he stopped you for speeding. And it wasn't the typical close SCOTUS vote—it was a 9–0 stinging rebuke of both the Bush and Obama administrations for operating on the premise that the label "national security" made all things okay. By anyone's reading of the actual text of the Fourth Amendment, I think it's pretty clear that it's *not* okay.

The Fifth Amendment to the Constitution reads:

> No person shall be held to answer for a capital, or otherwise infamous crime, unless on a presentment of indictment of a Grand Jury, except in cases in the land or naval forces, or in the Militia, when in actual service in time of War or public danger; nor shall any person be subject for the same offense to be twice put in jeopardy of life or limb; nor shall be compelled in any criminal case to be a witness against himself, nor be deprived of life, liberty, or property, without due process of law; nor shall private property be taken for public use, without just compensation.

It bears repeating: The purpose of the Bill of Rights was never to limit the rights of the citizen, but rather the power of the government. The burden of proof is on the *government* to show just cause for entering one's home, forcing one to answer questions, or in any way impeding a citizen's personal liberty.

When the government tells me I have to turn the lights off the flags that fly over my house, they're not only taking away *lights*, they're taking away my *liberty*. Granted, if the lights are shining in my neighbors' windows or blinding aircraft pilots, then turning them off honors someone else's liberty and safety. But what should be rare actions to restrict the use of property have become commonplace as government escalates its controlling demands and limitations on what I do with my property and how I exercise my personal freedoms.

Most people living in my world just want to be left alone. In

Bubba-ville, we don't need a lot of micromanaging; we already tend to see the good things around us as a blessing from God that requires good stewardship on our part. When *government* acts like an all-powerful God, the result is a serious breakdown that could best be described by that classic line from the film *Cool Hand Luke,* when the warden tells Luke (Paul Newman): "What we've got here is failure to communicate."

If the Founders who gave up so much to create liberty for us could see how our government has morphed into a ham-fisted, hypercontrolling "Sugar Daddy," I believe those same patriots who launched a revolution would launch another one. Too many Americans have grown used to Big Government's overreach. They've been conditioned to just bend over and take it like a prisoner. But in Bubba-ville, the days of bending are just about over. People are ready to start standing up for freedom and refusing to take it anymore.

11

Reality-TV Culture

THERE'S NO QUESTION THAT our society at large has been affected by the rise of "reality TV," both in the impressions it gives the world of what working-class Americans are like, and the influence it's had on the attitudes and behavior of American youth.

For many Bubble-ville elites, the only mental images they have of people who live outside their gated communities and high-rise Manhattan apartments are the ugly stereotypes they see on reality-TV shows: drunken, brawling New Jersey guidos; shallow, social-climbing suburban "housewives"; obese, illiterate Southern rednecks; and so on. I much preferred it when city slickers got their ideas of what we Southerners were like from *The Andy Griffith Show*. Or even *The Beverly Hillbillies*. At least the Clampetts were a hardworking, down-to-earth, God-fearing, loving family, with far more common sense and morals than their greedy, conniving banker, Mr. Drysdale. If you compared the typical Southern family of today to many of the Wall Street bankers of today, that old sitcom might seem like prophecy.

But wait, you protest, I can't possibly be saying that *The Beverly Hillbillies* was more realistic than reality TV! Yes, I am. And so were *Mork and Mindy*, *Bewitched*, and *My Mother the Car*.

Not since Obamacare was dubbed the "Affordable Care Act" has anything been so wildly misnamed as "reality TV." One thing that Michael Moore should have taught us by now is that just because something looks like a documentary and sounds like a documentary, that doesn't mean there's a lick of truth in it.

Reality TV is a genre of television that allegedly dispenses with the artifices of scripts and acting to give the viewer a glimpse of raw, real life unfolding spontaneously in front of the camera. In fact, it bears about as much resemblance to real life as the glop on your movie popcorn does to real butter. Reality TV doesn't do away with scripts, it just does away with *good* scripts. Good scriptwriters strive to create original, engrossing stories and complex, multilayered characters. Most reality-TV shows are just as scripted, except at a level of sophistication a notch below cave paintings or Three Stooges movies.

People who are desperate to get on TV will gladly follow crude scenarios for staged conflict and outrageous behavior that are assembled later in the editing room to create whatever impression the producers want to convey. Top writers of drama or comedy expect to be paid commensurate with their talent, but why pay their price when the lowest common denominator yields similar ratings at lower cost? That's why so many of the best writers, like *The Sopranos* creator David Chase and Matthew Weiner of *Mad Men,* are on cable channels that are willing to pay for quality to enhance their reputations. And it's working: in 2013, HBO garnered 108 Emmy Award nominations. The "Big Four" broadcast network ABC had 45.

It's no coincidence that the rise of reality TV ran parallel to the erosion in viewership and falling ad revenues of traditional television. If a struggling network can draw just as many viewers by serving up cheap garbage as by preparing expensive gourmet fare, then they'll be dumpster diving into reality programming every night of the week.

If I sound cynical about the big television networks, don't take my word for it. *Saturday Night Live* producer Lorne Michaels well remembers the day he lost his innocence. In 1979, fed up after five years of battling with NBC over what he saw as their constant blocking of his attempts to improve *SNL*, Michaels had a meeting with the then-head of programming, Irwin Segelstein. In Bill Carter's terrific book *The War for Late Night*, Michaels recalls that Segelstein listened quietly to his litany of complaints before setting him straight on how the TV business really works. He quotes Segelstein as telling him:

> If you read your contract closely, it says that the show is to be 90 minutes in length. It is to cost X. That's the budget. Nowhere in that do we ever say that it has to be good. And if you are so robotic and driven that you feel the pressure to push yourself in that way to make it good, don't come to us and say you've been treated unfairly, because you're trying hard to make it good and we're getting in your way. Because at no point did we ask for it to be good. That you're neurotic is a bonus to us. Our job is to lie, cheat and steal—and your job is to do the show.

After that meeting, Michaels was so dispirited that he quit *SNL* and didn't return to series television for four years. Since then, of course, with the rise of reality TV, the constant digging to find the lowest common denominator has reached fracking depths.

In 2008, at reality TV's peak of popularity, the producers of the Emmy Awards made spitting on scriptwriters the theme of the telecast. The awards for writing were relegated to the off-camera preshow ceremony while they added an award for Best Reality Show Host and even let the Emmy telecast itself be emceed by five reality hosts who were given ten minutes on live TV with no prepared material. That night, we discovered why cue cards are sometimes called "idiot cards." That telecast could have been repackaged as a reality show called "Prime Time's Deadliest Train Wrecks." But it did go down in history by chalking up the lowest Emmy rating ever and landing a spot on the TV Guide Network's *25 Biggest TV Blunders* special, which I'll bet had a script created by professional writers.

Reality TV wasn't always the celebration of lust, greed, pride, envy, wrath, sloth, and gluttony (and let's toss in stupidity and drunkenness, just to be thorough) that it is today. Its birth is usually traced back to the 1973 PBS series, *An American Family*, in which the upper-middle-class Loud family of Santa Barbara, California, allowed a TV documentary crew to move into their home and film their everyday lives. It became a cultural phenomenon when the cameras caught such intimate, never-before-seen-on-TV moments as the parents' marriage falling apart, their subsequent divorce, and their eldest son Lance coming out as gay.

But it sparked a backlash, with the Loud family complaining that the three hundred hours of video footage had been deliberately edited to create a negative impression of them. Critics also questioned whether the presence of the cameras and the pressures of the media fame that came along with them might have contributed to the family's dissolution, becoming not just a passive observer but an active force in distorting and destroying the family's lives. This was also the theme of Albert Brooks's satire, *Real Life*. It's since become one of the chief criticisms of all "reality TV" shows: that the presence of the cameras and the cast's knowledge that they're being filmed insures that what you are seeing isn't real. Social scientists call this the Hawthorne effect, when a behavioral experiment is worthless because people under observation behave differently if they know they're being observed.

Jump forward to 1992, and the premiere of what's generally considered the first reality-TV series as we now know them, MTV's *The Real World*. It was a show that followed a group of young people of widely varying backgrounds and personalities, chosen by the producers to share an apartment in a particular city. The cameras caught their struggles to find their places in the world, as well as to get along with their telegenically diverse roomies. At least, those were the original lofty ambitions that MTV trumpeted.

The show at first garnered praise for its frank discussions of drugs, sexuality, AIDS, abortion, politics, racial prejudice, and other hot-button issues. And the cast members generally came across as decent, thoughtful young people. But the show's success attracted thousands of attention-craving applicants who realized it was no longer necessary to possess any actual talent or wit to become a celebrity. Willingness to be an obnoxious jerk on TV had suddenly become a golden ticket to fame and fortune.

Despite cast members' claims that they were unaffected by the cameras, it wasn't long before *The Real World* was less connected to reality than the cartoon series, *The Real Ghostbusters*. Some roommates went public with complaints that they had to stage phony arguments and outrageous antics to spark ratings-generating controversy. After about twenty years, the format eventually degenerated into MTV's ultimate celebration of drunken hedonism, *Jersey Shore*.

The next big boosts to reality TV came with the introductions of *Big Brother* and *Survivor*, two shows that, like ABBA music and smallpox, originated in Europe (*Big Brother* in the Netherlands in 1999, and *Survivor* in Sweden in 1997), then spread worldwide, with local versions in many different countries.

Big Brother was essentially *The Real World* minus the youth and the world, as a group of obnoxious attention junkies, some of whom should have been old enough to know better, were locked together in a house full of cameras that recorded their petty battles and illicit couplings the way scientists might observe the breakdown into fornicating and cannibalism of an overpopulated rat colony.

Survivor seemed to have higher ambitions, but was basically *Big Brother* on a desert island. Imagine *Gilligan's Island*, if the castaways had been the aforementioned cannibalistic rats. Or *Robinson Crusoe*, if Crusoe had spent 90 percent of his time on the island scheming how to double-cross his sidekick, Friday. The show was immensely popular, with the selling point being the educational adventure of watching humans struggling to survive a hostile environment with only the barest of necessities (the fact that many of the female contestants were attractive women whose barest necessities included tiny bikinis also didn't hurt the ratings, and likely helped inspire the Discovery Channel to take it one step further with *Naked and Afraid*). From the very first season, it became apparent that the real key to winning on *Survivor* wasn't knowing Boy Scout skills, like how to build a fire or spear a fish, but knowing how to burn and backstab your fellow castaways. It hardly came as a surprise that the very first *Survivor* winner, Richard Hatch, later went to prison twice for scheming to evade taxes. How's that for a dose of reality?

The success of *Survivor* and *Big Brother* opened the floodgates—or more accurately, the sewer pipes—and soon, television was awash in allegedly unscripted reality shows, glorifying unknown no-talents who were trying to outdo one another in selfish, gross, antisocial behavior. Ironically, even as these shows decimated the market for quality scripted dramas, they trumpeted that they offered up plenty of "drama"—only in the case of shows such as the various incarnations of Real Housewives, "drama" was defined as egocentric, diva-like behavior that usually ended with a drink thrown in someone's face.

Scripted soap opera–style dramas such as *Dallas* and *Melrose Place* looked like the works of Shakespeare compared to the reality versions that replaced them, such as *Laguna Beach: The Real Orange County* and *The Hills*. Traditional game shows that tested people's knowledge were shoved aside by gross and/or mean-spirited, reality-based variations, such as *Fear Factor, Weakest Link, Married by America* (contestants agreed to marry a stranger selected by viewers), *The Swan* ("ugly ducklings" battled to win a complete plastic surgery makeover), *Who's Your Daddy* (adoptees competed to guess which contestant was their birth father and which was lying to win prizes), and *Temptation Island* (couples were transported to a tropical island and separated, and hot singles of the opposite sex competed to entice them into cheating on each other). As Ron Burgundy would say, "Stay classy!"

We used to think *The Dating Game* was too risqué for kids. But after eighteen seasons of *The Bachelor*, we now have a whole generation that was brought up thinking true love is something an oversexed hound finds by seducing a harem of scheming women in a hot tub of questionable hygiene. Cooking shows in which the worst violence was Julia Child boning a pheasant were replaced with shows like *Hell's Kitchen*, featuring amateur cooks stabbing each other in the back with salad forks as red-faced British chefs screamed profanity at them. (Perhaps because of Simon Cowell, all reality competition shows require a nasty Brit; but why anyone would consider a British chef to be the ultimate culinary authority is an eternal mystery.) There were also food shows featuring globe-trotting hosts scouring the world to uncover the most disgusting things and see if they could swallow them without vomiting. (Now, there's a perfect metaphor for reality TV!)

Then there were the celebrity reality shows, featuring people famous solely for being famous (Paris Hilton, the Kardashians) or talented celebrities a bit past their prime, like Joan Rivers, Lindsay Lohan, and the Osbournes, whose constant cursing and floors covered with dog droppings earned them high ratings, magazine covers, an invitation to the 2002 White House Correspondents' Dinner, and accolades as the new face of the American family. I can safely state they were nothing like my family, where both potty mouths and dirty floors got washed out with soap, and both the dogs and the kids were house-trained.

By now, you may be wondering why I went to all the trouble of tracing the birth and long downward spiral of reality TV. It's because like anything else in the mass media that's wildly popular, it's had an effect on society in general. Along with its attention-mongering, privacy-destroying, do-it-yourself cousin, online social media, it's been a particularly negative influence on impressionable young people.

Many of these so-called reality shows have been plagued by the same complaints: Cast members are secretly given scripts or at least "directed" to say and do certain things; shows are misleadingly edited to create heroes, villains, and conflict; they glorify and promote shallow, irresponsible behavior, such as promiscuity, exhibitionism, conspicuous consumption, substance abuse, violence, and mindless partying; they cruelly exploit people who don't realize they're being mocked (Anna Nicole Smith); they've eradicated the concepts of privacy and modesty; and by making instant celebrities out of no-talent attention addicts, they teach young viewers that fame is the highest goal you can aspire to, and that vulgarity and voyeurism, not talent, training, or hard work, are the easiest ways to achieve it.

The results of their mass-media "education" can be seen in a 2007 Pew Research survey of Millennials, age eighteen to twenty-five. It found that many young people's values had been so distorted that they resembled a *TV Guide* synopsis of a typical reality show. Asked what their most important goals in life were, eight out of ten young Americans said that getting rich was the most or second-most important goal in life. About half said that being famous was also a top priority. Large majorities believed that casual sex, binge drinking, illegal drug use, and violence were more common among youth now than twenty years before. And their constant posting of photos and updates about themselves to social network sites inspired the pollsters to dub them not the "Me" Generation but the "Look at Me" Generation.

These depressing findings were backed up by a 2013 survey by UCLA's Children's Digital Media Center. It focused on even younger Americans, age nine to fifteen. A full one-third of them said that being famous was somewhat important, important, or very important. Even among the very youngest, those under age thirteen, 23 percent were on a social networking site and 26 percent had their own YouTube accounts.

One child psychologist said it's nothing new: Kids have always had dreams of becoming famous. But what is new is that the Internet now gives them the opportunity to imitate the trappings of fame by posting their photos, videos, and personal information in front of the whole world. When you add that they've been taught by reality TV that the key to grabbing the world's attention is obnoxious, dangerous, antisocial behavior, you have a recipe for disaster.

A perfect example is *Buckwild*, a reality show about the self-destructive redneck antics of a group of nine young people in Charleston, West Virginia. It briefly took over *Jersey Shore*'s time slot, but proved to be too irresponsible even for MTV. It was canceled after just one season, during which various cast members were arrested on drug, DUI, and other charges, and young cast member Shain Gandee, his uncle, and another man were found dead. They'd gone off-roading in deep mud, which covered the tailpipe of their Ford Bronco and resulted in lethal carbon monoxide poisoning.

On December 7, 2012, before *Buckwild* had even premiered, West Virginia Senator Joe Manchin wrote a letter to the president of MTV requesting that it be canceled. Senator Manchin wrote, "This show plays to ugly, inaccurate stereotypes about the people of West Virginia . . . You preyed on young people, coaxed them into displaying shameful behavior—and now you are profiting from it. That is just wrong." All it had taken to repulse him was MTV's two-minute advance trailer featuring highlights—or more precisely, lowlights—of the upcoming series. Just two minutes from introduction to repulsion to calls for cancellation. That might be a new world record, even for a reality show!

To be fair, there have been some reality shows that aimed to educate viewers about something they might not otherwise have encountered. Many focus on people with unusual or dangerous occupations, such as *Ice Road Truckers*, *Deadliest Catch*, and the granddaddy of them all, *Cops*. *Time* magazine critic James Poniewozik noted that TV used to be filled with scripted shows about the type of blue-collar workers who make America run; but in the nineties, as the networks began chasing yuppie viewers with large disposable incomes, reality TV became the only place where viewers could learn about the lives of anyone other than attractive young urbanites working at hip lifestyle magazines and hanging out together at coffee houses.

Unfortunately, as I've already noted, what they learned from reality TV about people outside big cities is mostly a load of ugly, exaggerated, and downright false stereotypes. Shows about the tough, respectable jobs of fishermen and truckers quickly devolved into shows set in tattoo parlors and pawn shops, then into the condescending mockery of rural Southerners, as seen in *Buckwild* and *Here Comes Honey Boo Boo*.

Despite its popularity, *Here Comes Honey Boo Boo* has come in for sharp criticism for the producers' transparent attempts to depict the Thompson family as, to quote a reviewer for *Forbes*, "a horde of lice-picking, lard-eating, nose-thumbing hooligans south of the Mason-Dixon Line." Great Britain's *Guardian* newspaper noted the disconnect between the show's not-so-subtle attempts to "point and snicker" at the family, and the female family members, who stubbornly refuse "to hate themselves for their poverty, their weight, their less-than-urbane lifestyle, or the ways in which they diverge from the socially-acceptable beauty standard."

I suspect that a similar condescending attitude toward rural Southerners might have originally been behind the greenlighting of the A&E reality series, *Duck Dynasty*. But for once, the typical reality show story took a surprise twist. Who could have predicted that audiences wouldn't look down on and ridicule the tight-knit Robertson family of Louisiana, owners of a successful family business making duck calls and other hunting equipment? Instead, they embraced the Robertsons for their solid family values, their patriotism and love of the great outdoors, their work ethic, their common sense, and their unshakable, unapologetic Christian faith. Finally, there was a family on TV that actually resembled *us*! Well, us and ZZ Top. *Duck Dynasty* is a refreshing brand of reality TV, not because it's sophisticated or truly unscripted reality, but because it at least reflects and encourages the kind of wholesomeness that is all too rare on TV and for that matter, getting more rare in our communities. I think of it as *The Waltons* with beards and a more decidedly and unapologetic Christian faith.

Duck Dynasty fans don't mock the Robertsons; they want to emulate them. According to *Forbes*, as of the third quarter of 2013, the show had sold $400 million worth of merchandise and generated $80 million in ad income for A&E. The show's fourth season premiere drew 11.8 million viewers, beating the major network competition and breaking the record as the most-watched nonfiction cable series episode in history.

In another departure from the sordid and sleazy, TLC's hit show *19 Kids and Counting* features the real-life Duggar family of Springdale, Arkansas. Jim Bob (yes, that's his real name) and Michelle are cherished personal friends of mine. Jim Bob was in the state legislature during my tenure as governor, and he and Michelle and their very large brood of children really are amazing people.

Like the Robertsons of *Duck Dynasty* fame, the Duggars reflect all that is good and decent about family. They pray, go to church (and not just for TV), they work hard, they don't take handouts to care for their large number of children, but instead truly model the behavior of a family who helps each other, respects each other, and loves each other and whose entire family revolves around their deep and authentic Christian faith.

Jim Bob is a self-made millionaire, having dabbled in real estate and selling cars and being blessed by being very good at figuring out what would make money. He and Michelle believe that their primary role in life is to create the next generation (some might think they singlehandedly will do so by themselves) and train them to be their replacements. I've known this family since the kids were little and back when there were only four or five of them, if that. I've marveled at the exemplary manners and behavior of all of their children. They are every parent's dream in their attitudes toward each other, their parents, and their chores. They have endured relentless and vicious ridicule from the snobby and snotty sophisticates who exemplify their own jealousy of how well behaved the Duggar kids are compared to the little hellions and yuppie larvae created by the critics of the Duggars.

If all reality TV were the Robertsons and Duggars, I'd say, "bring more of it!" It would be like "Father Knows Best with Beards" or "Leave It to Beaver and His 18 Brothers and Sisters." Unfortunately, for every *Duck Dynasty* and Duggar show, we get fifty dumpster-diving, snuff-dipping, knuckle-dragging dopes.

Excuse me while I change the channel and catch a rerun of *The Beverly Hillbillies*.

12

Bailing Out the Big Boys

It was September 2007, and I was one of the Republican candidates for President participating in a debate on economics being held in Dearborn, Michigan, and moderated by Maria Bartiromo, then of CNBC and now of the Fox Business Network. The question posed was, "How is the economy doing?" One by one, my challengers all but read directly from talking points published by the Republican National Committee, saying that "we've had sustained economic growth over the past twenty-three quarters." In other words, the economy is churning along just fine.

When it was my time to respond, I did the unthinkable—I suggested that for people at the bottom, the economy wasn't doing that well. I remarked that if you're sitting in the corner office, life probably is pretty good, but for those folks working on their feet in the hot sun and sweating to do their work and lifting heavy things, life is a struggle. For being the contrarian in a lineup of lemmings, I paid the price.

My comments were lampooned and roundly criticized by the elites in the media, who live comfortably in their "bubble" and rarely socialize with the hoi polloi. The people I talked to every day on my campaign were not the folks from the donor class—who made seven-, eight-, and nine-figure incomes—but rather taxi drivers, hotel workers, food servers, airline attendants, and people from all walks of life at campaign events in small towns.

As with many other people in Bubba-ville, one of the most important ways I stayed connected to people from all walks of life was through my church. The church for me is first and foremost a place of worship and fellowship, but it's also a place where people are naturally congregated according to faith rather than finances, family tree, or friends in high places. Church is where people of all walks of life are truly equal. In my church, no one can just join and sit idly by and enjoy the services. Every person wishing to move beyond the status of a visitor or regular attender and who wishes to formally unite with the church must agree to volunteer for some time of service. At my church, for example, I work on the parking lot crew and drive a golf cart so we can transport people from the parking lot to the church doors, which is especially appreciated by young mothers and fathers trying to get several little ones to church or by our aging members and guests who might need some assistance if they park in the far corners of the lot. And sometimes it's just a lady who needs the ride because for reasons known only to her and God, she is wearing high heels so tall, they must have been invented by Satan to hurt women as they walk. I get quite a few questions from people attending for the first time, like: "Has anyone ever told you that you look a lot like Governor Huckabee?"

I usually will say, "I do hear that sometimes." Then comes the following: "And you even sound like him." When I tell them, "I look and sound like him because I *am* him," I will sometimes be met with, "No you're not!" I suppose people who watched my television show from New York on Saturday night aren't expecting to show up on Sunday morning and be driven around the church parking lot by the guy who hosted the show.

But it's at church that many of us in Bubba-ville stay connected. We interact with people from the military; with young and older and middle-age groups; with professional people who wear suits and ties to work to people who do manual labor and everything in between. Our church is quite diverse in that we have people from all races, biracial couples, and a wide array of people from all over the political and financial spectrum. What unites us is our common commitment to personal faith. In Bubba-ville, going to church is not required, but it's not "weird" or unusual. It's unusual to *not* attend church.

For all the talk about "tolerance" and "diversity" from the media, entertainment, and political elites in New York and D.C., have you ever wondered how many people you personally know and interact with regularly who lost their home in a foreclosure, who have never driven a car newer than ten years old, or who have never flown in an airplane, or who coupon shop at the grocery store? I rub shoulders with people like that every week. Church is the great equalizer in that people aren't accepted on what they have done for God, but rather what God has done for them.

In September 2007, a full year before the great financial collapse, I was aware that financial troubles were brewing, despite what my Republican colleagues were saying on command, directly from the talking points of the Republican National Committee.

It wasn't because I was an economist or a sociologist. I just traveled, met a lot of people, and listened. I asked them lots of questions, and I listened some more. The evidence was overwhelming and obvious to all unless one had been living "in a bubble."

One often hears of "trickle-down economics," a popular conservative notion that when the economy for the top earners in our society gets better, the effect will "trickle down" to the rest of the people. That's largely true. But what I never hear the pundits discuss is that the inverse is true; a good economy may start at the top and trickle down to the bottom, but a bad economy usually hits the poorest people first and hardest, and it eventually works it way up to the top. When it does reach the top, it's catastrophic because it completes the full circle of the citizenry in the collapse.

One of the comical observations I have made is that each month when job numbers and economic growth are reported, the economists always express "surprise." Being an economist must be interesting since they are paid handsomely to be wrong most of the time. If the economists were to spend more time in Bubba-ville, they wouldn't be so surprised. They would start seeing the economic turns more quickly. Instead, every month, we learn how surprised the economists are about whatever numbers they are reporting.

I well remember the derision I received from the *Wall Street Journal* editorial board and many of the TV commentators for my comments stating that the economy wasn't working that well for the people lifting heavy things and getting hot and sweaty to make a living. After all, officially, things were going "swimmingly well" for the swell. I was pretty much labeled a bumpkin, uninformed, and lacking in the sophistication that the better bred elements of our party were blessed with.

My vindication came exactly a year later, September 2008, when America's economy took a nosedive. It was in the heat of the 2008 Presidential campaign. By then, John McCain had long since surpassed me as the last man standing and gained the nomination. A young, energetic senator from Chicago, Barack Obama, had captured the nomination of the Democratic party. What had been a campaign largely about the war in Iraq suddenly became a campaign about the domestic economy. Major banks, huge insurance giants, and investment brokerage firms were said to be teetering on the brink of collapse. If they went down, we were told, the world economy as we knew it would go over the edge. It was the Apocalypse!

What was the remedy? To let the same people who engineered the train wreck drive the train and in fact even design the new train! Much to my chagrin, the Bush administration turned to Treasury Secretary Henry Paulson, former CEO of Goldman Sachs, who concocted a massive bailout for the nation's banks and major financial institutions, including his old firm, Goldman Sachs. No cronyism, I'm sure. But it was $700 billion worth of corporate welfare that all good conservatives were supposed to salute, even though the notion of the federal government stepping in to rescue the most heavily capitalized institutions in the world seemed completely unseemly.

I was stunned at the people who crowed during the 2008 campaign that *they* were so much more conservative than *me,* yet they thought a legitimate function of the government was to take the money earned by the middle class and paid in as taxes and redistribute it to the wealthiest and most powerful companies in America. Every attempt to protest the TARP (Troubled Asset Relief Plan) was countered with, *"We have no choice!"* I said TARP was misnamed. It should have stood for the Congressional Relief Assets Plan, or CRAP. It was just that.

Then and now, I believe there is *always* a choice to be made on the basis of principle. And Republicans miserably failed in 2008 to apply principles. Instead, we caved to pressure from the biggest political donors who dug their own hole by turning Wall Street into the largest casino on the East Coast.

To my knowledge, I was the first person to call the actions of Wall Street a "casino," where instead of investing in things of tangible value, investors instead wanted a quicker path to a bigger payday and began betting not on tangible goods and services, but on what a good or service *might* be worth in the future. The main difference between the Wall Street casinos and the Las Vegas casinos was that in Vegas, if you lose, you have to pay for your losses. In Bubble-ville, the government will offer other people's money in huge amounts to protect the guilty at the expense of the innocent.

I feel now as strongly as I felt then—government had ceased to be about solving problems, but had become all about a level of crony capitalism that if practiced in the private sector would result in jail terms. Instead, the very people who had crafted the destruction of the American economy were rewarded with government bailouts and bonuses. At the other end of the economic class, a lot of middle- and working-class people were punished with the loss of their homes, the complete devastation and devaluing of their pension funds and retirement accounts, and a sudden loss or drastic drop in income that meant that they were unable to purchase durable goods that would have kept the economy stable.

The sheer size of the bailout for the big boys was mind-numbing. Most Americans lose track of the bigness of the numbers, but let's put the $700 *billion* in perspective. When New York got a bailout in 1975, it was for $2.3 billion in loans; Chrysler in 1980 got $1.5 billion in loans. Even bailing out the *entire* savings and loan industry in the eighties was done at a cost of $292.3 billion. By contrast, in the bailouts of 2008–2009, Bank of America alone received $142.2 billion, AIG got $180 billion, Citigroup held its hand out for $280 billion, and Freddie Mac and Fannie Mae took $400 billion. All told, over $1 trillion.

Defenders of the bailouts attempted to tout the benefits, especially crowing that it had all been paid back and money was even made on the deal with interest payments. Right—tell that to the people at the bottom who *didn't* get bailed out and lost their homes to foreclosure. (In 2008 alone, there were 2 *million* foreclosure procedures launched and 1 million Americans lost their homes. From January 2007 to December 2011, there were more than 4 million completed foreclosures and more than 8.2 million foreclosure starts.)

Those with a 401K saw their nest egg become a 101K and the destruction of their funds forced them to work an additional ten years past what they had hoped would be their retirement.

All the while, commentators kept telling us that the bailouts for those who were "too big to fail" were absolutely necessary to keep things from getting worse. Tell that to the people who lost jobs due to the miscalculations of the wizards on Wall Street. The "smartest guys in the room" did some really dumb things, but the rest of America paid for it.

One might think that in light of the generosity of the taxpayers to the biggest companies in the nation, those companies would be contrite and seek to pass on the good will to their customers. One would be wrong. In the latter part of 2010, JP Morgan Chase quietly decided to end a program that allowed active duty military members to defer their student loan payments until they were safely home. Kerri Napoli got a call from JP Morgan Chase indicating that her husband, Andrew, a soldier in the U.S. Army, would have to start making payments again, even though he was at that very moment fighting in Afghanistan. After several conversations with the bank, she told them she'd called NBC News, and they decided to make a special exception for Andrew. Then NBC News called, and JP Morgan Chase decided that the student loan deferral program would be reinstated for all active duty military members.

While President Obama promised the "most transparent administration in history," the reality of his administration was as opaque and obtuse as any ever seen. It took a lawsuit by Fox News and Bloomberg News—one that went all the way to the Supreme Court in March 2011—to obtain the details of federal bailout loan agreements. The banks argued that releasing that information could harm their reputations. I think the banks getting the bailouts failed to understand that their reputations were already ruined. They should have been more concerned about ruining the lives of their customers who trusted them and were left homeless or had their businesses bankrupted.

I've been forthright in criticism directed toward my own party, but there's plenty of blame to go around. One of the more comical moments of political theater occurred when Debbie Wasserman Schultz launched her stint as chairperson of the Democratic National Committee in May 2011. In her first appearance at the podium in her new job, she slammed Republican Party Presidential candidates for not backing the Detroit bailout and said if it were up to them, we'd all be driving foreign cars. An astute reporter found out that Ms. Wasserman Schultz had driven to her news conference in her Nissan Infiniti. Oops! Of course, this is the same DNC chair who a few days after that embarrassing gaffe accused the GOP of wanting to make *illegal* immigration a "crime." I kid you not! As comedian Ron White brilliantly observed, "You can't fix stupid."

Make sure you understand, I'm an unrepentant and unapologetic capitalist. Free markets—real free markets—are the backbone of a strong economy. The problem is that some of the very people who pretend to be the "most conservative," believe in free markets until they don't. Free markets, but juiced with government handouts to take care of the donor class is not a truly free market. Sometimes it's hard to find out who really believes in free enterprise and who believes in having the government standing by in the event that big business needs a bailout.

In 2011, the Occupy Wall Street (OWS) movement was launched with the same level of media hype as a new Batman movie. It pretended to be a grass roots revolt of the excesses of capitalism, but was basically a "rent a mob" of professional protesters who shut down commerce and jobs for the very people they were supposedly fighting for. It was one of the most absurd political spoofs ever—unwashed protestors posing as aggrieved Americans who hated capitalists, but who very much enjoyed the fruit of capitalists like Steve Jobs, Mark Zuckerberg, Sergey Brin, and Larry Page.

If the Wall Street Occupiers had really been "fighting for the little guy," they wouldn't have been so boneheaded in their tactics that put many of those working people out of work. The owner of a New York City bakery reported $3,000 in damages to her bathroom. Many of the area restaurants and small businesses laid off employees because the OWS crowd had turned the neighborhood into a crime haven and people stopped going to the stores and businesses for fear of getting caught up in violence.

In the meantime, what happened to the one-percenters? The upper echelon of the financial world who were supposedly the targets of the movement? Did any of them lose their jobs? Their homes? Even their parking places? Nary a one, best anyone can tell. They did just fine.

Back in 2008, when I was running for President and dared to criticize the government bailouts of so-called "too-big-to-fail" Wall Street firms, it made me a lonely target among many fellow conservatives. I was accused of attacking capitalism, or even being a socialist, which is downright funny. What I thought I was doing was defending the classic free-market model that said when you risk capital, if you win, you deserve the profits, but if not, you take the loss. Our current model isn't capitalism, it's corporatism and cronyism. Real capitalism gives anyone with a good idea a chance to compete with the big guys and become big themselves. Cronyism unfairly stifles competition. Well, several years and trillions of dollars worth of bailouts and government sweetheart contracts to donors later, and suddenly, it's not so lonely out here. Even some of the conservative groups who attacked me in 2008 are now pressing Congress to rein in the lovefest between big business and Big Government. And now, even the intellectuals are finally catching on. In the summer of 2012, George Mason University kicked off a series of academic conferences on cronyism and government-and-business collusion, and how it's undermining our capitalist system. All I can say is welcome to the party . . . but where were you guys eight years ago, when I really needed you?

As one of the few Republicans who opposed the $700 billion TARP bailout from the beginning, I took a lot of heat from people who claimed that not bailing out those "too-big-to-fail" banks would plunge us into a depression. Look, I never said the government shouldn't take any action. But just shoveling money at banks that took stupid risks, without the government or taxpayers getting anything in return, did nothing but transfer their losses onto the backs of taxpayers. Many of those same taxpayers are still struggling with depressed 401Ks and underwater mortgages, and neither the government nor the big banks has rushed to bail them out. In its January 2012 issue, *Bloomberg Markets* published an eye-opening investigative report on what really happened behind the scenes during the Fed bailouts of the banks, how the Fed money dwarfed the TARP bill, and how much was kept secret even from Congress. It turns out that while the banks were assuring investors they were solid, the Fed was loaning them a total of $7.7 *trillion*—nearly half the annual GDP. The argument is that it prevented a depression and has all been paid back. The counterargument is that it preserved a "too-big-to-fail" banking system that's made no serious reforms since and has so far profited by $13 billion off the Fed's low rates while senior citizens watch their own investment interest dwindle to nothing. It's the type of cronyism that infuriates all Americans, from Tea Partiers to the Occupy Wall Street crowd. Some Congress members say if they'd actually been told the details at the time, they would've changed their votes. It's a long report, but well worth reading. Just be prepared to be furious when you're finished. Especially at the thought that it took two years of Freedom of Information suits just to find out what was being done with our own money.

I have repeatedly said that government has a role in the economy, but it's not to pick the winners and the losers. Government should be like the referee in the striped jersey. When he does his job well, neither team feels the referee's preference. He simply calls the fouls and makes sure the game is played fairly. He doesn't coach or correct, he makes sure that the rules are applied equally and fairly across the board. When the guy in the striped shirt puts on a team jersey and starts scoring points for one side against the other, he's no longer a referee, he's a player. Players are playing to win; referees should be indifferent to the outcome, but diligent about the process to insure it's fair.

Bailouts were not limited to Wall Street, of course. In fact, once President Bush had persuaded Congress to give the big bailouts to the big banks and brokerage houses, the inevitable happened. Everyone in need ran to the trough. Some of the first at the government teat were the big automakers from Detroit.

My wife and I had been loyal customers of GM cars exclusively for thirty-five of the forty years our marriage. The bailout changed that. I was beyond disappointed—I was angry that not only would I be making payments on my vehicles to GM, but that the tax dollars I coughed up to the "goodfellows" at the IRS would then be given to those same car companies some more. The standing joke (not so funny) was that GM now stood for "Government Motors."

In October 2013, President Obama seemed to have blurred the lines of common sense and political rhetoric when he tried to compare individual citizens to GM. It might just be the former college lecturer in him, but President Obama doesn't speak to his audiences so much as lecture at them. And sometimes, his lectures get so high-and-mighty, they bust loose and float away from reality. For instance, in December 2013, he compared America to its individual citizens. He said neither a nation nor a person should risk their credit rating, and for Congress not to pay the interest on the debt would be like thinking you're saving money by not paying your mortgage. He said if you don't pay your mortgage, "you're just a deadbeat."

And I couldn't help thinking: wait a minute. Isn't this the President who created a huge federal bailout to help people who borrowed more than they could afford and couldn't pay their mortgages? And his own program wouldn't even help those who sacrificed and kept up their mortgage payments. You had to stop paying and go into default before you qualified for help. And the cost of that bailout was added to the debt, and is now part of the reason why we have to raise the debt ceiling again. Where was all this tough love when he was running for office? I don't recall him ever giving a speech where he told upside-down homeowners, "Serves ya right, deadbeats."

Theories as to the problems in the Republican Party are as numerous as the suspects in an old *Perry Mason* show. We hear it's because they won't support Obamacare or gun control or immigration reform or gay marriage or abortion. But the problem with Republicans is not that they refuse to move farther left and become calorie-free Democrats. It's that they've forgotten to respect and reach out to the people who really make this country work—and here's a hint: It's not the guys in the big corner offices.

My wife and I were at Fenway Park in the summer of 2013, and I was watching the peanut and hot dog vendors, carrying heavy loads up and down the steps in the heat. When I see them, I see what makes America great: people working hard for a living, so that one day, they can be the ones in the seats. People who work with their hands have a gift. I can't fix a car or an air conditioner, and the people who can are valuable. Republicans need to communicate why Big Government and high taxes hurt the guys who are building the skyscraper, not just the guy who owns it. They need to explain why educational choice gives the kids of working single moms the same opportunities as kids going to the finest private schools. They need to make it clear what the Democrats' energy policies are costing people at the gas pumps and in their electric bills.

I grew up having a lot more in common with the people working in the kitchen than those sitting at the head table. If Republicans can explain to the waitstaff at the GOP fundraisers how conservative policies will help them, then they won't have to worry so much about the people who paid $10,000 a plate. Don't begrudge the underemployed family food stamps, and then justify bailouts for AIG, Goldman Sachs, and GM. The GOP's problem isn't that it's too conservative. It's convincing the masses and the majority that they aren't invisible.

13

Environmentalist Hypocrisy

THERE'S PROBABLY NO OTHER ISSUE that chafes the chaps of people in God, guns, grits, and gravy territory like environmental extremism. These are the folks who actually live on farms and ranches, where understanding fluctuations in weather patterns is a life-or-death skill. They know about "communing with animals" because they get up before dawn every day to milk the cows, feed the chickens, and, on occasion, play midwife to a horse. They're well aware of the conditions of marshes, waterways, and forests because they spend as much time as possible right in the middle of them, hunting and fishing (and knowing that despite what the EPA says, the mud puddle in their driveway or a ditch that's dry except in times of gulley rusher rains are *not* "wetlands"). They know that meat comes from animals, not from a Styrofoam tray, and that vegetables are pulled out of a garden, not a freezer. A group of schoolchildren in New York City were asked where milk came from. Most of them answered, "The store." They had no idea that a cow was involved. The Bubbas understand, even if the Bubble-ville elites don't, that humans are not the enemy of the natural world, but *part* of the natural world. They also understand that the word "conservative" derives from the same root as "conservation," and that it's their duty to be good stewards of the Earth that God has blessed them with so they can pass it on to their children and grandchildren.

When that's the way you've been brought up since you were knee-high to a duck (or a duck *hunter*), it's infuriating to be lectured about how you are destroying the planet when the one accusing you is an environmental pressure group attorney who lives in a Manhattan town house, whose bare feet haven't touched grass since he dropped his joint in college, and whose idea of getting close to nature is to let the nanny use the Prius to take the kids to Central Park.

Another leading source of noxious gas is Hollywood, which routinely burns vast amounts of gasoline, jet fuel, and smoke-producing pyrotechnics in order to make movies that harangue average Americans to stop their evil polluting ways. One classic example of the hypocrisy is the Leonardo DiCaprio movie *The Beach*. To film their cautionary tale about how man destroys a tropical beach paradise, the filmmakers found an actual pristine beach in Thailand, then set out to make it look even more "paradise-y" by moving some sand dunes and clearing away grass and coconut trees. Some Thai officials, along with 20th Century Fox, landed in the Thailand Supreme Court for damaging the environment with their environmental message movie. Ironically, the case finally made it to court two years after the 2004 tsunami wiped away all the moviemaker's "improvements" and reminded everyone of just what Mother Nature thinks about man's hubris in believing he can control the Earth's environment.

I freely admit that I am doing my part to destroy the atmosphere by flying on commercial airliners, often several times a week. This is a big no-no with the environmentalist lobby, which believes that nothing is worse than commercial jetliners spewing CO_2 into the upper atmosphere. It doesn't occur to them that there is something that might be harder to justify for an environmentalist: private jets carrying a handful of environmentalist celebrities and showbiz moguls instead of 200 or more passengers. But wait, they cry, commercial airliners are worse because they're giant, fuel-guzzling aircrafts. You mean like the Boeing 707 owned and piloted by environmentalist celebrity John Travolta?

Please understand, I don't mean to pick on Vinnie Barbarino. If he can afford to tote his family around in a jet that was made to carry up to 189 passengers—and which is merely the largest of the five jets he owns—then congratulations to him for achieving the American Dream. Maybe it's just the Hollywood version of buying the biggest model Winnebago. (Come to think of it, some movie stars are known for their gigantic luxury dressing room motor homes; I've heard Will Smith has the most incredible one of all, costing $2.5 million and about the size of an ocean liner. Wonder how many miles to the gallon that baby gets.) But please spare us the lectures about how the rest of us need to reduce our carbon footprints when, as the British government estimated, Travolta's flying generated over 800 tons of CO_2 in one year, creating a "carbon footprint" nearly 100 times greater than that of the average British citizen.

Travolta admitted that maybe he wasn't the best spokesman for cutting back on CO_2 emissions. But like all environmentalist hypocrites, he had a good excuse: "I use [jets] as a business tool, though, as others do. I think it's part of this industry—otherwise I couldn't be here doing this and I wouldn't be here now" [*Daily Mail*, "With Five Private Jets, Travolta Still Lectures on Global Warming," March 30, 2007]. Not as if noncelebrities didn't also have good reasons for getting where they need to go.

Like Oliver Hardy exasperated with Stan Laurel, environmental activists fumed at Travolta, "Stop trying to *help* us!" They blasted him for setting a bad example by preaching against flying while taking unnecessary flights himself. Funny they should mention that!

Probably the best-known environmental pressure group in the world is Greenpeace. That organization launched a campaign to convince people to reduce air travel to curb climate change. So it was pretty embarrassing when the *Guardian* newspaper revealed that one of the group's top European executives lived in Luxembourg and commuted to work a couple of times a month to Amsterdam by jet. The paper estimated that over the two years he'd held the job, the Greenpeace executive's commute had generated 7.4 metric tons of CO_2.

At the risk of giving you déjà vu, I should note that Greenpeace, too, had a feeble excuse. They insisted that the poor fellow felt just awful about all that flying but noted that making the same trip by train would have taken twelve hours, an inconveniently long stretch that would have cut into his work and family time [*The Guardian*, "Greenpeace Losses: Leaked Documents Reveal Extent of Financial Disarray," June 23, 2014]. Cue the violin!

So the official position of Greenpeace is that flying is destroying the planet, so *don't do it* . . . unless, of course, you do it only because it's faster and more convenient than taking less-polluting forms of mass transit. Say, isn't that the exact same reason all the rest of us fly? Yes, but the difference is that when environmentalists do it, they feel *just awful* about it, which makes them better people than us. In fact, if liberal guilt absorbed CO_2, we wouldn't have to think twice about greenhouse gases.

No wonder they feel so much guilt: A University of Exeter researcher found that people who described themselves as "committed environmentalists" actually flew *more* than nonenvironmentalists (to be fair, there are a lot of very important environmental conferences held in various resorts all around the world every year). They rationalized it by imagining that the recycling they did at home balanced out all the CO_2 generated by their jetting around. If only someone could invent a plane powered by self-delusion!

It's this type of hypocrisy that inspired law professor and blogmaster Glenn Reynolds of *Instapundit* to develop his rule for environmental scare stories, one that he has occasion to quote with surprising frequency: "I'll believe this is a serious problem when the people who claim it's a serious problem start acting like it's a serious problem."

Of course, environmental hypocrisy isn't confined to Hollywood stars and radical activist groups. It's also become a potent political issue for those who believe that every problem, including lousy weather, is a justification for ceding more power, freedom, and money to the government.

Like the Internet, environmentalism stretches back a long way, yet many people believe Al Gore invented it. There's no question that Gore's slideshow-turned-film documentary, *An Inconvenient Truth*, gave a huge jumpstart to the global warming . . . sorry, "climate change" . . . wait, sorry, "climate disruption" . . . no, hold on, "climate chaos" movement. (If the science is settled, why do they have to keep changing its name?) I won't bother recounting all the challenges to Gore's claims, as many others have already done so; or the widely noted disparities between the Spartan existence Gore prescribes for the rest of humanity and his own opulent, jet-set lifestyle. I'll just point out what I consider the most damning fact of all: While he was prophesying that global warming would cause a twenty-foot sea-level rise by the year 2100, flooding coastal areas and leaving hundreds of millions homeless (a claim debunked by a University of Montana study), he spent nearly $9 million on an oceanfront mansion in the limousine-liberal enclave of Montecito, California [*USA Today*, "How Green Is Al Gore's $9 Million Montecito Oceanfront Villa?" May 18, 2010]. If he truly believed in his own message, wouldn't it have been wiser to spend $1 million on a mansion in Phoenix, Arizona, and then just wait for it to *become* oceanfront property?

It's no surprise that the biggest proponent of expanding government to combat "climate disruption" is also among the biggest emitters of hot gas. On Earth Day 2014, President Obama issued a Presidential Proclamation listing the many dire consequences of climate change and the valiant ways in which he was working "to reduce greenhouse gas emissions around the globe." He also posted a "green" call-to-arms on the White House blog, declaring, "Our climate is changing, and that change is being driven by human activity. Every year, the United States pumps millions of tons of carbon dioxide pollution and other greenhouse gases into the atmosphere. Earth Day is about taking action."

And take action he did! To spread his message, Obama embarked on a whirlwind Earth Day promotional tour, flying from D.C. to Washington State to Tokyo to spread the gospel of reducing fossil fuel use and cutting CO_2 emissions.

Using numbers from the Department of Energy, the UK newspaper the *Daily Mail* calculated that Obama's Excellent Earth Day Adventure burned 35,600 gallons of helicopter and jet fuel, pumping out 375 tons of carbon dioxide "around the globe." That doesn't include all the fuel used for his motorcades, security, the cars of the people who turned out to see him, and the entire fleet of planes including at least two C-5 transport planes. That figure is just the carbon footprint for his Marine One copter and his 747 jet, Air Force One. It would take the average resident of the planet Earth 441 years to generate as much CO_2 as Obama did just to warn us about CO_2 on Earth Day.

By comparison, I also delivered an Earth Day message to millions of people. Granted, it was to point out the tremendous waste and hypocrisy of Obama's tour, but it did reach millions of people, and it caused far less damage to the environment than Obama did. It aired on my daily syndicated radio show, *The Huckabee Report*. Here's how a true conservationist spreads his message.

As usual, I communicated by e-mail with my writing and research staff. When we finished the script, I recorded it using a portable microphone and my trusty MacBook laptop. The recording was e-mailed as an MP3 file to my producer, who inserted the commercial and uploaded it to the Internet. Finally, over five hundred radio stations downloaded it and played it to millions of listeners nationwide. At no point did any of the people involved even have to step outside their homes or offices. The total CO_2 generated was probably no more than if I'd switched on one of those corkscrew-shaped, environmentally correct lightbulbs that make people look like they're in the morgue.

All those savings in CO_2 were due to modern technology that eliminated the need to travel to speak to a big gathering (which would also have required travel for the audience), to commute to an office or studio to write and record the show, or to ship it to the stations. And it's all thanks to the many companies like Apple, Intel, and AT&T that make it possible and affordable. These evil, capitalist, for-profit corporations, with their constant striving for greater efficiency, have eliminated far more pollution and greenhouse gasses than the environmental extremists railing against capitalism could dream of stopping with heavy-handed government edicts. Say, maybe someone should tell the President about capitalism, competition, and technology!

I believe in the old Boy Scout rule. As a Scout, I was taught to leave the campsite in as good or better shape than I found it. It's my deeply held conviction that the Earth and all its resources don't belong to me, but to God. He lets me use them, but doesn't permit me to abuse them. It should be my responsibility to be a good steward, or manager, of the natural resources. I want my children and grandchildren to enjoy them as much as I have.

At this point, I think it would be wise to set the record straight on one of the most unfair canards in the entire environmental movement: the attempt to tar anyone who questions apocalyptic predictions about man-made climate change as a "climate change denier," a scientific illiterate comparable to a Holocaust denier. This may surprise you, but I don't believe I've ever met a conservative who denies that the Earth's climate is changing. Most people are well aware that the Earth's climate is constantly changing. I've also met very few conservatives who think that humans have no impact on the environment. But as we like to say down South, the devil is in the details.

Those who question apocalyptic environmental claims have been given plenty of good reasons to be skeptical, including scandals over altered and hidden data and the blatant, thuggish suppression of dissenting scientists. Some environmental activists have openly admitted that they believe their cause to be so important that exaggerating the scary consequences is justified to achieve their desired results. Then there's the lockstep biased media reporting. Steven F. Hayward of the American Enterprise Institute noted that a recent UN IPCC report that was widely touted by the media as ironclad proof of cataclysmic, irreversible man-made climate change actually used the terms "uncertain" or "uncertainty" 173 times in its chapter on computer models [AEI.org. "Politics Posing as Science," December 3, 2007]. So far, those computer models have been about as accurate in their predictions as a drunken stockbroker with a Ouija board.

Even so, for the most part, people in the heartland who live close to nature want to protect and conserve it, and they are willing to err on the side of caution and make some sacrifices. They'd just like some honest answers to their legitimate questions. For instance . . .

Are the scary predictions really likely, or are they worst-case scenarios taken to the nth degree for propaganda purposes? How much of the changing climate is really due to humans and how much is due to naturally occurring climate cycles or other natural phenomena such as volcanoes?

Exactly how much money and personal freedom are we expected to hand over to the government in exchange for promises of environmental salvation, and are those costs being deliberately understated? Would the miniscule dent that such action might make in CO_2 levels make enough difference to be worth the tremendous cost to our economy, lifestyles, and freedom? Or would that money be better spent preparing to deal with whatever climate change might come anyway?

You'll notice that none of those questions is predicated on "denying climate change." If environmental activists really want to reduce global warming, it might help if they'd quit turning their flamethrowers on so many straw men.

Climate change isn't the only field in which the environmental movement has claimed to represent unassailable scientific truth, only to be brought up short by new data.

For years, we were told that biofuels were the future. Skeptics who questioned whether it took more energy to create a gallon of fuel from corn than was generated by burning it were dismissed. But as we devoted more and more of our food crops to energy production, we discovered yet again that for every action, there is an equal and opposite reaction. (Science!) In this case, so-called environmentalist policies hurt the poor when the supply of corn and other grains fell, causing skyrocketing food prices and shortages that led to riots in undeveloped nations. At this writing, the European Union has just agreed to limit biofuels, for those reasons and also because they were found to make some engines run *less* efficiently, to cause *more* pollution than expected, and to *harm* the environment and contribute to global warming, due to the need for clear-cutting more farmland.

Likewise, we were told that solar and wind power were the renewable energy alternatives to coal- and gas-fired power plants. Billions of our tax dollars were ladled out to well-connected cronies in those "green" industries—"green" meaning money. But solar and wind can't generate enough power on a consistent basis to meet demand, and electricity can't be stored. When the clouds appear or the wind stops blowing, the juice stops flowing as well, so we still need the coal- and gas-powered plants. The Germans nearly lost their lederhosen trying to convert to a wind-power society. Even though the program was already an expensive disaster, the German government pressed on after environmentalists insisted that the nation's nuclear power plants be shut down in the wake of the 2011 Fukushima nuke plant disaster in Japan. Apparently, nobody bothered to calculate the odds of a tsunami striking Germany. Or maybe they were just planning for that twenty-foot rise in sea levels that Al Gore predicted.

Here's another thing the environmentalists failed to anticipate: Spinning wind turbines are a landscape-sized Cuisinart for birds and bats, slicing and dicing them faster than Ron Popeil. It's a federal crime to shoot a bald eagle, our national bird, or for most of us to possess even one of its feathers, but environmentalists don't seem to mind very much when they're felled by windmill blades, in the interest of green energy and all that (when it became known that wind farms were Freddy Kruegering golden and bald eagles, the Obama administration took swift action to save the environment and granted wind farm companies a thirty-year exemption to the eagle-killing ban [*Los Angeles Times,* "Wind Farms Get Extended Leeway on Eagle Deaths," December 6, 2013]). Likewise, solar panels in the desert sun can flash-fry a bird crispier than Colonel Sanders ever dreamed. But if you want to make an omelet, you have to break a few eggs, and I guess if you want to protect Mother Nature, you have to kill a few million birds and bats.

Well-intentioned "green" forest management, which bans the use of firebreaks in forest areas and leaves dead trees and underbrush untouched to serve as kindling, contributes greatly to the sweeping damage done by wildfires. When a fire rages and equipment needs to be brought in, we should recognize that building a few roads through the woods might have been a good idea. Of course, the environmentalists responsible for piling up all that kindling and blocking access to fire trucks blame the growing number of wildfires entirely on global warming. As governor of a timber state like Arkansas, I can attest to the stupidity of many of the policies of the federal government to "save the trees!" Problem is, without some thinning out of the trees, there won't be adequate sun for trees to grow and much of the forest will die. After an exceptionally bad ice storm in 2000 which destroyed tens of thousands of acres of forest representing millions of board feet of timber, our state fought the feds continually to allow access to the federal forest lands so the dead trees on the ground could be hauled out for lumber, firewood, and to help preserve the forest itself. The presence of dead and rotting trees on the ground is not only extremely dangerous as a source of ready-made fuel for a massive forest fire, but bugs and beetles that inhabit dead trees can destroy the live ones. Getting those dead trees out of the forests was common sense to the folks in Bubba-ville; but in Bubble-ville, that would have meant "disturbing the natural setting."

I could go on and on, citing statements from people who claimed to have irrefutable scientific proof on their side ("Due to ocean depletion, tuna will cost eighty dollars a can by the 1980s!"), only to end up with egg on their faces when new data appeared or the planetary ecosystem proved to be more complicated than they realized. I well remember my college days in the early seventies how we were told that it was an absolute fact that we were experiencing global cooling, and the covers of *Newsweek* and *Time* touted the *imminent* danger of our planet becoming a big popsicle. Maybe this is why hyperenvironmentalists are so desperate to shut down any further discussion that might give rise to new, contradictory data (i.e., "science"). This attitude is nothing new. The progressive environmentalist movement had a spiritual forefather in the theologian Philipp Melanchthon, who wrote in 1541 that "wise governments ought to repress impudence of mind." He was suggesting that government power be wielded to silence the crazy claim by Copernicus that the Earth went around the sun instead of the other way around, as was the consensus of all learned men and governments at the time.

Recall, it hasn't been that long since the self-proclaimed scientific "experts" were telling us that chocolate, coffee, eggs, coconut oil, and butter were killing us. Now, they're practically considered health foods by many nutritionists, as long as we stay at a reasonably healthy weight. Even bacon is suddenly okay to eat, at least at this writing. And those "experts" may change their minds yet again. Remember, they're the ones who told us that oat bran would make us live forever. Luckily, those of us from Paula Deen country never paid any attention to the food alarmists in the first place. You may take away our plane tickets, our coal industry, and our SUVs, but keep your cotton-pickin' hands off our butter!

For those of us from the land of God, guns, grits, and gravy, being told we need to ride a bicycle and live in a tree stump by an environmental lobbyist in a Gucci suit or an aging hippie who hasn't been outside the San Francisco city limits since Jerry Garcia died goes over about as well as Pee-wee Herman lecturing George Foreman on how to throw a punch. While environmental activist groups lobby Congress to spend more of other people's tax money on protecting species and habitats, the people putting up their own money to do just that are the hunters and fishermen who have a vested interest in keeping forests thick, waterways clean, and wildlife plentiful.

According to the Congressional Sportsmen's Foundation, there are around 34 million hunters and anglers in America, who generate a total of $25 billion a year in federal, state, and local tax revenues. They spend over a billion dollars annually just on licenses, permits, stamps, and tags, much of it going to pay for conservation and management of wildlife habitats and waterways. If that's not enough, there are nearly 600,000 members of Ducks Unlimited, a nonprofit group for duck hunters that generates nearly $180 million a year, at least 80 percent of which goes directly to habitat conservation. Full disclosure here: I'm a Life Member of Ducks Unlimited, a Life Member of Bass Anglers Sportsman Society (B.A.S.S.), and a member of the National Wild Turkey Federation. In fact, maybe I should add another "G" to *God, Guns, Grits, and Gravy: Game*. Because God gives us game that we shoot with guns and serve with grits and gravy. *Gooood*.

I'm sorry if that sounds cruel to any vegan readers (And are there any? Raise your hands, if you have the strength), but that's what nature is really like. Humans are part of the natural world, just as much as the spotted owl and the snail darter, only our place is higher on the food chain. I feel a twinge of sadness before pulling the trigger and killing a deer or duck, but I know that my family and I will eat the meat and give thanks for it. It's far kinder to cull the herd with a quick lethal shot than to let overpopulation lead to slow death by starvation. (Some animal rights groups want to shoot deer with birth control darts instead, which can cost up to $1,000 per deer per season—but then, government-paid birth control is some people's answer to everything.) I also like to think that given the choice, game animals would prefer a quick death by a hunter to being ripped apart by some less humane predator, like a wolf or a mountain lion. Again, I hate to disillusion those who learned about nature from Disney cartoons, but the real natural world is often cruel and painful.

Out in Bubba-ville, the natural environment of the great outdoors isn't some abstract concept that we imagine we can control at long distance through legislation. We "interact" with it every day. It's the forests, the fields, the farms, the mountains, the lakesides, and the riverbanks where we grew up and where our children will grow up. It's sometimes beautiful, sometimes frightening; but it's our home, it's where we're closest to God, and we would no more let the EPA tell us we have to get off of it than we'd let someone come in and pave over it.

That bearded guru of backwoods life, Phil Robertson of *Duck Dynasty*, perfectly expressed our attitude toward Mother Nature in all her unpredictability in his book, *Happy, Happy, Happy*. He recounted the day a real estate agent took him out to see a house that was down a dirt road, deep in the forest, and next to a river, a location that many environmental lobbyists would recoil from (it was so remote, there wasn't even a Starbucks!), but which Robertson described as "absolutely perfect." He wrote:

> The real estate lady sensed my excitement and told me, "Now, Mr. Robertson, I'm required by law to inform you that this home sits in a floodplain."
>
> "Perfect," I told her. "I wouldn't want it if it didn't."

It's one of the reasons I love Phil Robertson. He makes sense to me, but the elites will never "get him." Give thanks to God, and pass the grits!

14

School's Out

MASS EXODUS FROM
PUBLIC SCHOOLS

BILL CLINTON AND I BOTH attended Miss Marie's kindergarten and started first grade at the Brookwood Elementary School in Hope, Arkansas. Clinton never finished the first grade there since he moved to Hot Springs, Arkansas, that year. That means Clinton was a dropout from the school where I spent six years. Okay, that sounds a bit harsh and unfair, but we both did have our starts in a public school in a small town. We were not alone. Most kids of my generation went to public schools. There was really no other choice in my community and frankly, there didn't need to be. The public schools of Hope, Arkansas, in the fifties and sixties reflected values that were bedrock American, Judeo-Christian, patriotic, and traditional.

We started each day with a prayer, and said another one on the way to the lunchroom. We recited the pledge of allegiance to the flag every day and heard a reading from the Bible. We had guest speakers in assemblies, some of them guest ministers doing a church revival in one of the local churches that week, and they would give us a spiritual message. The Gideons came to our school and handed New Testaments to every fifth grader. We were required to say, "Yes, Ma'am" and "No, Ma'am"; "Yes, Sir" and "No, Sir" to adults—whether it was teachers, parents, or the janitor. If we misbehaved, we got a paddling at school (yes, we really got those), and in my case, one at school meant an automatic repeat at home. We had cake and Jell-O on our plates in the lunchroom and whole milk. We had popsicles in the afternoon recess. But no one ever got shot and we didn't have armed guards on the campus.

I am a product of the public schools. My sister taught for thirty-eight years in public schools before retiring. Two of my aunts were public schoolteachers. And all three of my own children attended the public schools of Arkansas their entire first grade through twelfth grade. In fact, I was the first Arkansas governor in fifty years whose own children attended the public schools of our state exclusively. When the teacher's unions of Arkansas would oppose me and virtually everything I ever did for education, I would remind the public (especially some of the left-of-center partisan Democrats who doubted my support for education) of that fact.

I'm so very grateful for the public schools and the public schoolteachers I was blessed to have as a kid growing up. Because of the opportunity to have access to a good and challenging education, I was able to do something no male in my entire paternal lineage had ever done: I graduated from high school. That's right—upstream from me, no male in my paternal ancestry had ever finished high school, much less went to college.

After I tried a few teenage jobs such as stocking shelves and cleaning the local JCPenney store, or catching chickens and hauling hay with one of my friends who lived on a farm, or unloading a truck full of strawberries, I wanted to know, "What do I have to do so I don't have to do this for the rest of my life?" When I was told I would have to get a good education, I was *highly* motivated! And I was fortunate to be able to access a good education in the public schools, because my family would not have been able to afford an alternative. It's one of the reasons that I do understand the importance of good public schools. If we can't make them work, then we need to create options for the parents, whether through vouchers, tax credits, or another way, so every parent can make a good decision for the education of their children.

I wish I could say that the public schools are where my grandchildren will be great as well, but I can no longer say that what was perfectly fine for my generation and for my children's generation is perfectly fine for my grandchildren's generation. In some communities, perhaps; but in most of America's communities, parents cannot confidently send their children to a public school unless they are prepared to undo the damage done each day to values and mores the parents are attempting to instill in their children.

Parents are ditching the very schools that they once attended and, in many cases, spending large sums of money out of pocket to receive what they already have paid for in taxes to their state and local community.

Some of the reasons parents give up on the schools they are already paying for and opting to pay twice for their children to have an education is the sheer insanity of some of the policies the "educrats" create. Nowhere is this more pronounced than in the truly nutty attitudes some schools have adopted regarding violence and guns. Don't misunderstand—guns and violence are serious issues on a school campus, but I'm talking about something that defies common sense and makes one believe that morons are running the schools.

Fourteen-year-old Andrew Mikel did what every bored teenage boy has done since the dawn of time: In February 2011, he used his fountain pen tube to blow some small plastic pellets at three classmates during lunch period. Sure, his miniature blowgun was childish and annoying, but completely harmless. But not to school officials! Oh, no! Andrew was not only expelled for possession and use of a weapon, he's also charged with three counts of assault. The officials insist that under the federal Gun-Free School Zones Act, Andrew's pen tube was a "projectile weapon," "used to intimidate, threaten or harm others," and he had to be expelled to insure a safe learning environment [*The Washington Post,* "Plastic Pellet Incident at Va. School Ends in Expulsion, Assault Charges," February 1, 2011]. He's now being homeschooled, which sounds like a darn good idea. I guess he's lucky he didn't throw a spitball. He might've been accused of a biological weapons attack.

From a Pop-Tarts gun (there was actually a case [*New York Daily News*, "Boy Suspended for Chewing Pop-Tart into Shape of a Gun, Gets Lifetime NRA Membership," May 31, 2013] where a student was suspended because he bit his Pop-Tarts into the shape of a gun!) to a picture of a rifle on a T-shirt, schools have punished students for anything that even resembles a gun. But this may be the screwiest story of all. The Rutherford Institute is suing a Chicago-area school district on behalf of veteran second-grade teacher Doug Bartlett. He was suspended without pay by Washington Irving Elementary School for violating the zero-tolerance policy on "possessing, carrying, storing or using a weapon." And what was his crime? He brought his toolbox to school to give his kids a lesson on how pliers, wrenches, and screwdrivers are used. He didn't even have a nail gun. When he wasn't demonstrating the tools, they were secured on a high shelf, out of reach, and the students never even touched them. A spokesman called Bartlett's suspension a "zealous misapplication of misguided zero tolerance policies." [*The Christian Science Monitor*, "When Is a Tool a Weapon? Chicago Court Throws Out Teacher's Discipline Case," April 18, 2014]. But you know who I really feel sorry for? The kids in that school district's high school shop class. How do they cut boards? With their teeth?

Parents know that if you don't let a little boy play with a toy gun, he'll make anything into a pretend gun. That happened in Suffolk, Virginia, where two seven-year-old boys pointed pencils at one another and made shooting sounds with their mouths, as boys have done for generations. Only in this generation, it got them both suspended from Driver Elementary School. Officials say it violated the zero-tolerance policy because a pencil is considered a weapon if it's pointed in a threatening way [Washington.CBSLocal.com. "2 Va. Boys Suspended for Using Pencils as Guns," May 7, 2013] and gun noises are made. That also applies to pointing your finger. Funny, I thought fingers and pencils were only dangerous weapons when you use those fingers to pick up a pencil and write idiotic school policies.

But it isn't just imaginary weapons that make some school officials overreact. They get the vapors over love bombs, too. Hunter Yelton is a student at Lincoln School of Science and Technology in Canon City, Colorado. He likes a girl in his class, and she likes him back. So one day, he kissed her on the hand. Big mistake. He was accused of sexual harassment. He got off with a warning once. But Hunter is a repeat offender. He gave his crush a peck on the cheek. For that, he was charged with unwanted touching under the school's zero-tolerance policy on bullying and sexual harassment, and suspended for several days. He's back now, but asking a lot of uncomfortable questions. Questions like, "What is 'sex,' mommy?" You see, Hunter Yelton—that unrepentant serial harasser, who forced his lips onto both his girlfriend's hand *and* her cheek—is six years old. He's in the first grade. He doesn't know yet that expressing love is bad. But it sounds like that's one thing our schools are determined to teach.

On another front, New York City education bureaucrats have taken political correctness to new heights by banning dozens of words and topics from appearing on city-issued tests. For instance, dinosaurs can't be mentioned because it might upset fundamentalists. "Halloween" is banned because it suggests paganism. "Birthdays" are forbidden because Jehovah's Witnesses don't celebrate them. Even "dancing" is banned because some religions bar dancing, although it's still okay to mention ballet. The edict states that these and other subjects must be avoided because they could evoke "unpleasant emotions" in the students [*The Huffington Post*, "New York City Bans References to Dinosaurs, Birthdays, Halloween, Dancing in Standardized Tests," March 26, 2012].

Keep in mind that those are just crazy instances (and there are *thousands* of them) of some of the social aspects of modern school life. We haven't even started touching on the academic atmosphere of our schools today or the paranoia in many public schools that someone might hear something about God and die from it.

Despite nutty policies about the shapes of chewed Pop-Tarts, or forbidding the combination of green and red colors in clothing during December for fear that it might cause someone to "think" about Christmas (yes, this actually happened in December 2013 in an elementary school in Frisco, Texas, a suburb of Dallas ["School Bans Christmas Trees, the Colors Red and Green," Fox News, December 5, 2013]), the main reason that children go to school is to receive an education and to learn basic facts about history, math, language, science, art, and music. When parents lose confidence that their children will even be exposed to and participate in rigorous academic pursuits, they will run for the exits and find alternatives. And that's exactly what they are doing.

A generation ago, parents who homeschooled their children were probably considered religious extremists or leftover hippies from the sixties. "Normal" people just didn't do such things. Why, what kind of education would children get if they didn't sit for six hours a days in a classroom listening to a teacher and watching the teacher write with chalk on a big green board at the front of the room? Turns out, a pretty good education could be had at home!

The first-ever perfect score on the SAT exam up through my tenure as Arkansas governor was achieved by a young lady who was homeschooled. (Her dad, in fact, worked for me in our Department of Human Services.) It was a source of great pride to her parents, but a source of great embarrassment for the educational establishment.

While there have always been private prep schools and parochial schools, the rapid growth of the homeschool movement is nothing short of stunning. Just how many students are being homeschooled is a difficult number to pin down. The National Center for Educational Statistics says this:

> Approximately 3 percent of the school-age population was homeschooled in the 2011 to 2012 school year. Among children who were homeschooled, a higher percentage were White (68 percent) than Black (8 percent), Hispanic (15 percent), or Asian or Pacific Islander (4 percent).

Parents gave a number of different reasons for homeschooling their children. In the 2011 to 2012 school year, 91 percent of homeschooled students had parents who said that a concern about the environment of other schools was an important reason for homeschooling their child, which was a higher percentage than other reasons listed.

Education News reported almost 2.4 million homeschooled children in the United States as of 2011, with the number growing between 7 percent and 15 percent per year. Since 1999, the number of children who are homeschooled has increased by 75 percent, and the number of children whose parents decide to homeschool is growing at an astonishing rate, seven times faster than the number of children who attend K-12 of public schools.

Some of our close friends began homeschooling their children when doing so was still fairly rare. Many factors contributed to their decision, one of which was indeed wanting to be able to undergird their family's faith rather than have the public schools undermine it. But there were other practical reasons, such as being able to have flexibility in the school calendar to accommodate their desires to travel and tailor their school lives around their family rather than have their family life built around the school schedule. And the argument that kids who were homeschooled don't get enough socialization is laughable for those of us who personally know homeschool families, because their children are typically very involved in numerous activities, from sports to music to theater to forensic debate. And in at least one recent year, both the winner and runner up in the National Spelling Bee were homeschooled kids.

My first appointment to the Arkansas State Board of Education was a homeschooling parent. She was the first homeschooling parent in the United States to be appointed to a State Board of Education. The teachers union was apoplectic as was the rest of the board, all of whom had been appointed by my Democrat predecessors Bill Clinton and Jim Guy

Tucker. The very idea that one of those "homeschool moms" would be allowed to sit on the State Board of Education!

But the educational establishment never thought it inappropriate for them to regulate homeschooling, so why would they be so afraid that one out of seven members of the state board would be one of "those people?" She was incredibly effective, fair-minded, and within two years, was highly respected and regarded for her contribution to the board.

Per pupil expenditure continues to soar even as standardized test results languish or decline. Some states and school districts spend more per year on K-12 students than other states spend for a year in a university! New York averages over $19,000 per student; Alaska, $17,390; New Jersey, $17,266; and Vermont, $16,039 [*USA Today*, "States Spending the Most on Education," June 7, 2014].

As outrageous as that sounds, a 2010 report by the Cato Institute argued that the costs of public schools are vastly underreported. The study looked at the five largest U.S. metro areas plus the District of Columbia and found that on average, public school spending was 44 percent higher than officially reported. The highest was in New York, where per-student spending actually reached $27,000. The study found that public schools were spending an average of 93 percent more than the estimated median private school in the same area.

But wait: Cato researcher Andrew Coulson later found that they'd overlooked some line items in the D.C. budget, and in fact, public schools there spend a mind-boggling average of $29,409 per pupil per year.

For that mountain of money, Washington, D.C., public school students get one of the worst educational experiences in America. Crime, drugs, gang violence, and depressing, dilapidated facilities. The district has been trying to correct the latter by building and refurbishing schools, like a $130 million makeover for Cardozo High School. But even with the much-improved facilities, sophomores' reading proficiency in 2013 was under 20 percent, a drop of nearly 6 percentage points from 2012. D.C.'s public schools have been so bad for so long, and so resistant to reform, that even *The Washington Post* did a series of articles exposing the decline.

My favorite story from the *Post* concerns a couple of D.C. school officials who worked for D.C. Afterschool for All, a program that provides extra instruction and afternoon supervision for thousands of impoverished children. Over a two-year period, they spent over $13,000 on expensive meals and drinks (including $82 bottles of wine at an upscale Italian restaurant) and entertainment (including a $225 tab at the Camelot Show Bar, one of D.C.'s fanciest strip clubs, expensed as a "school planning meeting") and charged it all to the Shaw Junior High School activity fund.

It's no wonder that D.C.'s public elementary and high schools are under capacity and its middle schools are literally half-empty (52 percent utilization of facilities). Much of that is due to birth rates and changing demographics, but I have to assume that fleeing also plays a major role.

Say, here's a suggestion for getting the D.C. public school population back up! Why don't all the liberal politicians who champion public schools (or more precisely, public schoolteachers' unions) and fight tooth and claw against vouchers or any other idea to give parents more control and kids a better education and hopes for a better life, take their own kids out of private schools like Sidwell Friends and put them into D.C.'s public schools? That would fill a lot of empty desks!

It doesn't help at all that some of the attempts to improve public education get hijacked by those with agendas that are not about the students. It's what Ray Simon, who was State Director of Education during a good part of my tenure as governor, used to call the difference between "school people" and "kid people." I came to realize that some people are about protecting the *school* as an institution and those who are employed by it. Sadly, much of the money and energy are gobbled up by the school people. Too little is done to actually benefit the kids.

A great example of a good idea gone bad is Common Core, which has become the whipping boy of the left and the right. I'm not sure who hates it the most, but the very mention of it gets the veins on people's necks bulging. If there is anything less than a primal scream demanding that anyone who does or who has ever supported Common Core should be burned at the stake, then that person is the same as a Communist sympathizer or child molester, not worthy of his or her next breath of air.

Common Core is dead, and because of what it has become in most states should be. But the origins were pretty simple and straightforward and were actually launched by conservatives to keep education standards under the control of local school boards and states and out of the hands of the federal government.

The concept grew from an effort that conservative Republican governors like Jeb Bush of Florida, Tommy Thompson (Wisconsin governor who pioneered school vouchers in Milwaukee), John Engler of Michigan, and I all supported. It was an initiative called "Achieve," and an effort of the National Governors Association to do three things: raise academic standards to be rigorous and consistent; measure the performance of students to determine how well they were doing against those standards; and hold the stakeholders (teachers, administrators, students, and yes, even politicians) responsible for the results.

Many of us feared an increasing role of the federal government in education mandates and were strenuously opposed to that both on constitutional grounds and practical ones. The federal government has no role to play in education. It's the purview of the states and the local communities through their elected school boards. Further, most every governor I've known believes as did the Founders that states are the laboratory of democracy where ideas and innovations get created and tested. If they work, other states will adopt them. If they don't work, we don't end up making a fifty-state mistake. Experience had also been a cruel teacher to governors as to what happens when the federal government wants to get in the middle of local school decisions. The Individuals with

Disabilities Education Act (IDEA) hatched in the 1970s proved to be a financial trap for states who were promised money by the feds to pay for fully integrating all persons, including those with developmental disabilities, into the regular classrooms, replacing the traditional "special education" model. The states have been left holding the bag ever since and the federal government never fulfilled even a fraction of its commitment to fully fund it. It's why those of us who went through that nightmare in the 1990s were adamantly opposed to Obamacare mandates for Medicaid, despite big assurances that the federal government would cover the cost for the first three years. We'd all heard that song before. And it ends on a very sour note!

Common Core was the natural outgrowth of the standards sought from back in the late 1990s. It was pushed by the National Governors Association, and forty-four states initially signed on because it would keep authority and control at the state level but would establish a cooperative set of standards for two (and *only* two) subjects: math and language arts. There was not one bit regarding curriculum, data collection on students or schools that would go to the federal government, and nothing with Common Core would involve science, history, the arts, or any area of study other than math and language arts, period.

As I tried unsuccessfully to explain to parents the intent (not, however, the outcome), I used a sports analogy. If an eighth grader plays on a basketball team in Oregon, and moves to South Carolina, he should have a reasonable expectation that the basic rules of the game will be the same. The rim of the goal will be ten feet from the floor; the court will measure eighty-four feet long by fifty feet wide, and the free throw line will be fifteen feet from the point on the floor directly beneath the backboard. If every state, every district, and every team could make up its own standards, imagine the chaos in a state tournament when one team shot the ball toward a goal ten feet off the floor, while another played on a court where the goal was only seven feet off the floor. Those boys used to a seven-foot goal probably thought they were all pretty amazing players to be able to slam dunk the ball at will, but they will be creamed when they play the team that is used to playing with much more rigorous standards.

No matter how many times I've repeated that analogy, I am utterly frustrated that what was supposed to be state-controlled standards in two areas has morphed into a federal behemoth. Even now I get e-mails and posts on my Web site that say, "Mike Huckabee supports Common Core; I'll *never* vote for him or even listen to him, *ever*!" Okay, that's your prerogative, but while I agree that Common Core has become an unmanageable Frankenstandard kidnapped by the federal government, please tell me that you do insist on standards to be clear, that measurements should be taken to see if we're achieving them, and that if the enormous amount of money we're spending isn't effective, we'll fire people, hire new ones, and get the job done.

The controversy over Common Core may have had an unintended benefit for those of us who believe that education decisions should be made by Mom and Dad, not Uncle Sam. If it's further driven a wedge between the freedom of parents and the force of the federal government, then good! We need to keep the federal fingers off our kids.

It's increasingly evident that parents throughout America are no longer willing to drive up to the school each day, drop off their children, and assume that everything will turn out all right. Parents are voting with their feet and taking their children out of government-run schools. While affluent families have had and have exercised that option for years, working-class families know that for their children to have a shot at making it to the next rung on the ladder, they have to have schools that are run by "kid people."

Regulation + Taxation + Litigation = Job Migration

ONE OF THE CHERISHED BELIEFS of so-called "progressives" is that their policies don't cause economic stagnation because businesses and individuals will simply lie there and absorb whatever new taxes and regulations are dumped on them ("Please, sir, may I have another?"), and won't take any evasive action. You can see a good example of that mind-set in their claims that there's no evidence that many businesses are cutting workers to part-time and holding down their staffs to under fifty employees to avoid the Obamacare mandates. I hear they also have a plan to pay off the national debt with Tooth Fairy money and rides on unicorns.

Outside of Bubble-ville, where the rest of us have to deal with the reality of their misbegotten policies, the migration of businesses from highly taxed and regulated states and nations to those that offer lower taxes and more freedom is as obvious and predictable as the migration of mallard ducks from Canada to the rice fields in east Arkansas.

It's said that most new trends start in California and spread eastward, and California has been leading the nation for years in electing far-left politicians who love raising taxes, growing government, prosecuting and suing entire industries, and turning every crackpot suggestion for how to improve the world into a state regulation. There are many people across the United States who think the "progressive" model of California should be adopted by other states in the same way that the federal government has been embracing it. So, to paraphrase that great philosopher, Dr. Phil, "How's that workin' out for them?"

In 2014, California achieved the dubious distinction of being named by *Chief Executive* magazine as the worst state in America to do business for the tenth year in a row. It was followed by New York and Illinois. (Hmm . . . what do these states have in common?) California's chief rival, Texas, was ranked the best state to open or run a business for the tenth straight year, although Florida was nipping at its heels, largely by copying Texas's winning formula of cutting taxes and actively promoting itself as a corporate relocation destination.

Chief Executive conceded that in recent years, California Governor Jerry Brown has improved the state's situation somewhat by eliminating its staggering budget deficits. But that came at the cost of enacting even higher taxes. The editors noted that California's top marginal tax rate of 33 percent "is the third-highest tax rate in the industrialized world, behind only Denmark and France. This situation creates a bias against savings, slows economic growth and harms competitiveness."

But it's no great feat to get California legislators to agree to higher taxes and to get the state's voters to approve them, providing they're assured that only rich people—generally defined as "anyone with a dollar more than you"—will pay them. The second part of the equation for encouraging businesses to open and expand and create jobs is to eliminate burdensome regulations. That's harder in California than talking a surfer dude into wearing a necktie and not using the word "dude" for more than an hour of waking time.

For instance, the magazine found that in Texas, if you want to open a restaurant, complying with all the required regulations takes just six to eight weeks from first permit filing to grand opening. In California, it involves a descent into the Ninth Circle of Bureaucratic Hell that takes an average of three years to navigate, if you're lucky enough to come out of it with enough money left over to open a restaurant. I hope your customers weren't too hungry! No wonder people in California are skinnier than the rest of the country—they're reduced to eating sunshine while the eating places are trying to get the government to give them a permit.

And just try getting California politicians to cut the bloated public workforce or scale back the lavish union benefits and pensions that are driving cities as large as Stockton and even San Bernardino County to seek bankruptcy protection. It was a sweet deal while it lasted: Union negotiators hammered out ever-more-generous contracts with political officials who were dependent on union support for their reelections, and sent the bill to all the poor suckers—oops, sorry, "taxpayers and business owners"—who weren't even allowed in the room. Then one day, the politicians found themselves deep in debt, looked around, and discovered that the taxpayers and businesses weren't just out of the room, they'd moved out of the state entirely. Here's a rule of thumb for governing from my personal experience: When two parties are negotiating a deal that neither has to pay for, it doesn't end well for the sucker who does have to pay for it.

A study by Dun & Bradstreet found that over 2,500 California businesses with three or more workers relocated to other states between 2007 and 2011, taking more than 109,000 jobs with them. Since then, the exodus has escalated. Texas Governor Rick Perry earned the scorn of liberals in California, New York, and other blue states for his unapologetic promotional tours, selling their states' companies on the benefits of moving to Texas. He's been accused of "poaching" their tax bases. But they should ask their buddies in the animal rights movement to define that term for them. Perry isn't shooting anything, except maybe fish in a barrel. It's not "poaching" when a free-range animal decides to move to a greener pasture. That's just "migration." Businesses and workers are migrating from a number of blue states, not just to Texas, but to Florida, Tennessee, the Carolinas, and other more business-friendly locales.

Here's my favorite shorthand way of determining how good a job a city or state is doing at encouraging people to stay there. Just go to www

.uhaul.com and check out the going rate to rent a U-Haul truck to and from Dallas. As of this writing, renting a fourteen-foot truck, big enough to move a two-bedroom apartment, in Los Angeles and dropping it off in Dallas will cost you $1,602. Renting the same truck for the same time period from Dallas to LA costs just $946. U-Haul has so many moving vans heading one-way from California to Texas that they'll subsidize your move by $656 (that's a 41 percent discount) just to drive one back to LA for them.

The tragedy is that there's no good reason at all for Californians to have to update Horace Greeley's famous advice and cry, "Go east, young Californians!" For most of the twentieth century, California was a solar-powered magnet, attracting people from across America and around the world. It earned its nickname the "Golden State" for more reasons than the gold nuggets in its mountains. And all of those assets are still there, in abundance: a near-perfect climate, gorgeous scenery, an 840-mile coastline offering both pristine beaches and busy seaports, vast mineral and timber resources, and some of the finest farmland in the world—if the environmentalists would just let farmers plow it without arresting them every time their tractors run over a field mouse. The great Backward California Gold Rush is best described by the euphemism that the Obama administration created to replace the word "terrorism." California's problems are a "man-caused disaster." Gold flakes enticed settlers to rush to California, and now left-wing flakes are driving them out.

Speaking frankly (and anonymously) to ChiefExecutive.net, a number of CEOs explained why their companies were fleeing California. Here are some of their comments:

> "The government is the worst in every possible way."
> "California's taxes and ongoing changes for regulations are devastating. One never knows from day to day what new interpretation of an existing regulation or new regulation will befall your small business."

"Too much government (with) nothing better to do than to harass businesses in the state. They need to cut the size of their regulatory bodies in half."

"State politicians feel business and commerce are 'necessary evils' that provide the funds to enable pursuit of their misguided agendas."

"California regulations, taxes and costs will leave only tech, life sciences and entertainment as viable."

That last comment is worth exploring in more detail. Whenever conservatives point out the ways in which California's politicians are driving away businesses, jobs, and middle-class workers, liberals always point to Hollywood and Silicon Valley to refute it. They say that California is actually doing great because of the billions of dollars the entertainment and high-tech industries are bringing into the state. That's true—for the moment—but it's an economic foundation built on quicksand.

California politicians have been very lucky that at this particular moment in history, events have converged to create an unprecedented business climate in which very young people can create a new piece of hardware or software that makes them wealthy overnight, before they've had enough life experience to knock their youthful flirtation with socialism and progressivism out of their heads. Nothing so thrills a liberal California politician as seeing a shaggy-haired young billionaire in a Che Guevara T-shirt. (And never mind that a naïve young billionaire is likely one of the first people that a Communist revolutionary like Che would put before a firing squad.)

Of course, Hollywood has been a fundraising goldmine for left-wing politicians ever since the Young Turks overthrew the big studio system in the sixties and seventies. Barack Obama probably spends more time at Harvey Weinstein's house than at the White House. Actors are particularly vulnerable to arguments about the unfairness of capitalism because in Hollywood, the "winners of life's lottery" argument seems especially convincing. While some stars are making $10 million a movie, they know there are countless struggling actors with just as much talent who are still waiting tables. Some of these wealthy celebrities can even be persuaded by politicians to feel guilty about their success (*Kaching!*). Add to that the fact that these days, actors have to get started on their careers at such a tender age that many drop out of school before they've had a chance to take Econ 101. A few of those who achieve early success do take a break from making movies and complete their education, but they typically matriculate (enroll, for those in Bubbaville) at very expensive bastions of liberal indoctrination such as Harvard, Yale, or Brown.

But there are ominous signs for California liberals that the Hollywood/Silicon Valley gravy train might be slowly pulling out of the station. Hollywood still churns out countless movies portraying business people as heartless villains who want to shaft the workers and avoid paying their "fair share." But if you sit through the end credits, you'll notice how many Hollywood movies and TV shows are now shot in states such as Texas and Louisiana that offer nonunion labor and tax breaks to filmmakers—even New York offers enticing tax incentives—or in cheaper, less regulation-bound locations outside the United States such as Canada, Mexico, or Australia. Hollywood likes lecturing the rest of us about how greedy we are to want to keep more of our own money, but they don't like having to pay a lot of taxes for the privilege.

These movies and TV shows have been very aptly dubbed "runaway productions." They're increasing so rapidly that Chris Baugh, location manager for the Oscar-winning film *Argo* (which actually *was* shot in Hollywood—but then, it was made by Ben Affleck, a liberal actor with reported political ambitions) was quoted in *Variety* as saying, "I am starting to see people who have never made a feature film in Los Angeles. In fact, they are afraid to. They are concerned that it is too expensive and too difficult."

In 2013, Los Angeles Mayor Eric Garcetti declared the outbound stampede of movie and TV productions to be a "state of emergency" and called on California officials to do something to combat the incentives being offered by out-of-state shooting locations. But the trend is only accelerating. A 2014 study by FilmL.A. found that for the first time, the number of TV pilots filmed in Los Angeles had dropped below the halfway mark, to just 44 percent. These days, "greenlighting a pilot" means hiring someone to fly the plane that takes the entire production out of California.

One thing that's making it easier than ever to shoot a movie or TV show outside of LA is the advent of cheap, top-quality digital, audio, and video equipment and computer software to handle the video editing and special effects. These days, a teenager with a video camera and a laptop can part the Red Sea faster and more convincingly than Cecil B. DeMille did.

It's ironic that much of the high-tech innovation that's making Hollywood studios obsolete is the product of California's other liberal cash cow, Silicon Valley. But as those tech companies grow from garage startups to global giants, even some of them are starting to notice that intrusive government and high taxes are bad for their businesses, not to mention a real buzzkill, dude.

When you get rich overnight from a piece of software you created in your bedroom, and you're used to being able to reach anyone in the world instantly by cell phone or to access any data online within seconds, you eventually start to chafe at the type of regulatory restraints on innovation that make it impossible even to open a hot dog stand in under three years. The information superhighway is speeding up while the bureaucracy is stuck in a traffic jam.

Likewise, the founders of Internet companies that lavished money, adoration, and free publicity on Obama in 2008 are finally starting to realize that no matter how cool the figurehead may seem, oppressive government is not the friend of those who make a living off the free flow of information (though the NSA has used a little "friendly persuasion" to get them to let private information about their users flow into government data banks). Sure, it's nice to have cronies in D.C. who'll stifle your domestic competitors. But in a rapidly changing global industry, getting fat and complacent is a ticket to oblivion. Once those hip, young CEOs mature a bit, it's very likely that many will get tired of paying the bill for their own straitjackets and start looking for greener pastures. After all, who is more aware that people in the tech industry who have computers and the Internet can work from *anywhere*?

Some early sounds of dissent are already starting to be heard from Silicon Valley. After Governor Brown got his big package of tax hikes, including Prop 30, a retroactive tax hike on income dating back to 2012, ex-Google executive and Redbeacon co-founder Ethan Anderson penned an angry op-ed for AllThingsD.com. He wrote, "Given the inherent risks entrepreneurs take just to start a new company, will they want to now take on additional tax and regulatory risk?" He said that tech founders won't quit starting new businesses, they'll just do it somewhere else, and California will lose "the wealthy and productive classes we need to stay and rebuild the Golden State to its former glory."

Anderson's warning, like the warnings about Obamacare suppressing hiring, were dismissed as nonsense by the left-leaning media. *New York* magazine's Kevin Roose said it was the "same kind of veiled threat— 'If you raise our taxes, we'll move'—that Wall Street millionaires and billionaires have been making for years." And *The Huffington Post* quoted Mark Cuban as once saying, "Entrepreneurs who create something out of nothing don't care what tax rates are," and scoffed that studies have shown "there is little evidence that the rich flee high-tax states."

Maybe they were out drinking with Harvey the giant invisible rabbit and missed the study of IRS data by the nonprofit Tax Foundation. It showed that between 2000 and 2010, high-income earners fleeing New York took $45.6 billion in personal income out of the state's economy. The second biggest loser was California, whose wealthy expatriates took $29.4 billion with them. Illinois was third, with a loss of $20.4 billion. Where did they all go? Some moved to Arizona or Texas, but most moved to the Sunshine State, Florida, bringing along carpetbags filled with flip-flops, sunscreen, and $67.3 billion worth of personal income. As someone who makes part of my living by having to go to New

York City, I often wonder why any business domiciles there. The cost of relocation would be recovered fairly soon with lower taxes and lower cost of living.

The wealth migration deniers might also check out the Bank of America–Merrill Lynch analysis of the results of Maryland's 2008 "millionaires' tax." Even though Maryland has a high percentage of wealthy residents, thanks to its proximity to the ultimate money trough, Washington, D.C., its deep-blue leaders couldn't think of any way to bring down their budget deficit other than raising taxes on higher incomes. But the expected revenues from the millionaires' tax never materialized. Instead, revenues tumbled as wealthy people moved out, reducing Maryland's net tax base by $1 billion.

To those who insist the tech industry will never leave Silicon Valley because that's where all the best talent is, I'd respond that the best talent migrates to where the best jobs are, and the best jobs tend to be in places that don't punish the people who figured out how to create the jobs. If you don't believe it's possible that California's high taxes and onerous regulations could eventually drive away even the tech industry, then I invite you to tour the construction site of Apple's planned $300 million "America's Operations Center." When finished, it will be a million square feet in size and serve as headquarters for 3,600 employees. And it's in . . . wait for it . . . Austin, Texas.

Those of you who happen to be reading this book in California—or, more likely, listening to the audiobook while stuck in traffic—please understand: I am not wishing ill on your state. Like most Americans of my generation, I still get a thrill hearing The Mamas & the Papas sing "California Dreamin'," or thinking about my teen years listening to the Beach Boys and wishing they "all could be California Girls." I love the Golden Gate Bridge, Disneyland, Palm Springs, the Hollywood Walk of Fame, Monterey and Carmel, the great music and friendly people of Bakersfield, the forests, the beaches, the rugged coastline, the high desert. From the mountains to the prairies to the ocean white with foam (or in some places, Styrofoam), God bless California! (Also those giant redwoods you can drive a car through. Can you imagine drilling a tunnel through a redwood tree today? Environmentalists' heads would explode!) Most of us here in God, guns, grits, and gravy territory aren't pulling for California to fail. We're praying that its people will wake up to the way their elected officials and unelected bureaucrats have misled and mismanaged the state, toss the bums out, and turn California back into the Golden State we all grew up dreaming about moving *to*.

In the meantime, if you find yourself forced to leave California—or New York or Illinois or wherever—and move to our states to find a job (or even if you're a liberal Hollywood actor who's only here temporarily because your hit TV series about the zombie apocalypse is filmed in Georgia), please rest assured that we'll greet you with open arms and Southern hospitality. We ask only three things in return:

1. Please don't move here and start voting for the same failed leftist policies that made you flee the last place you lived. We don't want to be the next Colorado.
2. Don't ask Lurleen down at the truck stop to bring you a kale salad, unless you want it deep-fried. No, come to think of it, not even then. Ask for the grits. And if it's dinner, ask for them with shrimp, garlic, and cheese. And get gravy for your biscuits.
3. Before you eat, bow your head and thank God for your food. You don't have to do it out loud. But if you do it, you won't stand out like some outsider who wasn't brought up right.

16

The United States Is Falling Behind Other Nations

Posterity! you will never know how much it cost the present Genera-
tion to preserve your Freedom! I hope you will make good use of it. If
you do not, I shall repent in Heaven, that I ever took half the Pains
to preserve it.   —JOHN ADAMS

MY WIFE, JANET, AND I celebrated our fortieth wedding anniversary in May 2014 by taking a trip to China. It was a fantastic tour: the
Great Wall, Forbidden City, and Tiananmen Square in Beijing; the Terra
Cotta Warriors near Xi'an; the stunning skyline of Shanghai; the Sich-
uan Province and Chengdu. It was there Janet held and fed a baby
panda. And no, I didn't bring a real one home for the grandkids!

As I traveled across China, it was impossible not to notice the rapid
growth and modernization that's taking place since the Communist government loosened its grip a bit on entrepreneurs. Now, many Americans fear that China might grow too strong. I must confess that I'm
not too worried about China getting too strong. I'm more worried that
America might be getting too weak.

It's not bad for the United States if other nations have a strong economy. One fewer hungry-mouthed country wanting us to take care of it and its people is great news. If they have money, maybe they will buy the things we innovate and make. Instead, we need to fear that we will *quit* innovating and making things because excess taxation, regulation, and litigation will drive the jobs and the money away from American working men and women.

I was stunned that China is becoming more like America used to be, while America is becoming more like China used to be. Even more frustrating, they're doing it by emulating the free-market, entrepreneurial capitalism that made America great, even as we seem to be abandoning it. While America's infrastructure crumbles, China is busy building roadways, bridges, airports, and utility systems. China is still a Communist-governed country, and we're still a constitutional republic, but they are allowing more and more free enterprise and personal ownership. Meanwhile, we're watching our government take away land rights and personal and religious freedoms at a stunning rate. I certainly don't want what still remains of Chinese communism, but maybe we could loan them our Constitution. It doesn't appear that we're using it much these days anyhow.

Of course, America still has some advantages over China. The Chinese government exercises strict control over the Internet, blocking Facebook, YouTube, and a host of Web sites, including the *New York Times* site, because they feel it's propaganda. But then, we have members of Congress pushing for greater control over the Internet as well. And I'm not so sure the Chinese don't have it right about *The New York Times*.

The Chinese scrub their history books of moments like the brutal killing of protesters in Tiananmen Square in 1989. Good thing we don't rewrite *our* history to ignore parts of it that aren't politically correct! But wait, have you seen an American history textbook lately? They leave out the great and inspiring parts of our history and concentrate solely on the negatives. Can you find a history book that extols the spiritual dimensions of our nation's history? Do you often hear of the intense and protracted prayer meetings that preceded the writing of the

Declaration of Independence and the Constitution? Of the worship services held in the Capitol in the early days of our nation's history? Schoolchildren read that America is an imperialistic aggressor, but do they read how we rebuilt countries like Japan and Germany after they tried to destroy us?

If China were like us, their history books would have one paragraph on the Ming Dynasty and five hundred pages on the Tiananmen Square massacre. Instead, they have scrubbed their history books of any mention of the 1989 massacre at Tiananmen Square. When we asked our young thirty-year-old guide about the events there as we stood in the square just days before the twenty-fifth anniversary, she looked at us with bewilderment because she had no idea what had happened there.

China is notorious for spying on its citizens and using the full force of government to monitor its people and minimize dissent and religious expression. Thank God the United States would never do that! Unless you count our government collecting our phone calls and Web searches, reading our e-mails, tracking us through our cell phones, and systematically scrubbing God from the public square.

China's government regulates much of daily life for its citizens, from housing and health care to education and personal artistic freedom, but one can still see a lot of personal freedoms in public parks, where people can sing, dance, or do Tai Chi. I'm pretty sure that if people used personal amplification devices in New York's Central Park, the nanny-state city government would send in the cops to confiscate both their microphones and their Big Gulps.

China has a history of dealing harshly with those it perceives as its enemies—some simply disappear. We have strict constitutional protections in America to guarantee civil rights, such as being able to face our accuser and not having our homes searched or our property seized without a warrant. No government agency can find us guilty without a trial and seize our property. Well, except the IRS. And the DEA, if we're suspected of having anything to do with drugs. And we can lose our right to life if we happen to be sitting where a drone drops a bomb or fires a missile at (or near) us. But, hey, at least it saves the cost of a pesky trial.

Sometimes the people we kill aren't even our enemies. Sometimes, they are our veterans, who thought we'd give them protection and health care. They gave us our liberties; by mistreating them and killing them, we take away theirs. The scandals of the Veterans Affairs (VA) system are shocking and disgusting, knowing that VA employees falsified documents to make it appear that our veterans were scheduled for appointments they never had. Senator Tom Coburn found that as many as one thousand veterans died from the shoddy treatment. Veterans should get the first fruits of our treasury—not the leftovers.

That's why I say I don't fear that China is becoming more like the United States used to be. I fear America is becoming more like China used to be.

But China is hardly the only nation that's starting to look at America in the rear view mirror. Each year, the Heritage Foundation issues its "Index of Economic Freedom." They define economic freedom as the "fundamental right of every human to control his or her own labor and property." They rank 186 nations based on various aspects of four categories: the Rule of Law (whether or not the law protects property rights and is administered free of corruption), Limited Government (including freedom from ruinous government spending), Regulatory Efficiency, and Open Markets.

In the 2014 ranking, Hong Kong (which is under the jurisdiction of China) was rated number one in economic freedom. It was followed by Singapore, Australia, Switzerland, New Zealand, and Canada. So where was America, the "Land of the Free"? In twelfth place, just behind Estonia. The Heritage Foundation placed the USA in the "mostly free" category. I guess we should count our blessings that we're still "mostly free."

Of course, this hardly means that American business owners will be closing their factories and fleeing to Estonia (well, some of them in California might). But it does mean that when it comes to five areas in which America should be leading the world—fiscal freedom, government spending, monetary freedom, financial freedom, and property freedom—America now trails behind eleven other nations. Some of the criteria may be debatable; for instance, the freedom in some nations to fire workers without a lot of paperwork or legal exposure might not seem like a positive if you happen to be a worker. But if you're the person deciding where to locate the corporate headquarters, there's no question that it puts a check mark in the Estonia column.

Sadly, there are a number of other international rankings where the United States has to settle for the "Honorary Mention" ribbon. The World Economic Forum ranks 148 nations for competitiveness, defined as "the set of institutions, policies, and factors that determine the level of productivity of a country," which measures its economic growth potential. In the 2013–2014 rankings, the United States came in fifth, behind Switzerland, Singapore, Finland, and Germany. The World Economic Forum now ranks the United States, land of Thomas Edison and Steve Jobs, seventh in the world in innovation. And in the nonpartisan Legatum Institute's annual Prosperity Index, the USA has fallen from fourth in 2008 to eleventh out of 142 nations in 2013.

How is it possible that the United States, a nation founded by immigrants who came here seeking more freedom, opportunities, and prosperity than they could ever dream of in their native lands, could have fallen behind so many of those nations in those very same areas? Again, it's because as more nations have adopted at least some aspects of what made America great, we are rapidly abandoning those same winning principles. Can we fix it? Of course! But not by doing dumb things like electing people to lead the country who are clueless about how jobs are created.

For decades now, progressives have drilled into young people's heads the notions that America is the source of all evil; that capitalism harms the lower and middle classes while socialism uplifts them (history teaches us that the exact opposite is the case); that successful people get rich not by creating products that other people want but by stealing from everyone else; that everyone is entitled to all sorts of things just by virtue of being born and that someone else should pay for them; that people who achieve success aren't smart and hardworking but "winners in life's lottery"; and that if you have a business, no matter how much you worked and sacrificed to create it, "you didn't build that." (Gosh, who told them *that*?)

In the 2008 election, American voters, angry at Republicans over the Middle Eastern wars and panicked by the economic meltdown and the insanity of rewarding the people who caused it with big fat bailouts, took one of the biggest gambles in history. They entrusted the reins of government to Barack Obama, the least experienced and most liberal person ever elected President, and gave his party unstoppable control of both Houses of Congress. They pursued a classic liberal agenda on steroids: the biggest expansion of government power in decades (Obamacare), along with ballooning government, taxes, regulations, and deficit spending to stimulate the economy. To be fair, that big stimulus ("porkulus" as I like to call it) was precipitated by the Republicans pushing the Wall Street bailouts. I mean, once you forked over $700 billion to a bunch of inept Ivy League–educated executives who gambled their companies' and their clients' assets into the dirt, how can you say that it's a bad idea to throw some more money out there for everyone else—even if "everyone else" never saw it because it went to the President's cronies for their windmills.

But the $800 billion–plus from the stimulus bill that was touted as creating "shovel-ready" jobs largely went to keeping government employees from suffering the same layoffs as private sector workers, while also rewarding crony corporations. Even Obama had to admit that there *were* no "shovel-ready jobs." Of course, that was mostly thanks to the environmentalists who supported him; every time someone gets near a shovel these days, EPA attorneys descend on him like a swarm of mosquitoes on a summer night in a rice field. We needed a shovel all right—to scoop up the horse manure substituting for policy.

All this Big Government and big spending acted less like a stimulant than a tranquilizer, as the jobless economy struggled on for years past the point when history would suggest it should have recovered and even boomed. With no concrete accomplishments to point to, Obama's supporters had to invent some out of thin air, claiming that without all this government intervention, why, it would have been even worse! With few new jobs to point to, they instead started counting "saved jobs," as if anyone who miraculously still had a job should thank the government for "saving" it.

The American people, many of them by now working three part-time jobs to survive, gave those claims the same fish-eye that people gave Jimmy Stewart in the movie *Harvey* when he introduced his giant, invisible rabbit pal, and promptly voted the Republicans back into power in the House of Representatives. But by then, the damage was done, and with Senate Majority Leader Harry Reid blocking every House attempt to undo it, it's continued to fester year by year.

We now have a plethora of government leaders who are happy to scold business owners and corporations for not hiring more people or building factories in America, but who would never dream of changing the government policies that punish those very things. For instance, the United States now has the highest corporate tax rate in the industrialized world: 39.1 percent (35 percent federal tax plus the average state tax). Even in Sweden, it's only 22 percent. In France, it's 34.4 percent—and their leaders are actual, card-carrying socialists!

If that's not enough to scare corporations away from building factories in America, consider all the other disincentives placed on them: the Obamacare mandates; the explosion of government regulations from the EPA, the FTC, and the whole alphabet soup of federal agencies; the fact that if they want to move money they made and had already paid taxes on in other nations back to America, where it could create jobs, we tax it again, eliminating their profits.

The private research firm Audit Analytics calculated that between 2008 and 2013, American-owned corporations amassed over $2.1 trillion in profits overseas that were not brought back to the United States to be reinvested because they would be subject to double taxation. Imagine how big a "stimulus" it would be to job creation here at home to inject $2.1 trillion of nonborrowed money directly into private sector investment. Companies used to run *to* America; now they run *from* America.

The leaders of other nations must sometimes marvel at the way America is tying its own hands as it competes with them on the economic playing field. Many of those other nations have already been down that Big Government "progressive" road and know it's a dead end.

Not long after the 2008 global recession, President Obama tried to push progressivism on other nations, such as Germany. He wanted them to follow America's lead and okay even more stimulus spending to help debt-ridden European Union nations stay afloat. Because if history has taught us anything, it's that you can't spend your way out of debt. German Chancellor Angela Merkel, however, considered the meltdown to be *caused* by unregulated bubble markets and out-of-control government spending. She saw no reason why more government spending should be used to reinflate the bubble, or why German taxpayers should be bled dry to pay for it. Her response was to propose tighter regulations on banks and to cut government spending while putting strict conditions on the use of bailout money loaned to struggling nations (aka "imposing austerity"). In my world growing up, it was simply called "living within your means." My mother used to say when I wanted something we couldn't afford, "Boy, you've got a champagne appetite and a Coca-Cola pocketbook!"

There were massive protests in debtor nations such as Greece, and Obama indirectly lectured Merkel that austerity policies might destroy the fragile recovery. Some nations agreed with him, such as France, which went "all in" by electing an outright socialist, François Hollande, as President and giving him a socialist Parliament.

Hollande imposed the predictable economic solutions of punishing the successful, including a controversial 75 percent millionaire's tax. These measures caused capital to flee from France and even led French film icon Gerard Depardieu to give up his French passport and move to Belgium and be granted citizenship by Russia, which charges him a 6 percent income tax rate. (I hear that in exchange, he must appear in every movie made in Russia, the way he did in France.) Panicking at the public revolt, Hollande promised to enact some market-based reforms, such as cutting spending to reduce the deficit, enacting some pro-growth policies, and capping government worker salaries. But it was too little too late. The voters took a sharp right turn in the next election. Sound familiar?

The results of these two competing economic philosophies were stark and revealing. In the first quarter of 2014, weak consumer spending and business investment caused France's economic growth to grind to a standstill at zero (it could've been worse; at least it didn't shrink 2.9 percent, as ours did). Meanwhile, Germany, which ignored Obama's fiscal policy lecture, is now the "economic powerhouse of Europe." In the first quarter of 2014, Germany's GDP grew 0.8 percent. Their unemployment rate was 5.1 percent, while America's was 6.3 percent. And our jobless rate could be achieved only by massaging the numbers harder than a German masseuse.

Our underemployment rate (which includes the jobless; "discouraged workers" who've been jobless so long, they've given up looking; and people working part-time because it's all they can find) was 13.4 percent. The U.S. Bureau of Labor Statistics (BLS) reported that, as of April 2014, a record 92,594,000 Americans were not working. That translates to just a 62.8 percent labor force participation rate, which matches a thirty-six-year low.

For those who try to claim that's just due to baby boomers retiring, the BLS also noted that in April 2014, the labor force participation rate for Americans aged 25–29 was 79.8 percent, the lowest level since 1982 when the BLS started keeping records.

The pity is that many Americans outside the elite bubbles know exactly what's wrong, but our leaders seem determined to do nothing about it. Any attempt to cut the government chains and anchors off businesses

so they can get back to growing, innovating, and creating jobs is dem-
agogued as "tax breaks for the rich" or "favors for the one-percenters."
Never mind that many of those who would benefit are small-business
owners who've been decimated over the past few years, first by the economic meltdown, then by government policies put in place to "fix" it.
The money printed by the Fed to keep the economy pumped up flows
to Wall Street, not Main Street, so small businesses aren't borrowing
it to pay for expansion. Even if they wanted to expand, about a third of
all U.S. workers are employed by businesses with fifty or fewer employees, and Obamacare insures that if they hire a fifty-first, they'll face
crippling new costs for mandated health care.

I remember when I was a kid seeing books that imagined what the
world would be like if Germany had beaten America or if China took
over the world. The authors of such wild, speculative history never imagined that one day, those scenarios might seem shockingly plausible. Except that Germany and China wouldn't defeat America by military force.
They'd surpass us by copying the fundamental tenets of the American
economy—free markets, rewarding innovation, limiting regulation, letting people keep the fruits of their labor—that the elites in Bubble-ville
seem to have forgotten all about. In Bubba-ville, we still think the United
States is the greatest country in the history of the world, but we know
it won't be if we don't return to the principles we were built on. And it
starts with a God who gave birth to this nation and miraculously preserved us through battles we should have lost.

17

Grenades in Our Tent

THE EXPRESSION "DON'T AIR YOUR dirty laundry in public" doesn't make sense to many Millennials because most of them never hung their laundry on a clothesline in their backyard. When and where I grew up, a clothesline in the yard was as much a given as a roof on the house or gravy on the potatoes. But frankly, the part about airing "dirty" laundry never made sense because no one would place *dirty* laundry on the line—the whole point was to place the freshly washed and clean laundry on the clothesline so it would dry and be sanitized by the sun. There were few secrets in a neighborhood where people put their underwear on a clothesline for the world to see, and whose houses had open windows with screens that kept out flies and mosquitoes, but also let the conversations be heard. Since we only could get three channels on the old black-and-white TV on a good day off the rooftop antenna, when TV was boring, one could just sit near a window and catch up on what the neighbors were saying. And if they were on the phone, we could still keep up because in the days before the NSA listened in and taped our every call, most of us had "party lines" for phone service. That meant that several families in the neighborhood shared a line. Each family had a distinct ring so we knew whether to officially pick up or just pick up and listen in without saying anything. Party lines were much cheaper than private lines, so naturally, we had one.

In the summer, when it way too hot to sit indoors on an August night in Arkansas until well after sundown, most folks would take to the front porch. The porch usually had some chairs, a ceiling fan of some kind, and ideally a porch swing hung from the rafters or ceiling of the porch. If you were lucky, the porch was screened, but if not, there would be several flyswatters and everyone took turns swatting at flies and mosquitoes or wasps or yellow jackets. If insect repellant products like OFF! had been invented, we certainly couldn't afford to buy them, and a flyswatter would last for several summers and usually was given for free at the hardware store when you bought some stuff. I don't think we ever had a flyswatter at my house that didn't remind us that we could buy lumber or tools at Duffy Hardware. And all of our yardsticks (three-foot type) and twelve-inch rulers let us know that Lagrone Williams Hardware had paint and pots and pans.

As we sat on the front porch, it was a time to talk, hear stories about the "good ol' days" from my relatives that didn't seem all that good to me given the way they described the hardships of the Depression and World War II. We'd break out guitars and play music and hear the same old family stories that we'd all heard a thousand times before. In the sweltering hot nights of the summer, everyone who wasn't playing a musical instrument had to shell purple hull and black-eyed peas that had been bought that day from the back of a farmer's truck that would pass through the neighborhood selling peas by the bushel. Shelling peas made one's fingers turn purple so I hated shelling peas, and thus one of my many reasons for learning to play the guitar!

Sometimes the neighbors or relatives came to sit on the porch and sometimes when things were quiet on our porch, we just listened to what the neighbors were saying on theirs. Many nights, it was for sure better than TV.

The culture I grew up in created a sense of community, but also a sense of accountability. The openness of our lives with our laundry visible to God and all His creation and conversations being heard without the whiz bang electronic surveillance devices we would come to despise meant that we lived with our families, but within a neighborhood and community. And out of a combination of courtesy, old-fashioned manners, and the need to survive by having neighbors you could count on, we didn't talk "ugly" about neighbors too much. There was a good chance they could hear us. That meant they'd never help shell our peas again.

I miss the front porch culture. Communities where people looked after each other and where we never expected the government to do so had a real strength about them. We were too closely tied together, working-class people struggling to make it paycheck to paycheck, to afford the luxury of losing the friendship of those around us.

As I ponder the current climate in my own political party, I wish we were "front porch Republicans" where we spent time getting to know each other, helping each other, and seeing ourselves as a neighborhood and community where we dared not put our "dirty laundry" on the clothesline for all to see and smell.

Since the summer of 2008, I've had the privilege of working for Roger Ailes at Fox News. Roger is a genius. He has his share of critics, but that's because nearly all of them are insanely jealous of his success. For those of us who have worked for him, it's clearly understood that the reason he's been incredibly good at what he does is because of two things:

1. He really is the smartest guy in the room, and it doesn't matter who's in the room.
2. He understands that the success of an organization is that the people in the organization feel bonded by a common goal, share an esprit de corps, and that each member of the team builds the others up.

The basic rule of working for Roger is, "Don't pee inside the tent." (Although Roger is known to use the more earthy and graphic term.)

It's one of the many reasons I truly admire and respect him. That attitude is evident pretty much up and down the entire food chain, from the highly paid stars who anchor shows, to the production crew, to the makeup artists, to the people who clean the building. He enjoys heart-felt respect because one thing that everyone in that building knows is that Roger stands with his team and protects them. He is fiercely loyal to those who are part of his empire, and he has no tolerance for the destructive infighting that plagues most high profile, ego-driven media entities. He has created a truly collegial atmosphere in which to work and a place where the peer pressure is to excel. That breeds a spirit of healthy competition where everyone wants to succeed, but not at the expense of others at the network. If someone does well, we all celebrate that success because it floats our entire boat higher in the water.

I wish the Republicans were only guilty of peeing inside the tent. Sadly, some are intent to bring grenades, pull the pin, and toss them under the chair of another Republican. If we would operate by Roger's rules instead of allowing suicide bombers to determine our direction, we'd have no trouble winning elections at the local, state, and national level.

I watch with sadness when self-proclaimed conservative outside groups raise and spend millions of dollars not to defeat the far left, but to blow up and destroy other conservatives that aren't deemed "conservative enough." Having highly contested primaries can be healthy when based on legitimate contrast and competition, but much of the heavy money spent on behalf of anonymous donors too timid to ever run for office themselves ends up giving mortal wounds to people wearing the same uniform. When Major Nidal Hasan opened fire on his fellow soldiers at Fort Hood, killing fourteen people (thirteen personnel and one unborn child) and wounding over thirty in November 2009, the horror of the shooting was magnified by the fact that at the time, he was wearing the same uniform as the people he was killing. Many of them had survived combat against the enemy in Iraq and Afghanistan only to die from the wounds inflicted by someone who supposedly saluted the same flag, but who thought that his view of the world was superior.

When conservatives viciously attack other conservatives and label them "RINO" (Republican in Name Only), they are presuming to have been given the power to determine exactly what the "real" Republican looks like. That always has seemed a bit audacious, to essentially say, "God died and left me in charge."

I was in the green room backstage at the NRA Annual Convention in Pittsburgh, Pennsylvania, in May 2011, where I was to speak. Michael Reagan, the son of President Reagan, was also on the program that night. Michael is one of my favorite people as he has so many of the great qualities of his father: articulate and witty, a man of true courage and conviction, and yet who hasn't made his mark by condemning people, but by expressing the ideal. As we visited, we talked about the brutal atmosphere in the GOP and he remarked that he wasn't sure his father could get nominated in today's GOP climate. I had said the exact same thing before and found some degree of comfort in knowing that the very son of Ronald Reagan felt the same way.

It's the great irony that many of those seeking to invoke the name if not the mantra of Ronald Reagan and claiming to be "more like him" than others would probably have a hard time supporting the Gipper if he were running for President in 2016 instead of 1980 or 1984. Here was a man who had "evolved" in his view on abortion, but who ultimately was a strong voice and force for the sanctity of life. He didn't run from the "social issues" or those who espoused them, believing that those were principled views not only of many in the Republican base, but also among Democrats who were Catholic or evangelical. Although he was known for firing the union air traffic controllers (PATCO), he was far from anti-labor or anti-union, having been the president of the Screen Actors Guild himself. He indeed believed that lower taxes were a stimulant to the economy and did lower taxes, but there were taxes he raised both as governor of California and as President, most notably the Tax Equity and Fiscal Responsibility Act (TEFRA) of 1982. He was responsible for the greatest immigration amnesty act in America's history, essentially waving the wand of forgiveness and welcome to over 3 million illegal immigrants in 1986, and he was opposed to a fence. It's been noted that Reagan granting amnesty to the 3 million probably encouraged the next 8 million to come. And in his personal life, he was a divorced and twice-married man. In today's culture, such a thing seems utterly insignificant, but there was still some stigma to divorce during that time and there were some in the faith world who had to be convinced that it was okay to vote for a man who had been married more than once. He was noted for his ability to meet with, work with, and compromise on legislation with liberal Speaker Tip O'Neill of Massachusetts.

In this day and age, he would be labeled a "RINO" by conservative bloggers and talk show hosts. I can just imagine that he would be routinely called "Ronald RINO." He would be yelled at in town hall meetings for promoting amnesty and raising taxes and compromising with Democrats.

Yes, if Reagan were just arriving on the national scene now, or if he were in a hotly contested primary and carried with him the record he had as both a governor and a President, groups like the Club for Growth and the Senate Conservatives Fund would be raising millions of dollars to run attack ads on the man who is considered the gold standard of conservatism in our lifetime.

This stunning trend of Republicans throwing grenades inside their own tent has taken the party from a place of winning to losing key elections. Dave Levinthal of the Center for Public Integrity analyzed donor data and found some startling realities of the "eat your own first" movement:

> One in five dollars spent by all super PACs, nonprofit groups and the like on election advocacy came from identifiably

conservative groups attacking Republican congressional candidates, according to a Center for Public Integrity analysis of federal campaign disclosures covering Jan. 1 to Feb. 28, 2014.

Liberal political groups, in contrast, didn't spent a dime roughing up Democrats during this time, focusing their efforts exclusively on promoting Democrats or bashing Republicans.

In all, conservative groups spent more than $2.3 million on negative ads targeting Republican candidates, according to FEC records.

That's more than the $2.1 million conservative groups spent overtly advocating against the election of Democratic candidates.

Their activity also represents a dramatic shift in political strategy from the same block of time during 2010 midterm elections, when conservative organizations didn't spend cash attacking GOP hopefuls at all, federal records from the time show.

Granted, people can do with their money whatever they want, and some clearly are more interested in destroying other Republicans than beating liberal Democrats, but it never made sense to me to spend more money to tear down the people on your own team than to defeat the real opposition. It's the equivalent of some members of an NFL team trying to cause injury to a teammate because they don't like the way he plays, instead of saving their toughest play for Sunday's opponent.

Abraham Lincoln quoted Jesus and reminded us that a house divided against itself can't stand. Come to think of it, I'll doubt ol' Abe himself could secure the GOP nomination in today's climate. Why, as I reflect on his record, that lily-livered liberal is nothing but a poser! A real RINO who cuts deals and won't "take a stand!"

You think I'm kidding? Lincoln was a staunch advocate for public education and public funding of infrastructure that would build rail lines, roads, and water transportation. He supported raising taxes to pay off the increasing debt, and was a compromiser. For sure, he was principled in his commitment to abolish slavery, but he needed to balance the method and time frame to do it and the scope of the implantation of abolition with the political realities of the time. Yep, I'm afraid Abraham Lincoln himself would be branded a "RINO" by those who have deemed themselves the "purer version" of Republicanism.

Is there any Republican who can withstand the extremely narrow, laser-like focus on a few tenets of the conservative movement and be anything but a RINO? I hate the term and have publicly urged people not to apply it. Creating false narratives and labels for fellow conservatives is more an ego trip for those who engage in the name-calling than the mark of those who truly want to restore America to its greatness. I'm quite certain that I'm closer to any Republican in the party than I am to Harry Reid, Nancy Pelosi, and Barack Obama. Of course, I have my own picks in a primary and sometimes choose to endorse and campaign for one candidate over another. But I'm very careful not to say something about a candidate in a primary that I'd have to explain away in a general election should the other candidate win. If I demonize a Republican candidate in a primary and that candidate wins, and then I'm expected to be a good team player and help the very person I shredded, any endorsement or effort seems transparently phony.

Some of my angst with the "suicide bombers" comes from my personal experience with them. The Club for Growth spent about a million dollars against me in 2008 just in Iowa and almost that much again in South Carolina. They distorted my record as a governor and were quite creative in how they defined what "conservative" really meant. I found out that most of the ads were funded by and inspired by an extremely wealthy Arkansas donor, who inherited a boatload of money. He was upset over my failure to support an initiative he backed that would have immediately eliminated the long-standing sales tax on groceries. I loved the idea of getting rid of the grocery tax, but he was proposing it in 2002 when we were in a deep recession nationwide and when the state was struggling to meet the essentials of the budget. I was never given credit for cutting about 11 percent of a state budget, 91 percent of which was spent on education, prisons, and Medicaid, none of which

afforded leeway unless we violated our own state law regarding education funding, turned loose thousands of inmates, and violated the state
Medicaid charter by not paying for the legitimate health-care costs of
children, the elderly, and the most impoverished in our state. I was rather
proud of the fact that I cut over ninety-four taxes, took the state from
almost a billion-dollar deficit to almost a billion-dollar surplus, rebuilt
the road system that was crumbling, brought innovations to health-care
policy that were heralded nationally, and greatly increased test scores
in K-12 and dramatically upped the number of people attending college. Oh, and did I mention that I did that with a legislature that was
the most lopsided and blue in the nation? Eighty-nine of a hundred in
the Arkansas House were Democrats and thirty-one of thirty-five members of the Senate were Democrats. The state General Assembly was
more Democrat than those of Massachusetts, Vermont, Maine, or Oregon. I can assure you that it was tough sledding to work with a legislative body in which my party didn't even have the votes to sustain a
governor's veto or even block a budget bill (which required seventy-five
votes), much less pass one!

But the hostile legislative environment I faced turned out to be valuable in teaching me how to actually govern. I can assure you that it's
much easier to campaign than to govern. And even easier to just talk
about it as a commentator. I've done all three—which puts me in a pretty
rare position to know the difference.

Groups like Club for Growth are basically "pay for play." If you have
a lot of money and want to destroy someone running for office, regard-
less of the reason, you can anonymously write a check to the "Club"
and it will do the dirty work for you. The donor can hide behind the
skirt of the organization and never come out to be accountable for the
attacks. It's a coward's way to fight. Well, a coward with a lot of cash
and ill will toward Republicans. After the 2008 election, I was persuaded
to sit down with the leaders of the Club for Growth to try and find
common ground. One of the original charter members was a wonderful friend and strong pro-life advocate and a leader in the Fair Tax move-

ment, which I strongly support and pushed hard for in my campaign. The late Leo Linbeck was one of those rare people one meets in politics who was in it for all the right reasons. Highly principled and a man of deep faith who was very active in his Houston, Texas, Catholic church, he arranged for me to go to D.C. for a meeting, supposedly to clear the air. It didn't go well. The club staff couldn't give credible reasons for attacking the fact that revenue in Arkansas had to be raised in order to build roads; an initiative that had been approved by 80 percent of the voters, when both Mitt Romney in Masschusetts and Ronald Reagan in California had done the same as governors. Pat Toomey, then a former congressman from Pennsylvania, and currently a U.S. senator, was the head of Club for Growth at the time. I left the meeting feeling as if I had wasted my time because it didn't appear that the CFG was driven by facts, but by checkbooks of those who wanted to target someone for character assassination. Later, when Toomey joined with a Senate Democrat to pass some gun control legislation in the wake of the Sandy Hook school shooting tragedy and got pummeled by conservatives for "becoming a squish" on the Second Amendment, I wondered if he ever thought about the many broadsides he had leveled against other Republicans. I heard him on TV lament how he was being misunderstood and how unfair it was to paint him as not supporting the Second Amendment. Forgive me if I was not moved to tears. "They that take the sword shall perish with the sword," said Jesus in Matthew's Gospel, chapter 26, verse 52.

Some Republicans have failed to heed those critical words of warning, and instead wake up each morning and look for the sword. It's the same as throwing a grenade in your own tent. I really don't think Nidal Hasan is the role model the GOP wants to emulate. We should leave the kind of Sunni/Shiite fights for the real jihadists. The goal of conservatives should be to build up America—not blow up the Republican Party.

18

Rules for Reformers—(Redneck Remedies)—The Difference Between Killing Pigs and Making Sausage

YOU'VE HEARD THE SAYING, "Two things you should never watch being made—a law and sausage." I don't agree with half of that. I've been involved in lawmaking as a lieutenant governor presiding over the State Senate and as a governor negotiating every step of the process with a legislature that was 90 percent Democrat. I've also seen sausage made.

I still eat sausage.

For the faint of heart and those without a strong stomach, seeing the process of politics become the process of governing can result in serious reactions. It's not a pretty process. It can be tedious, exasperating, and embarrassing. But let me let you in on a little secret—it's supposed to be!

As hard as it may be to believe, making a law was never designed by our Founding Fathers to be quick and simple. When they wrote and approved the Constitution, it was intentional that the passage of a bill to become law would be a hard slog. They feared that passion would overwhelm reason and thoughtfulness, and so they built in plenty of speed bumps to make sure that a bill never whizzed through Congress and got signed by the President as hurriedly as Lindsay Lohan gets through another round of rehab. Now, I'm pretty sure that the Founding Fathers didn't design total gridlock like we have today in Congress, but as much as it may surprise you, they would prefer gridlock to haste. Why? Because they feared government about the way I fear snakes, spiders, and sharks. They knew that the sheer power of it is an intoxicant and that most of the people who enter government will be like sixteen-year-old boys with keys to the liquor cabinet whose parents are gone for the weekend. It will be *Ferris Bueller's Day Off* on steroids (and boozed up). In fact, watching Congress make laws and oversee regulation is a lot like watching sixteen-year-olds with booze and a BMW. You get the distinct impression that they have no business with either one.

While I've sought to explain the differences in the way people from Bubba-ville *think* vs. the folks from Bubble-ville, I want to point out the solutions to how we change our culture and country and restore things to a constitutional republic, instead of a nation of narcissist numbskulls from the Northeast creating a plutocracy.

I will be fine with it should you choose to call these ideas "Redneck Remedies." For many of us in rural America, being called a redneck isn't a slur or an insult. I don't get my shorts in a wad when someone labels me one. I consider it a compliment! I know for sure that if I were to be broken down on the side of the highway, I'd much rather a couple of rednecks in a pickup pull over than a Wall Street banker wearing a $4,000 Italian suit and driving a Porsche. The rednecks could change the tire, jump start the battery, or fix a carburetor; whereas if the banker were out of cell phone range to call AAA, I'd be left on the roadside.

We have an expression in the south that "if duct tape or WD-40 can't fix it, it can't be fixed." Duct tape (commonly mispronounced as "duck tape") and WD-40 are basic staples in any rural American's garage or tool kit. Consider these proposals for governing to be the duct tape and WD-40 for reform.

TERM LIMITS

It's ironic that politicians want to limit everything under the sun—the size of our sodas, the speed and number of miles we can drive, the amount of water and electricity we can use, where we can send our kids to school, and the list goes on and on and on—but the one thing they think should never be limited in any way is their own political careers.

Term limits are not a recent invention. The concept stretches back to Ancient Rome and Greece, where holders of certain offices were limited in how many terms they could serve consecutively. The great Greek philosopher Aristotle observed, "It is not so easy to do wrong in a short as in a long tenure of office" [*Politics* by Aristotle. Translated by Benjamin Jowett. http://classics.mit.edu/Aristotle/politics.5.five.html].

Of course, the most famous explanation for the need for term limits was made by English historian, politician, and author Lord Acton, who said, "Power tends to corrupt, and absolute power corrupts absolutely. Great men are almost always bad men." And he said that long before Watergate, Whitewater, and the IRS scandal of the Obama era.

Term limits were also a part of the Founders' earliest plans for the U.S. government. As Robert Struble notes in his book on constitutional history, *Treatise on Twelve Lights*, in June 1776, "the Continental Congress appointed a committee of thirteen to consider a frame of government. Among the proposals the committee considered was one from the State of Virginia, written by Thomas Jefferson, and urging a limitation of tenure, 'to prevent every danger which might arise to American freedom by continuing too long in office the members of the Continental Congress . . .' A month later the committee made its recommendations, which as regards the rotation of congress were incorporated unchanged into the Articles of Confederation (1781 to 1789). The fifth Article provided that 'no person shall be capable of being a delegate [to the Continental Congress] for more than three years in any term of six years.'"

Incidentally, serving as President didn't soften Jefferson's views about the need for regular rotation in government positions. In 1807, half-way through his second term, he wrote that "if some termination to the services of the chief Magistrate be not fixed by the Constitution, or supplied by practice, his office, nominally four years, will in fact become for life."

Struble notes that the American preference for turnover in leadership was so deeply ingrained that it took until the twentieth century for the concept of career politicians to take hold. The popular novelist James Fenimore Cooper summed up the prevailing attitude in 1838 when he said that "contact with the affairs of state is one of the most corrupting of the influences to which men are exposed."

Unfortunately, among the many bad ideas that arose in the twentieth century, like Nazism, socialism, and letting movie actors talk, came the argument that "experience" in government was a far more valuable asset than a fresh perspective or a knowledge of business, farming, or other fields in which the vast majority of Americans work. (It's funny that the same hothouse academics who mock the idea of those hayseed Tea Partiers having enough experience to make legislation also hailed Barack Obama, the least experienced President ever, as not only the most qualified person in America to be President, but the most qualified in all of history, more qualified than Jefferson himself.)

Not everyone swallowed that argument, including twentieth-century Presidents of each party. Republican Calvin Coolidge said:

> When a man begins to feel that he is the only one who can lead in this republic, he is guilty of treason to the spirit of our institutions . . . It is difficult for men in high office to avoid the malady of self-delusion. They are always surrounded by worshipers. They are constantly, and for the most part sincerely, assured of their greatness. They live in an artificial atmosphere of adulation

and exaltation which sooner or later impairs their judgment. They are in grave danger of becoming careless and arrogant.

Coolidge must have been passionate about this subject because I believe those are the most words he ever said in one sitting.

I especially appreciate the view held by Coolidge that the presidency is not an office so extraordinary that there is only one person on earth who can "pull the sword from the stone," so to speak. I was interviewed by Karen Tumulty of *Time* magazine in 2011 as I contemplated running for President in 2012. I remarked that I didn't think that in a country of over 300 million people there was only one person capable of being President, and that anyone who thought he was the "*only* one" wasn't fit to be President. She took that to mean that I didn't have the proverbial "fire in the belly" to make a go of it. My reasons for not running in 2012 had nothing to do with lack of "fire in the belly." It had to do with having more than "mush in the brain" and "ego in the gut." I truly fear the megalomaniac who believes he's the "last hope for America!" That is a dangerous person. To run for President, a person needs to believe he or she can do the job and have the inner peace and strength and resolve to take on the responsibility, but God help us all when a person is so filled with himself to believe that he's the only one who can do it. Spare us from the haughty horrors that comes with such hubris!

In 1953, after deciding not to run for a third term, Democrat Harry Truman said:

> In my opinion, eight years as President is enough and sometimes too much for any man to serve in that capacity. There is a lure in power. It can get into a man's blood just as gambling and lust for money have been known to do.

Interesting quote, considering that he became President because he was Franklin Roosevelt's Vice President when FDR died in office shortly after being reelected to his fourth term. Truman saw FDR from as close a vantage point as anyone alive, and that was his impression of what the lack of term limits did to a person. *Hmmmm* . . .

Truman's successor, Eisenhower, originally opposed the Twenty-second Amendment, but later changed his mind. He and Truman both thought it should be extended to Congress, too, limiting members of both houses to twelve years. Eisenhower said that if a Congress member were limited to twelve years, he "would tend to think of his career as an important and exciting interlude in his life, a period dedicated to the entire public rather than as a way of making a living or making a career of exercising continuous political power." But he recognized that Congress would never pass term limits on itself, so it would be up to the states to pass an amendment forcing it on Congress.

In his 2007 book, *A More Perfect Constitution*, University of Virginia political science professor Larry J. Sabato promoted the idea of federal term limits modeled on the popular state-level limits. He agreed with Eisenhower's prediction that it would take a new constitutional convention to force Congress to limit its own power.

FDR was the first President to be reelected more than twice, but he wasn't the first to try to break the tradition set by George Washington of voluntarily stepping down after at most two terms. Grant and Wilson both tried to win third terms but lost their party's nomination, and Cleveland and Theodore Roosevelt sought nonconsecutive third terms. But FDR was the first to win more than two terms. His success at becoming President for Life alarmed Republicans, and anyone else who thought that America was founded on the principle of not having a king, and inspired the passage of the Twenty-second Amendment. It was passed by Congress in 1947 and ratified by the states in 1951, limiting Presidents to two terms. One of its early supporters was New York Governor Thomas Dewey, the GOP nominee against FDR in 1944, who announced his support for the amendment during his 1944 campaign, saying that for one person to be President for "four terms, or sixteen years, is the most dangerous threat to our freedom ever proposed."

For the record, my support for term limits has not diminished with my own service in government. I was a term-limits advocate from my very first run for public office in 1992 when I ran for the U.S. Senate. That year, I first met Paul Jacobs, who was then the president of U.S. Term Limits. I officially joined the fight and haven't quit since. I believed then and now that when people elected to public office become more focused on holding office than on making the tough decisions of governing, our great Republic is sunk.

Most people believe in term limits when they are "outsiders" running for their first office, but the longer they stay in office, the less support they espouse for the end of their own careers until they finally determine that we can't do without them and their wealth of experience.

Horse hooey! William F. Buckley once said, "I am obliged to confess I should sooner live in a society governed by the first two thousand names in the Boston telephone directory than in a society governed by the two thousand faculty members of Harvard University." In a bit of plagiarism from the distinguished Mr. Buckley, I have likewise said that if we randomly selected 535 names from the phone directory to install in the House and Senate, we probably wouldn't do any worse than we are doing now.

The longer I served, the *more* I believed term limits would improve the quality of government. I regularly heard from members of the legislature who had been elected believing in and supporting term limits, "I just can't learn the budget process in a mere six years in the House and eight in the Senate." In other words, if they stayed 14 years by spending all the time allowed in both the House and Senate (two 2-year terms in the House and two 4-year terms in the Senate), they still couldn't understand the state budget of Arkansas. If so, then they aren't smart enough to be in the legislature, and believe me, there are some folks that made it there that were probably kept back a grade or two. A person can become a neurosurgeon in less time than these guys thought it would take them to understand the budget, and having developed and balanced a bunch of state budgets, I can assure you that neurosurgery is much more complicated. I got pretty good at the budget—balanced every one of them and took a $1 billion deficit and left the state with almost a $1 billion in surplus, but I wouldn't get near scrubbing in to do brain surgery!

While windbags like Dick Durbin claim they're protecting the Constitution by keeping their own rear ends in the seat of power until the dawn of doomsday, the American people beg to differ. A January 2013 Gallup poll found that "75 percent of adults nationwide back term limits for members of the House and the Senate, while 21 percent say they would vote against term limits. Term limits received bipartisan support in the poll: Republicans would back such a measure 82 percent–15 percent; independents would do so 79 percent–17 percent and Democrats favored term limits 65 percent–29 percent."

What about term limits for the Supreme Court, or as I like to say, the "Extreme Court." There are currently no limits on how long a Supreme Court Justice can serve. All the Constitution says is that Justices serve during "good behavior," which implies that the only ways ever to get rid of one are retirement, impeachment, arrest, or death. (Also the only way to get rid of a Democratic congressman from Chicago.) University of Virginia political science professor Larry Sabato has proposed a limit of fifteen to eighteen years for justices.

The argument against term limits for the SCOTUS is that lifetime tenure insulates them from political concerns and allows them to render fair and impartial decisions. In reality, the rise of activist judges and the evolution of the hyperpartisan vetting process have given us a Court that constantly teeters between being stacked either left or right, with an endless series of 5–4 decisions decided by one or two "swing justices" who aren't predictably liberal or conservative.

Another recent development that's complicated lifetime judicial appointments is that people are living so much longer. Between 1971 and 2006, the average SCOTUS Justice served for 26.1 years. That leads to court decisions being imposed on young Americans by judges appointed by Presidents and approved by Congresses that were elected long before the people affected were old enough to vote. Just as passing down the national debt to future generations is a form of taxation without representation, rulings by these Justices is adjudication without representation.

Another thing unlimited terms lead to is the embarrassing and dangerous spectacle of rulings on complicated cutting-edge topics such as cell phone privacy and net neutrality being made by octogenarian judges who don't even know how to turn on a VHS player and still have a windup alarm clock. The same argument could be made about our ancient senators who make laws that affect, say, cable TV. In America, the walking dead regulate *The Walking Dead*.

A poll released in May 2014, by Greenberg Quinlan Rosner, a Democratic polling firm, found that by a 60–36 percent margin, Americans think SCOTUS Justices often make rulings influenced by their personal or partisan opinions rather than rendering an impartial ruling based on the facts and the law. That opinion held across party lines.

The same poll found that 74 percent of Americans support ending lifetime SCOTUS appointments and limiting Justices to one 18-year term; 54 percent "strongly" support it. Support remained high across partisan lines (Democrats 80 percent, Republicans 72 percent, Independents 73 percent).

Michigan Representative John Dingell, who has served in the House of Representatives since 1955, announced his retirement from Congress in February 2014. Dingell's legacy over the long run will be his tenure. He is already the longest-serving member in the history of Congress, with the closest runner up, Michigan's John Conyers, trailing him by almost a decade. Dingell served since the Eisenhower administration, since—for scale—the first McDonald's opened. He replaced his father in the seat to which he first won election; between the two of them, the Dingells will have served Michigan nearly half of the length of time that it has been a state. Part of the reason Dingell offered for retiring at this point was that he didn't want "to be carried out [of Congress] feet first"—as his father was.

One of the defining issues of Dingell's career has been his close relationship with the auto industry. His district, though it was redrawn several times, consistently overlapped with the suburbs of Detroit, meaning that a fair number of his constituents were current or former auto workers. Normally, that's not a problem for a Democrat, but when the industry and the push for new environmental regulations came into conflict, Dingell found himself at odds with his party.

In 1975, he helped draft the original automotive fuel-efficiency standards, known on Capitol Hill as CAFE (Corporate Average Fuel Economy). Repeated efforts to raise the minimum number of miles-per-gallon cars and trucks were expected to be met with opposition from Dingell, who worried that increases would harm auto sales and, therefore, employment. In 2009, *Mother Jones* outlined the case against Dingell on CAFE—but when President Obama in 2012 reached a deal to increase fuel-efficiency standards with the automotive industry, Dingell supported the move.

In other regards, Dingell has been staunchly liberal, repeatedly introducing single-payer health-care proposals.

While congressional retirement announcements appear to have been coming fast and furious of late, a reminder: This crop of retirements is not unusual. The only thing unusual about the retirement of John Dingell is that one would be forgiven for thinking that it was never going to happen.

So, if most of America really believes we ought to limit terms served by the legislative and judicial branches just like we limit terms in the executive branch, why don't we? Because we, the people, aren't really the bosses anymore. Elected officials believe it's about *their* ideas and not ours. Power was supposed to derive from the people and government was only to be by the consent of the governed.

DEVOLVED POWER TO THE STATES

The best government is the most local government, because it's the closest to the people being governed. The toughest jobs in government are
school board, city council, and county commissioner. People have your
home phone number, and don't mind coming up to you in the store or
at church and asking about trash pickup, potholes, or PTA meetings.
The higher up the food chain, the more insulated if not isolated one is
from the "boss"—that is, the people you serve.

The original notion of the federal government was that it would be
very limited in its scope. Its powers were narrowly defined in the Constitution and then, just to make sure the message about limiting the
power of the federal government was as clear as a Lady Gaga gown,
the Founders added ten amendments we know as the Bill of Rights.
Every last one of them put an ironclad restriction on the government
and gave it explicitly defined limits. It basically told the government
that it couldn't make us shut up, sit down, open our houses to them, let
them "TSA us" without a warrant, tell us to stop praying or preaching,
couldn't take away our guns, make us tell the cops something that might
send us to jail, and to finish it all off, they added one that said that if it
wasn't a power that was absolutely clear in the Constitution, then only
the states had the power to deal with it.

Has anyone in D.C. actually read the Constitution?

If they have, they don't seem to be concerned that they will be held
accountable for ignoring it. And that indifference may be due to the
fact that D.C. is driven by donors to the campaigns, not by the passions of the people.

One of the really colossal mistakes made by our government is one
that few people today even understand: the passage of the Seventeenth
Amendment, which after decades of effort, passed in April 1913. Are
you even aware of the Seventeenth Amendment and what it did? Well,
prior to 1913, senators were appointed by their respective state legisla-
tures and not directly elected by popular vote. At first glance, it might

seem that having the voters directly elect the senators would be a great idea—they would enter office in the same way as members of the House. But the results have been anything but stellar.

The Founders intentionally separated the functions of the House and Senate as well as how the members got there. The House members, elected every two years, would bring the passions of the people with them, being directly accountable to the voters. The Senate was sometimes called the "saucer" of legislation, where the passions were cooled by thoughtful debate. Originally, the Senate's focus was on how legislation affected the states, since senators were appointed by the states to make sure that the executive branch of D.C. wasn't stepping beyond the Tenth Amendment and the rest of the Constitution and getting into areas it wasn't allowed to enter. But once senators started getting elected by direct vote, they became wholly connected to D.C. and pretty much disconnected from the impact of their legislation on their state's budget or borders.

During my ten and a half years as governor, I often wished that those in D.C. knew or cared about the impact of their actions on the states. But it was hard to get anyone that worked up about it, because the concern of senators and House members is the *federal* budget. Even some who had served as governor or in their state legislature would end up defining their main objective as to keep power in D.C. for themselves, and to heck with how it impacted their state budget back home or the rights of the citizens at the local level. This line of thinking has led to a major shift in power from where *you* live to where federal bureaucrats, lobbyists, and federal politicians live. Did it not occur to you how strange was the fact that during the entire economic meltdown of 2008–2009, the *only* place in America where property values kept going *up* instead of down, the only place unaffected in per capita income or spending by consumers, was Washington, D.C.? It's because the people living and working there had the power and ability to take care of themselves, even if at the expense of everyone else in the country. Why do we put up with it?

MAD MONEY OF POLITICS

Every time Congress or the courts try to "fix" the unholy influence of special-interest money to politics, the worse they make it. I say that as a practitioner of politics and not just a spectator. Here's what we basically have today, thanks to the irrational hodgepodge of campaign finance laws and rulings: If you are an actual candidate for office, you are very tightly restricted in where your money comes from, how much you can take, and what you can do with it, and every bit of that money has to be reported in minute detail so your critics and opponents can pick over every line and misconstrue it and try to make you look like a crook or at least fairly corrupt. If you don't have the guts to actually run for office and put yourself and your family through the sausage grinder of elective politics, then you can create an organization through which you can pour unlimited amounts of money, beat the living daylights out of the people who were willing to do what you were too cowardly to do, and in many cases, never even have to tell anyone that you were behind the savage attacks on the candidate.

Here's my simple solution: Prohibit nothing. Disclose everything. For *everyone*. If you give money to express your views, then stand up and be counted for it. Give as much as you can or want. Just tell us who you are. If you want to give $10 million to a candidate, do it. The rest of us may wonder aloud if a candidate is a wholly owned subsidiary of his donor, but at least we'll know where the money comes from and can figure out if your actions in office give special attention and benefits to your benefactor. Another reason not to limit direct contributions to the candidate is because the current system favors the wealthy who decide to run for office and self-finance their campaign.

If a person who has the ability to spend $50 million of his own money and not miss it runs against a person who has no personal money to invest and in fact has to give up all income in order to run for office, then why shouldn't the candidate without means be able to receive any amount one wishes to give? Should a wealthy candidate be allowed to give $50 million to his own campaign, but the less affluent candidate be limited to soliciting donations of $2,600 or less—the maximum permitted for individual donations?

And we should add another provision in election law. If you currently hold office and wish to run for any office other than the one you currently hold, you must resign from that office in order to file for a different office. On this, I speak from experience!

When I ran for President, I looked around on the stage and saw that I was running against some people who could give themselves unlimited amounts of money to make themselves instantly "credible," because their campaign reports showed sizable amounts in the kitty. I saw others who were sitting members of Congress or the Senate, who would still receive the paycheck plus all their benefits that I helped pay for, and yet never had to show up for work to get the check! Nice work if you can get it. Those candidates enjoyed federally paid staff who, while they couldn't do direct political work, could be engaged in development of policy and the coordination of scheduling, and if an "official" reason for travel could be conjured up, you and I would be helping to pay for that as well.

I know that as a contributor for Fox News, if I failed to show up for my duties for months on end while at the same time I was standing over at CNN begging them for a job, I'd find out pretty quickly that I was really going to need that CNN job because I'd get tossed from the one I had at Fox. Can you not show up for work and spend your time applying for another job and still get paid? Then why should your congressman or your senator?

EMPOWERING PEOPLE INSTEAD OF ENSLAVING AND IMPOVERISHING THEM

One of the most surreal moments in my life came when then–Virginia Governor Mark Warner (now senator) and I appeared before the Senate Finance Committee on behalf of the National Governors Association, presenting a proposal for reforming Medicaid that had come from forty-nine of the fifty governors. (Only Rod Blagojevich of Illinois refused to sign on and we know how things ended up for him.) We were actually proposing that the governors of the states—Democrats and Republicans—be willing to take *less* money from the federal government in exchange for greater flexibility as to how we spent it. If you think that seemed like a slam dunk, then you wouldn't understand Washington, D.C. After I had outlined our proposal, I was subject to lectures from Ted Kennedy, John Kerry, and Jay Rockefeller about people in poverty. I had heard about all I could take and finally said, "Gentlemen, as someone who grew up one generation away from dirt floors and houses without plumbing or electricity, and as one who is the first in his long impoverished family to even graduate from high school, I never thought I would be getting a lecture on what it's like to be poor from a Kennedy, a Kerry, and a Rockefeller!"

Such is the arrogance of many making policy that supposedly is designed to help people out of the trap of poverty. They don't have a clue. Not *one clue*. The ignorance of those who tailor anti-poverty programs was one of the primary motivators that pushed me into politics. Not only had I grown up closer to the bottom than to the middle, much less the top, but in my role in church work and serving as a volunteer in community organizations to help people in poverty, I understood that these guys knew about as much about being poor as I knew which fork to use when eating caviar.

The fact is, since America's "War on Poverty" was launched a little over fifty years ago, the poverty rate in America is exactly where it was then. The main difference is that today, even poverty isn't as dire for most people as it was fifty years ago. Michael Tennant, writing in *The New American*, said: "Fifteen trillion dollars: That's how much American taxpayers have forked over in the name of helping the poor since 1964. And what do we have to show for it? A poverty rate that has barely budged, an entrenched bureaucracy, and a population—like that of Greece and Portugal, two welfare-state basket cases—increasingly dependent on government handouts."

Michael Tanner is the director of health and welfare studies for the libertarian Cato Institute, and has researched and written extensively about the well-intentioned but miserably failed efforts of the government to end poverty.

Tanner points out that when LBJ launched the War on Poverty "the poverty rate in America was around 19 percent and falling rapidly." Tanner reports that "Government spends $20,610 for every poor person in America, or $61,830 per poor family of three. Given that the poverty line for that family is just $18,530, we should have theoretically wiped out poverty in America many times over."

Think about that—instead of spending all that money for government programs to end poverty, if we'd just handed out checks without the programs, the people wouldn't be in poverty at all and we'd be saving a lot on bureaucracy!

But as Tennant points out, there are now 126 separate anti-poverty programs administered by seven different cabinet agencies and six independent agencies. Then there are the hordes of social workers and government employees who administer the various programs. All of these people have a vested interest in the programs' continuation and expansion.

Here's the dirty little secret about poverty programs: They aren't about ending poverty—they are about perpetuating government programs and private sector enterprises that make up what I call the "industry of poverty." Yes, poverty is a condition for poor people, but it's a career for those who administer the programs and who would be put out of business if they were actually successful in eradicating poverty, so rest assured, they will *never* eradicate it. Trust me on this—the biggest fights I ever had as governor were trying to take money from a "provider" that should have gone to someone who was actually poor and needed it.

Federal welfare spending has risen 375 percent (in constant 2011 dollars) since 1965 and total welfare spending has climbed almost as much, writes Tennant. If money solved the problem, we wouldn't have a problem.

THE FORCE OF THE FAMILY

The real secret to eliminating poverty is not a secret at all. It's amazingly simple, but it makes the people living in their tony little bubbles seethe with rage. Ready for this?

Marriage.

Sounds too simple to be true, but here's a fact—the Beverly LaHaye Institute researched data in 2012 to discover that if a family has two married parents, the poverty rate is about 7.5 percent. If a family is headed by a single mother, the poverty rate is almost 34 percent.

While Hollywood celebrities make it seem quite normal to have a baby now, and think about a husband later (if at all or ever), most young, single women having babies aren't Hollywood starlets with millions of dollars to afford full-time live-in nannies, private jets, and private schools. And the War on Poverty we discussed earlier was launched fifty years ago when most children were raised by two married parents.

The Heritage Foundation has done extensive and admirable research on the economics of the family and found that the poverty rate for white, married couples in 2009 was 3.2 percent. If it was a white nonmarried family, the poverty rate jumped to 22 percent. For black couples who were married, 7 percent were in poverty; if a nonmarried black family, that number soared to almost 36 percent!

There are mountains of evidence to support the fact that a child growing up with both a mother and father who are married to each other and stay married, and have at least a high school education and are employed, will most likely live beyond poverty for their entire lives and be less likely to use drugs, drop out of school, or go to prison.

Television, movies, novels, and the lifestyles of those who create them would make us believe that the glamorous life doesn't include a father around. Reality says fathers do matter. Not just biological sperm donors, but *Dads* who join with the mother in not only creating the child, but responsibly raising the child.

Robert Maranto and Michael Crouch of the University of Arkansas Department of Education Reform penned an insightful look into this reality for *The Wall Street Journal* in April 2014. According to Maranto and Crouch:

> Abuse, behavioral problems and psychological issues of all kinds, such as developmental behavior problems or concentration issues, are less common for children of married couples than for cohabitating or single parents, according to a 2003 Centers for Disease Control study of children's health. The causal pathways are about as clear as those from smoking to cancer.

PREVENTION INSTEAD OF INTERVENTION

I've long maintained that our health-care system is messed up not because we don't spend enough money on it—we spend more of our GDP on health care than virtually any nation on earth. Our problem is that we spend most of our health-care resources—between 75 and 80 percent—to treat chronic diseases that are mostly the result of eating too much, exercising too little, and continuing bad habits like smoking. Lifestyle issues and genetics are driving the costs, but we spend mostly to treat illnesses after they become catastrophic. It would make far more sense to focus on preventing diseases first, curing them if we don't prevent them, and treating them if we have to. My friend Jim Pinkerton has done the best research on what he calls a "Cure Strategy" and reveals that if we focused just on Alzheimer's disease alone, the financial benefits would be staggering. We already spend $200 *billion* a year on this dreadful curse, and by 2050, that figure will jump to $1 *trillion* a year! That doesn't even begin to account for the painful toll the disease takes on the caregivers and the loss of social capital a family suffers from the intense care necessary for a loved one with Alzheimer's.

If we said with determination that we would focus on finding a cause and cure for Alzheimer's, cancer, and heart disease (the three big cost factors of health care) in the same way we focused on eradicating polio when I was a child, we would not only change lives, but we would genuinely change our economy.

It's been incredibly shortsighted for us to pull back from focused and fact-driven scientific research. We've made the disastrous mistake of gutting the space budget. As one who grew up seeing the many side effects of the dollars we spent developing the exploration of space, I am appalled that instead of ramping up our efforts to find the cutting-edge of technology, we have reduced ourselves to hitchhiking to the space station on a Russian spacecraft. John F. Kennedy would be ashamed of our dismantling not only *his* dream, but my dream and the dream of every "space age" kid who has lived better thanks to the innovations that came from our NASA programs.

STOUT STATECRAFT

A question I've posed to my Democrat friends and especially those who supported Barack Obama and plan to support Hillary Clinton should she run for President in 2016 is this: "Name *one* country on this planet with which we have a better relationship today than we did in January 2009, when the two of them 'reset' our foreign policy." Silence. Sometimes there is some hem-hawing and throat clearing and defenses like, "Well, they inherited a real tough situation. . . ."

Spare me! Here's the skinny: There is not a nation on earth with whom our relations are better now than before the policies of Obama/ Hillary were launched. One could argue they are better with Iran, but that's only if you really believe the Iranian government can be trusted, gives a rat's rear what we think of it, or has any intention of acting responsibly as a part of the world. Our friends (Israel, the UK, Germany, France, Japan, Egypt, even Canada) don't trust us and our rivals (Russia, China, Syria, et al.) don't fear or even respect us. Our word is dirt and our reputation is mud.

In the world of God, guns, grits, and gravy, we were raised to live by the code, "A man's word is his bond." That was drilled into me from

the time I was a tot. My Dad was not an educated man and as I've mentioned, he never finished high school. But while he may have lacked
education, he didn't lack in being smart and honest. He would say, "Son,
if you tell the truth, you don't have to remember what you said." And as
to living up to obligations, he always said, "Don't ever have to be asked
but once to do what you said you would do, whether it's to pay a bill or
show up for work on time."

My late Dad could have run the foreign policy of this country more
effectively than the current administration, and I doubt he could have
named the leaders of three countries other than the United States or
found many nations on a world map. What he did understand was that
if you want to avoid a fight, you make your opponent afraid to start one.
No one picks a fight with someone they think will whip their butt. They
pick on someone who is either weak or unwilling to engage. America
ought to have the most effective army, navy, air force, coast guard,
and marine corps on the globe and it should be so incredibly well-
trained, well-equipped, and possess such overwhelming capacity that
it would never have to go to war and use its superior strength. We should
not start fights, jump into other nations' fights, or flex our military
muscle provocatively just because we can. Its purpose should not to be
"export democracy," or "nation build," because that's the work of diplo-
mats. Our military should be trained and ready to turn loose a living
hell on any nation or terrorist organization that hurts an American or
attempts to breach our borders.

Real rednecks don't like to fight. But if someone challenges their
honor, their family, or their property, then Buddy Boy, you better come
with an army, because you've just picked one heck of a fight. That gun
cabinet is not there to display force, but to deliver it if necessary. No
one I know would like to get something from the gun safe other than
to go duck hunting or deer hunting or turkey hunting. But threaten a
man's home or family, and the ducks and deer get the day off, but it
will be a bad day for the person who didn't understand that a country
boy doesn't helplessly call 911 and hope help arrives before he gets killed

or his wife and daughter get assaulted. He calls 911 to tell them where to come and pick up the carcass of the one who tried to break into his home.

If America were run by rednecks, we wouldn't go around waving guns at nations and threatening anyone. It's just not proper to do that. But God help the "sumbitch" that would hurt a hair on the neck of an American—because, to paraphrase that great military strategist Merle Haggard, "Partner, you've gotten on the fightin' side of me."

19

Beyond the Bumper Stickers

(YES, THIS IS THE
CONCLUSION, BUT BE
SURE AND READ IT BECAUSE
IT'S GOOD STUFF!)

HUGH ALBRIGHT IS ONE OF the best fishing guides in Arkansas, where he works on Lake Ouachita near Hot Springs. He's not only expert at finding and catching fish, but he's a good friend and I've had the joy of fishing with him and enjoying the fish and the fellowship. He's what those of us in the South call a true "good ol' boy." That's like a Jew calling you a mensch. It's a term of endearment. Hugh is also a great storyteller and if a person didn't even enjoy fishing, hanging out in the boat amid the beauty of Lake Ouachita and listening to him tell his tales is well worth the time and money.

Hugh tells the story of a client who had traveled from Minnesota every year for about seven years to fish with Hugh on Ouachita. His client usually would go out several consecutive days and return home with a freezer full of fresh fish. On the last day of his seventh-year trip, his client said, "Hugh, we've fished together for several years now, and

I feel like we've become friends." Hugh answered, "Yeah, I sure feel that way and glad you do."

His guest then said, "Well, Hugh, I don't want to say this wrong, but it seems like people down here [in the South] might just be a little slow. People talk slow, don't seem to be in a hurry to get places, and aren't as well-educated generally. Are folks here just a bit 'slow'?"

In his characteristic *slow* drawl of a voice, Hugh asked, "Before you leave today, are you going to fill up some of those plastic jugs you have with our fresh spring water?" The guest replied that he would because it was the best and purest water he'd ever had and he knew that people actually came from around the world to drink it and bathe in it for its mineral qualities and healing powers.

"And," Hugh continued, "are you going out to the rock shop on Highway 70 and load up with some of the beautiful crystal rocks that are sold there?"

His client responded, "Oh, yes, Hugh. My friends back home love getting those rocks—they've never seen anything quite like them and I always take a lot of them back."

Hugh then said, "Well, I don't reckon if I know if we're all that slow or not, but I do know that some of us make a pretty good living selling water from our ground, rocks from our yard, and taking Yankees fishing." Bang!

I'd rather eat barbecue with Hugh Albright than Chateaubriand with a Wall Street banker; I'd rather sit in church with Nancy the makeup artist who had a pizza and herself delivered to her house than sit in an opera with European royalty; and I'm more comfortable in Walmart than at Tiffany's. Yes, I've learned to sit at the head table, but I enjoy being with the folks in the kitchen even more.

As difficult as it may be for folks in the urban power centers to understand, real power for folks in the land of God, guns, grits, and gravy is having family and neighbors you can count on when you're in trouble, a church that keeps you centered around what's really important, a table where good food and laughter are always on the menu, and the self-reliance to take care of your home and your family should someone ever try to violate either one. I don't know anyone I live around who is ashamed of that.

The less contact we have with government, the better. We especially feel a disconnect with the people who live and work in our nation's capital.

Before getting into the particulars of the differences between the LA, D.C., and NYC elite and the rest of America, it's worth noting that D.C. has become an island unto itself, and I do mean a Treasure Island. Big money lobbyists are a plague that affects both parties, but the excesses are particularly egregious when liberals are in charge because their entire philosophy is built around more government and more spending, which means lobbyists are working overtime either to protect their industry bosses from the regulations or snap up those fat government contracts and stimulus bucks. Obama took office on a promise that lobbyists would have no place in his administration. He then not only threw open the gates to lobbyists, he actually gave a $510,577 government contract to Chatman LLC, a registered lobbying firm, to sign up Obamacare navigators. In fact, Chatman lobbies the government on behalf of a private hospital and even lobbied Congress during the writing of Obamacare. So their unusual government contract put them in the unique position of lobbying on behalf of a law they'd lobbied. I'm tempted to call that a "loblolly."

The explosion of government and spending under Obama insured that while the rest of the nation continued to suffer stagnant job growth and slow housing sales long past the time when a recovery should have been underway, one city was booming like a five-year-long Led Zeppelin drum solo: Washington, D.C.

According to the 2014 *Forbes* ranking of the ten richest counties in America, none were in New York, California, or Texas. Before Obama took office, five of the richest counties surrounded Washington, D.C. Now, seven years after Obama took office on his promise to rid the place of big money lobbyists, and Democrats assumed complete control of the White House and Congress for two years, *six* of the richest counties surround Washington, D.C.

Bear in mind that unlike Texas or California, where money is generated by creating products people actually need, such as oil or computers, Washington, D.C., produces nothing but government. In other words, six of the ten richest counties in America got that rich by being parasites. A case could be made that under the current leadership, crony capitalism is more rewarding than actual capitalism. And with all that government around business people's necks, it's certainly a heckuva lot easier.

Many Americans might not realize just how drunk with power and money, and how out of touch with regular Americans, the people in the nation's capital have become. After all, politicians love to show up at factories, wearing blue work shirts that still sport the creases from being folded inside the plastic wrapper, to laud the working person and vow that they are focused like a laser beam on creating jobs. Then they go back to D.C. and pass another tax or expensive mandate (i.e., "tax") on business owners. The only jobs they seem to have the slightest idea how to create are jobs for lobbyists and IRS workers.

Two quick examples:

1. The IRS budget request for fiscal year 2012 showed they planned to hire 1,269 full-time employees at a cost of $473 million to help implement the Patient Protection and Affordable Care Act. People in D.C. must also have a totally different definition of the word "affordable" than the rest of America does.

2. The founders of the Internet giant Google, whose informal slogan is DON'T BE EVIL, were big supporters of Obama and famous for their disdain of government lobbying. In 2004, Google opened a tiny office in D.C. with just one lobbyist. But *The Washington Post* reports that by 2012, Google had grown such a massive, active lobbying organization that their spending on lobbying was second only to General Electric, and they were preparing to move into a new D.C. headquarters spread over

55,000 square feet, about the size of the White House. My
question: Why not just move into the White House?

Well-connected D.C. insiders now live in a bubble of decadent luxury that rivals the titans of the Gilded Age. Some are elected officials,
like Nancy "I'll fly my grandkids home on a military jet" Pelosi or the
Obamas themselves, whose vacation videos resemble an episode of Robin
Leach's *Lifestyles of the Rich and Famous*. The *Washington Examiner* analyzed Air Force records for Air Force One and Two and found that
just the air travel expenses for the Obamas' and Bidens' vacations added
up to over $40 million since they took office. Two Obama golf outings
in 2014 cost $2.9 million in travel expenses alone. I wonder if we could
cut that down to $2 million if he took up miniature golf?

But if our elected leaders live like Rockefellers, some of the influence
peddlers surrounding them live lifestyles worthy of Cleopatra or Scrooge
McDuck. They try to keep it hidden behind gated communities and
dark-suited security guards at fundraisers inside luxury hotel ballrooms.
But glimpses occasionally leak out. Like when Democratic super-
lobbyists Tony and Heather Podesta went through a contentious divorce, and the legal battle over splitting their property was made public.

National Review's Kevin Williamson dubbed it "Lifestyles of the
Rich and Odious," as details spilled out about the estranged couple's
multimillion-dollar mansion, their expansive wine cellar, their second
home in Venice, and their museum-quality, 1,300-piece art collection.
The Washington Post reports that the Podestas held lavish mixers for
power players in their Washington, D.C., manor and opened it up for
tours to proudly show off their artworks, including an eight-foot pho-
tograph of a naked man in the living room and photos by an artist
famous for photographing naked teenagers in suburban homes. They
reportedly found the shocked looks on guests' faces amusing.

The differences between these folks and the rest of America are as
stark as the way we *give* as the way we *live*.

According to the stereotypes promulgated by those in politics and the media out of D.C., LA, and NYC, conservatives are greedy, mean, and uncaring, while liberals are openhearted, compassionate, and generous (also brilliant, witty, and superior lovers—see the advantages of owning the media?). But absolutely none of these tropes withstand objective evidence.

In his 2007 book *Who Really Gives*, Syracuse University professor Arthur C. Brooks looked at the real numbers behind charitable giving in America. He found that of the top twenty-five states where people gave an above-average percentage of their income to charity, Maryland was the only blue (liberal) state. While rich people gave the most dollars to charity, the highest percent of income was given by the working poor. They give almost 30 percent more as a share of their income than the rich do. Even though liberal-headed families make more money on average, conservative-headed families give 30 percent more of their income to charity. The most likely people to donate to charity are married, conservative churchgoers. The least likely to give are secular, young liberals under thirty—the group most likely to point the finger at others and call them greedy for not sharing enough of their wealth.

Critics tried to discount Brooks's numbers by saying he shouldn't count contributions to churches as charity giving. I'm not certain why that shouldn't be considered charity giving, but okay. Brooks checked the numbers and found that even if you factored out all the donations to churches, conservatives still give more than liberals. And not just to nonprofits aligned with their political or religious views, but to all types of charities. That includes money given to homeless people on the street. Conservatives were even 18 percent more likely to give blood than liberals. Brooks said that "people who believe it's the government's job to make incomes more equal are far less likely to give their money away." They're like a college student buying rounds of drinks for the house with their dad's credit card. Nothing is easier than being generous with someone else's money.

When John Stossel was on ABC's *20/20*, he tested Brooks's claim by setting up Salvation Army collection pots in San Francisco and Sioux

City, Iowa. One would think that the San Francisco pot would have all the advantages. Sioux City is filled with conservative churchgoers, the type of people gleefully caricatured as greedy, selfish hypocrites by liberals. San Francisco is filled with secular liberals with a far higher average income than Sioux City, and it's so crowded that three times as many people passed by the pot. And that's exactly what they did: passed it by. At the end of two days, the Sioux City collection pot held twice as much money as the San Francisco pot.

And for the New York and Hollywood centers of news and entertainment, to borrow a phrase from the once senator and Presidential candidate, but always sleazy John Edwards, there really are two Americas.

Liberals in NY and LA love to scoff at Fox News, or as they all call it (as if they thought of it themselves), "Faux News." Meanwhile, the rest of the nation respectfully disagrees.

From Mediabistro, April 30, 2014:

> Fox News finished its 148th consecutive month as the top-rated cable news network. FNC's hold on total viewers remains particularly strong, with the network beating CNN and MSNBC combined in every hour.
>
> The ratings for April 2014 (Nielsen Live + Same Day data):
>
> * Primetime (Mon–Sun): 1,614,000 total viewers/296,000 A25–54
> * Total Day (Mon–Sun): 960,000 total viewers/201,000 A25–54
>
> ... [Also] it was a milestone month for "Fox & Friends," which marks 150 consecutive months as the top-rated cable news morning show.

While the coastal media elites would have us believe that Americans are endlessly fascinated with the salacious doings of the Kardashian clan and their various divorces, pregnancies, and exposures of their bodies, the highest-rated episode ever of their reality show drew 3.7 million viewers in 2010. Meanwhile, the tight-knit, God-fearing, Bible-believing Robertson family on *Duck Dynasty*, alternately mocked and scorned by the coastal elites, drew 11.77 million viewers to their season four premiere in August 2013. It not only beat all competition on the major broadcast networks, it still stands as the highest-rated telecast in the history of the A&E cable channel.

When married producers Mark Burnett and Roma Downey tried to sell the idea of producing a miniseries called *The Bible*, they met resistance in Hollywood. Focus on the Family's president Jim Daly, who acted as a consultant on the series, told *The Denver Post* that "when they first proposed the project they were told to try and tell the story without mentioning Jesus. They refused." If ever there was a perfect summation of the Hollywood mentality, this is it: "We love your idea of turning the Bible into a movie, but does it have to include Jesus? Couldn't we make it Tom Cruise instead?"

Again, the Hollywood elites were wrong: *The Bible* was a major hit. Its premiere episode drew 13.1 million viewers to the History channel, beating the broadcast networks and setting a record as the highest-rated cable show of 2013. Subsequent episodes also drew huge audiences. The footage on the life of Jesus became the basis of the theatrical film, *Son of God*, which despite largely negative reviews has made nearly $60 million as of this writing. It became one of a wave of faith-based films (including *God's Not Dead* and *Heaven Is for Real*) to surprise Hollywood by unexpectedly hitting big at the box office. Somehow, liberals always find it unexpected when Christians turn out to see a faith-based movie or when Obama's economic numbers are disappointing. They are as easily surprised as bunny rabbits.

This trend should only grow stronger, for two reasons:

1. Studio executives may be liberals, but when it comes to box office grosses, they're unrepentant capitalists. Now that they're

finally seeing that religious audiences will pay to see a movie that appeals to them, they're starting to get on board. *Noah* was a big studio production aimed at churchgoers, but it alienated a lot of them because its director, Darren Aronofsky, just couldn't help himself: He had to rewrite the Bible to insert liberal and environmentalist messages. But *Heaven Is for Real* got it right, and it's a TriStar Studios release featuring mainstream star Greg Kinnear.

2. Even as the studios finally start creating movies that appeal to conservative Christians, new advances such as digital cameras, computer video editing, and crowd-sourced funding are empowering conservative indie filmmakers, who no longer have to depend on Hollywood to green-light movies and screen out anything that isn't filled with left-wing messages. They can now shoot movies on a shoestring that can compete in quality with major studio releases.

HUNTING VS. HEALTH CARE, OBAMA STYLE!

By the end of November 2013, only 269 people had enrolled on the Obamacare Web site in New Hampshire. The state gave out 281 moose-hunting permits, so I joked on my daily radio commentary *The Huckabee Report* that more New Hampshire residents wanted to shoot a moose than buy into Obamacare. Well, a self-proclaimed fact-checking site called PolitiFact accused me of telling a "half-truth." They claimed "it's possible" that more people wanted Obamacare but couldn't get through. And "it could be argued" that anyone who completed an application wanted it, even if they didn't buy it yet. That's a lot of weasel words for people who claim to deal in facts. Well, I don't like being accused of telling a half-truth when even they admitted that my numbers were correct. So let me give you just a few more details.

They claim that the number of "potential customers" in New

Hampshire who filled out an application for Obamacare was 7,817. We don't know how many of those are legitimate, or would ever have bought insurance, but I'll give them that number. Now, the moose-hunting permits are on a lottery system. They gave out 289 permits, but the number of applicants who filled out a form and definitely wanted one was 13,469. Even with my backward, red-state math education, I think that 13,469 moose-hunting applicants outnumber 7,817 potential Obamacare enrollees. Of course, I could argue that even more people wanted to apply to shoot a moose, but couldn't get through. But I trust the people who set up the moose-hunting lottery application site to have done it right. After all, that job is important.

I think maybe PolitiFact needs to learn the difference between an assumption and a fact. They might also want to look up the definition of the word "joke." And the word "opinion." As in, "It's my opinion, from personal experience growing up poor, that most families would find a pot of moose chili to be a lot more useful than an overpriced insurance policy their doctor won't take."

If you've had the misfortune of spending all your life in the tony, uptown enclaves of Manhattan, the Washington Beltway, or in Beverly Hills, I truly feel for you. Granted, it might not be your thing to wade in chest-deep water to hunt mallards in flooded timber, or to order a bowl of cheese grits for dinner (*never, ever* call them "cheesy grits" because "cheezy" means fake and cheap, not "cheese-filled") and know what you were getting, or to attend a revival meeting in which people held up their hands during the singing in praise to God. But don't be so smug about what makes us tick or keeps us happy. We like the simple life. Status is a Ford F-150 truck; luxury is crawfish étouffée and slaw on your pulled-pork sandwich; and privilege is front-row seats at a Lynyrd Skynyrd concert. Speaking of Skynyrd, their album *God & Guns* is the greatest collection of songs about Bubba-ville culture ever. I love every song on it, and the signature song "Simple Life" from the album says it better than I ever could:

Simple Life

Hey when was the last time you sat down
and had dinner with your kids?
Talked about what's goin' on in their lives
Hey when was the last time you just stopped and helped somebody
*   out?*
I bet ya can't remember

Well a lot of people are saying it's changing for the better
But that don't interest me

I like the simple life
The way it used to be
We left our doors wide open, we didn't need no key
I've been around the world
Seen all there is to see
I'd trade all those memories
For one more day of how it used to be
I like the simple life

I want to get up Sunday mornin' and go fishing with my boy
Watch the sunset and kick back in my yard
Take my Harley on a real long lazy Sunday drive
And do a little more of nothin' once in a while

Yeah maybe kick my feet up, watch an old rerun on TV
Laughing with old Barney, Andy and Aunt B.

I like the simple life
The way it used to be
We left our doors wide open, we didn't need no key
I've been around the world

Seen all there is to see
I'd trade all those memories
For one more day of how it used to be
I like the simple life

Everything's moving by so fast
I swear sometimes we just can't see
So caught up on where we're trying to get
Life as we know it can be gone in a minute

I want the simple life
The way it used to be
We left our doors wide open, didn't need no key
I've been around the world
Seen all there is to see
I'd trade all those memories
For one more day
I like the simple life
I want the simple life

INDEX